London: A Living Guide is the result of a project conceived in mid 1988 at a time when life in London was becoming increasingly difficult for many of its inhabitants. With the Greater London Council abolished and similar plans well under way for the Inner London Education Authority, control over people's lives was passing more and more into the hands of central government and out of the hands of Londoners themselves and their elected representatives.

On one level then, *London: A Living Guide* is an attempt to paint a picture of early 1990's London in all its aspects: a growing crisis in housing and mass homelessness, uncertain futures for health and education, pollution, racism, discrimination and violence.

Yet in the midst of the negative, positive aspects abound. Hundreds of organisations, both statutory and voluntary, struggle against the odds to provide vital services to Londoners from all walks of life, from housing advice to cleaning local ponds; from legal aid to meals on wheels.

London: A Living Guide is the most comprehensive resource currently available for people who live in London. It offers hundreds of addresses and phone numbers and more than 400 pages of practical information on every aspect of life in the capital in fifteen easy to follow chapters, covering housing, health, education, ethnic minorities, women, disability, lesbians and gay men, green London, social services and much more.

London: A Living Guide is published by Unwin Hyman Ltd in association with Books for a Change, 52 Charing Cross Road, London WC2H 0BB.

GW00578147

LONDON

A Living Guide

Edited by John Grounds
and published in association with
Books for a Change

UNWIN
PAPERBACKS

LONDON SYDNEY WELLINGTON

First published in paperback by Unwin ®Paperbacks, an imprint of Unwin Hyman Limited, in 1990.

Unwin Hyman Limited
15–17 Broadwick Street
London W1V 1FP

Allen & Unwin Australia Pty Ltd
8 Napier Street, North Sydney, NSW 2060, Australia

Allen & Unwin New Zealand Pty Ltd with the Port Nicholson Press
Compusales Building, 75 Ghuznee Street, Wellington, New Zealand

---

British Library Cataloguing in Publication Data

Grounds, John
  London: a living guide.
1. London. Social conditions
942.1085′8
ISBN 0–04–440527–8

Disc conversion by Columns Typesetters of Reading
Printed in Great Britain by Cox & Wyman Limited, Reading

CONTENTS

FOREWORD

The five years from May 1981, when I became Leader of the Greater London Council, were the most fulfilling and exciting of my life. As someone who had been born and raised in London, I found that the ability to reach out and change things for the better there was electrifying. It was not just that the new Labour administration could improve the services and cut the fares on bus and tube or build more homes for the homeless, or put on popular music and arts festivals which could attract over a quarter of a million people. It was more than just that – it was because we were doing these things in a city which had a history, personality and character unlike any other in Britain.

For London is unique. Long before the Romans created their camp of Londinium in AD 43, the Thames basin had been settled and was criss-crossed by Stone Age trade routes. The earliest evidence of habitation is found in Stoke Newington and dates back to the early Palaeolithic period, over 100,000 years ago. The remains of birch stakes wound with clematis and ferns there show that hunter-gatherers had struck a permanent camp site.

Although the last ice age drove humankind from the Thames area, this was only temporary and the hunter-gatherers had returned by the start of the Mesolithic (Middle Stone) Age, some 14,000 years ago, and settled along the banks of the Thames.

This city has grown from and been developed by the struggles of its peoples. Pagans, Romans, Dark Ages, Black Death, Peasants Revolt, Civil War, regicide, greatest port, the rise to global power and seat of one of the world's greatest empires – all that history was built on the labour and imagination of the unknown millions of people who lived in what was, until this century, the largest concentration of humanity ever assembled in one place.

We can still see the evidence of these Londoners' lives and history around us today in the slums and palaces or the great parks and the imperial banks. It is almost as though the end result of all the human effort and imagination which went into the creation of our city is greater than the sum of the total. It is no surprise that such a city attracts people from all over the face of the planet to make their homes and fulfil their potential within its bounds. Like other capital cities, London has always been a clearing house for newcomers and the last GLC survey showed that half of all the people living in London had been born somewhere else in the world.

It is for all Londoners, newcomer or old cockney, that John Grounds has written *London: A Living Guide*. This is a book that is long overdue for London is unique in another way. It is the only capital city in Western Europe in which the citizens are denied the right to elect (and sack) the people who run their city. Since the abolition of the GLC on April Fools' Day 1986, the decisions that affect the lives of Londoners, whether it be on where to build new roads, the cost of a bus ride, the protection of the green belt or the rights of women, are now taken by unelected bureaucrats meeting in secret on government appointed quangos.

And it shows. Like imperial administrators ruling some rebellious colony, they are chauffeur driven from their home counties mansions to their ministries. They don't travel on the buses or trains they run or educate their children in the state schools whose funds they restrict, or use the hospitals they plan to close. It is not their children who sleep in Waterloo's cardboard city or sell their bodies in the amusement arcades at Piccadilly. They keep their limousine windows firmly closed against the pollution and noise that their neglect breeds, and their only contact with real Londoners is when they are served by them in the exclusive restaurants and brothels of Mayfair.

John Grounds has produced a useful guide on how to survive in these circumstances and he has charted how much Londoners have really forfeited when they lost the right to elect a city-wide authority.

In the year this book appears, the people of Eastern Europe will have their first chance to elect democratically the people who run their cities. Perhaps, one day, we will have a government in Britain which no longer fears to give Londoners the same right.

Ken Livingstone

PREFACE

Two things prompted me to write this book: anger and necessity.

The anger grew from a bursting need to say something about what is happening to the capital. London is a mess. There's no point in trying to pretend otherwise. To an outsider it may seem like a fountain of culture, action and fun, but the other side of the coin is a grey and crumbling image of degeneration and despair. More depressing still is the speed of this decline. In only a few years Londoners have had to face an assault on their rights, living standards and expectations.

Homelessness and vagrancy, especially among young people, is rocketing, as an evening stroll around the West End or any park or tube station in the capital will soon testify; hospitals are overworked and underfunded; schools and colleges are crying out for help and support but instead are set upon the road towards market management; public transport is impoverished, splintered and overcrowded; London's rivers, streets and atmosphere are severely polluted.

Yet behind the mounting crisis literally hundreds of organisations are working twenty-four hours a day to help people cope with the problems forced upon them by government policy, poor planning and inefficiency, and to make the most of the help, advice and leisure facilities that are available to everybody.

Hence my second reason for writing this book: necessity. How do you find all the information you need and all the organisations which exist to help you survive and even enjoy the city? After all, London is still a cosmopolitan city full of possibilities. Millions of people wouldn't dream of living anywhere else.

In a sense, I compiled this book for myself. It is full of the kind of information I would have liked to have in my pocket when I first came to London and which I will continue to carry next to my *A to Z* to help me through the 101 problems and queries that used to take hours on a telephone or in someone's office to solve. Laws, regulations, rights, advice, addresses; it's all here. I hope you'll use it as much as I will.

Please note the following:

1.   The addresses given in this book have been checked as far as possible and are correct to the best of my knowledge at the time of going to press. For those organisations that for some reason could not be checked, the most recent known address is given.

2.   In many chapters I refer to 'Citizens Advice Bureaux, Law Centres or other independent advice centres'. The central bodies for such agencies, who will tell you about your local advice centre, can be found in the Appendix.

John Grounds
December 1989

ACKNOWLEDGEMENTS

Adrian Howe (for the idea); Harold Howe, Chris Hansford, David Cameron (Books for a Change); Michael Pountney, Janet Clayton, Val Pidgeon, Elizabeth Sich, Francesca Clarke, Mark Stevens (Unwin Hyman Ltd); Chris Edmondson, Helen Bladon and Paul Lowne (NACAB); Michael Turner, Anne Copestake, Liz Appleton, Caron Young (GLAD); Paul Walentowicz (SHAC); Judith Hanna (Transport 2000); Chris Gittins, Pippa Hyam, Martin Jones (Friends of the Earth); Frank Walsh (Ecology Centre); Jeff Cooper (London Waste Regulation Authority); Leigh Thornton (London Wildlife Trust); Gita Sheth (Corporation of London); Cathy Roberts, Standing Committee on the Sexual Abuse of Children (SCOSAC); Mary Wright, Stephen Chappell (Greater London Arts); Marjorie Thompson (RCN); Bill McAlister, Carol-Ann Allen (ICA); Marie Gabriel (Wesley House London Women's Centre); Griffith Vaughan-Williams (Campaign for Homosexual Equality); Malcolm Hurwitt, Chris Jones (NCCL); Michael King (Help the Aged); Kevin Barrett (NSPCC); Tony Price (Central London Social Security Advisors Forum); Pete Marshall (COHSE); Lionel Morrison, Cynthia McCaulsky (Commission for Racial Equality); David Mallen (ILEA); Christine Thornton (Federation of Independent Advice Centres); Gerry McManamon (Portobello Project); Alison Macnair (Legal Aid Head Office); Diana Breadmore (Haringey Alcohol Project); Eileen Lanigan; David Bellamy; Fay Weldon; Jane Wynborne; Sarah Sawyerr (Talawa Theatre Company, Africa Centre); Elaine Jay (Third World Foundation).

Special thanks to Elaine, Tom, Adrian, Karen, Edwina, Mum and Dad, my family and friends.

1

ARTS AND LEISURE

London is one of the world's great cultural capitals; most of what you could possibly want to do is here: the challenge, however, is to find it.

Negotiating London's information networks is the first skill to acquire. If you are only passing through town then consult *Time Out*, *City Limits* and the nearest taxi driver. Our taxi drivers are the best trained, most honest and knowledgeable in the world. If you are here for the long haul, there are many other useful information resources. A publication called *Floodlight* lists all the adult education workshops and classes in music, dance, theatre and the arts.

Currently, our great national museums are in various degrees of convulsion. The British Museum is running out of money and the Director is threatening to resign if museum charges are brought in. The Victoria and Albert, 'where the message is the logo' has become a sponsor's puppet. The new British Library rises hideously on the King's Cross horizon. The National Gallery is about to have a splendid extension thanks to J. P. Getty and Sainsbury's. There is a gleaming new Design Museum funded by Conran and one of the Saatchi brothers offers us the Saatchi Museum for Contemporary Art.

Sponsored art is the 'ism' of our day. Commercial ventures in theatre, music, cinema, even opera are thriving but those places previously supported by government to provide something different are in trouble.

For my money, the arts scene in London has had two really positive injections in recent years. First, foreign influences. There are more possibilities to see great films from China, Africa, Eastern Europe. Similar developments in theatre and the arts have widened our choices. Most encouragingly, the influences of recent immigrant communities – West Indian, Asian and Moslem – are now surfacing in British art. All this is good. The other great injection has been the impact, largely through television, of taking seriously the influences of popular culture. A new radio station for London dedicated to jazz is about to come on air and there has been an exciting revival of circuses with fresh new material. The street culture of London remains vital and idiosyncratic, although you will increasingly have to dodge the ubiquitous BMWs.

Bill McAlister
Director, Institute of Contemporary Arts (ICA)

GENERAL INFORMATION

There are a number of publications with listings of arts venues. The most comprehensive are *City Limits* and *Time Out* but there are also many free magazines, local newspapers and arts magazines with listings sections. *Time Out* also produces a series of guides to different aspects of London such as clubs and restaurants. It is therefore not the purpose of this chapter to list all venues, but to give some of the major contact addresses for organisations based in London. Borough Leisure Departments or local Arts Councils can provide local arts information.

London's three major arts complexes are the South Bank Centre (incorporating the National Theatre, Royal Festival Hall, Queen Elizabeth Hall, Purcell Room, National Film Theatre, Museum of the Moving Image and the Hayward Gallery); the Barbican Centre (including the Barbican Theatre and Barbican Art Gallery); and the Institute of Contemporary Arts (ICA), which presents all kinds of exhibitions as well as music, theatre, workshops and discussions. All three are good sources of information on what is happening in the arts.

I should emphasise that the purpose here is not to offer an exhaustive list of organisations active in the arts. This is done thoroughly elsewhere in a number of hefty publications, some of which are mentioned where relevant. The reason for including this chapter in *London: A Living Guide* is twofold: on the one hand, to show that the arts are as much a part of daily life in London as housing or education, and on the other, to point people towards organisations and publications that can provide much greater detail than space permits here.

Arts Centres
Greater London Arts (see below) have a list of local arts centres in London.

The Arts Council
105 Piccadilly
London W1V 0AU
629 9495

Arts Media Group
90 De Beauvoir Road
London N1 4EN
254 6256

Artsline
5 Crowndale Road
London NW1 1TU
388 2227/387 5911
Information and advice for Londoners with disabilities on all aspects of arts and leisure activities in London. Also publish Disability Arts in London.

Asian Women's Arts Group
Building D
Macbean Centre
Macbean Street
London SE18 6LW
854 1188

British Arts Festivals Association
c/o 23 Orchard Road
London N6 5TR

Greater London Arts
9 White Lion Street
London N1 9PD
837 8808
*Supports and funds the arts in
London. Can provide various
resource lists, including information
on borough Arts Councils and
general information.*

Minority Arts Advisory Service
28 Shacklewell Lane
London E8 2EZ
254 7295

**National Association of Local Arts
Councils**
c/o Walcot Avenue
Luton
Beds LU2 0PP
0582 30775
*Promoting local arts councils and
improving relationships between
local arts councils and The Arts
Council of Great Britain.*

National Campaign for the Arts
Francis House
Francis Street
London SW1P 1DE
828 4448
*Works to inform the public, brief the
media and alert politicians to the
need for greater public funding of
the arts.*

**Organisation for Black Arts
Advancement and Learning
Activities**
Obaala House
225 Seven Sisters Road
London N4 2DA
263 1918

Shape London
1 Thorpe Close
London W10 5XL
960 9245
*Aims to develop and expand ways
in which people with mental or
physical disabilities, people with
mental ill-health and elderly people
can enjoy and participate in the arts
in London. Also operates a West
End ticket scheme.*

Publications

British Performing Arts Yearbook (Rhinegold, £15.95), ed.
Sheena Barbour.
*A complete guide to venues, performers, arts centres, festivals,
supporting organisations and services for the arts professional.*

Arts Festivals in Britain and Ireland (Rhinegold, £7.95), ed.
Sheena Barbour.
*A guide to promoting events, including a calendar of festivals and
their subjects.*

Voluntary Agencies Directory (Bedford Square, £8.95), National
Council for Voluntary Organisations.
London Art and Artists Guide (Art Guide Publications, 1989,
£6.95).
Arts Address Book (Peter Marcan).
Directory of Arts Centres (Arts Council of Great Britain).
Directory of Local Arts Councils (Arts Council of Great Britain).

A number of specialist arts magazines are available, either from good newsagents and specialist shops, or via specific organisations. GLA receive most relevant publications and might provide you with a list on request.

THEATRE

Apart from listings magazines, information on the London theatre can be picked up from most theatres, especially on the South Bank, or from ticket agencies. Greater London Arts (see above) have a list of small-scale touring theatre venues in Greater London, such as the Almeida Theatre, Battersea Arts Centre, Drill Hall, Half Moon Theatre, and Tricycle Theatre.

Black Theatre Forum
6 Lissenden Gardens
London NW5 1LX
482 4596

British Actors Equity
8 Harley Street
London W1
637 9311
The actors union.

British Theatre Association
Regent's College
Inner Circle
Regent's Park
London NW1 4NW
935 2571
Information about training, library facilities, etc.

Children's Theatre Association
4 Enfield Road
London N1
254 3119
Promotes the work of theatre for children and stimulates its growth and development.

Fringe Theatre Box Office
Duke of York's Theatre
St Martin's Lane
London WC2
379 6002

Independent Theatre Council
Unit 129 West
Westminster

Business Square
Durham Street
London SE11
820 1712
The managers association and representative body for small-scale theatre.

International Amateur Theatre Association
c/o British Theatre Association (see above)

International Theatre Institute
4th Floor
St George's House
15 Hanover Square
London W1R 9HA
486 6363

National Theatre
South Bank
London SE1
928 2252
928 8126 (24 hour info)

National Youth Theatre
443–445 Holloway Road
London N7
281 3863

Royal Shakespeare Company
Barbican Centre
Whitecross Street
London EC2
638 8891

Society of West End Theatres
Bedford Chambers
Covent Garden
London WC2
836 3193

Spotlight
42–43 Cranbourn Street
London WC2
437 7631
Professional organisation advising on agents and contracts and producing an important directory of addresses.

Publications

British Theatre Directory (Richmond House).
Guide to venues, performers, festivals, organisations and services.

British Theatre Yearbook (Croom Helm, £9.95).
British Alternative Theatre Directory (Conway McGillivray, £9.95), David McGillivray.
A comprehensive guide, covering theatre companies (including small- and middle-scale touring companies, community theatre, producing venues, dance, performance art and mime), young people's theatre, puppets, the fringe register, rehearsal rooms, cabaret venues, theatre venues, theatre training, arts councils and regional arts associations, festivals, organisations, services and suppliers.

Contacts (Spotlight).
Massive publication giving contacts addresses and/or agents of working performers.

ART GALLERIES

The following are the major mainstream art galleries; borough council leisure departments or local arts councils can provide information on local galleries.

Courtauld Institute Galleries
Woburn Square
London WC1
580 1015/387 0370
Collection ranging from old masters to post-impressionists.

Dulwich Picture Gallery
College Road
London SE21
693 5254
Collection includes Rubens,

Rembrandt, Poussin, Gainsborough and Canaletto.

Hayward Gallery
South Bank Centre
London SE1
928 3144
Specialises in major temporary exhibitions.

Institute of Contemporary Arts (ICA)
Nash House

The Mall
London SW1
930 3647
Mainly temporary exhibitions, but the ICA also offers many other kinds of arts events (see above).

Iveagh Bequest
Kenwood House
Hampstead Lane
London NW3
348 1286
Collection includes Vermeer, Gainsborough, Reynolds, Van Dyck and Rembrandt.

Leighton House
12 Holland Park Road
London W14
602 3316
Collection includes pre-Raphaelites and High Victorian paintings.

National Gallery
Trafalgar Square
London WC2
839 3321
London's major collection covering thirteenth century to the present.

National Portrait Gallery
St Martin's Place
London WC2
930 1552

Queen's Gallery
Buckingham Palace Road
London SW1Y 1AY
930 4832
Paintings from the royal collection.

Royal Academy of Arts
Burlington House
Piccadilly
London W1
439 7438
Small permanent collection. Specialises in temporary exhibitions of major artists.

Tate Gallery
Millbank
London SW1
821 1313
London's main collection of modern painting and sculpture. Includes the Clore Gallery, housing the Turner collection.

Wallace Collection
Hertford House
Manchester Square
London W1
935 0687
Includes Canaletto, Boucher, Fragonard and Reynolds.

Publications

Directory of Exhibition Spaces (AN Publications, £12.50), ed. Susan Jones.
A directory of spaces including each venue's policy on exhibiting and a description of the venue, including access. Actually intended for people wishing to exhibit their work, but equally useful to the individual wishing to visit contemporary galleries. Covers the whole country but has about 450 entries for the London area.

MUSIC

General

British Music Information Centre
10 Stratford Place
London W1
499 8567
*Talks, recitals, library relating to
new music.*

Community Music Ltd
1 Hoxton Square
London N1 6NU
729 5600
*Training courses, educational
outreach service placing
professional musicians in
community venues and schools,
general information and
consultancy.*

**Electro-Acoustic Music Association
of Great Britain**
10 Stratford Place
London W1
499 2576
*Concerts, equipment hire,
information.*

London Musicians Collective
c/o Diorama Community Arts Centre
18 Park Square East
London NW1
487 2896/722 0456

Musicians Against Nuclear Arms
The Premises
201 Hackney Road
London E2 8JL
729 0885
*Associated names include John
Williams, Michael Tippett, Leonard
Bernstein, Charles Groves, Jessye
Norman, Neville Marriner. Concerts
and fundraising.*

**National Federation of Music
Societies**
Francis House
Francis Street
London SW1
*Umbrella organisation offering
information on amateur music
making activities.*

National Sound Archive
29 Exhibition Road
London SW7
589 6603
*Reference collection of sound
recordings from end of last century
to present day.*

**Society for the Promotion of New
Music**
10 Stratford Place
London W1
491 8111
*Publishes free monthly guide to
contemporary classical music and
promotes concerts and workshops.*

Women in Music
c/o Battersea Arts Centre
Old Town Hall
London SW11
223 6557
*Membership organisation aiming to
raise the profile of women in all
areas of music.*

Youth and Music
78 Neal Street
London WC2
675 6207
*Membership organisation offering
discounts and special ticket deals
for 14–30 year olds, as well as
information and merchandise. Also
promotes the annual 'cushion
concerts'.*

Classical and Opera (venues and information)

Barbican Centre
Silk Street
London EC2
638 4141

Blackheath Concert Halls
Lea Road
London SE3
318 9758

English National Opera
London Coliseum
St Martin's Lane
London WC2
836 3161 (Box Office)

Fairfield Halls
Park Lane
Croydon CR9 1DG
688 9291

Royal Festival Hall/Queen Elizabeth Hall/Purcell Room
South Bank
London SE1
928 3641

Royal Opera House
Covent Garden
London WC2E 9DD
240 1066

St John's, Smith Square
Smith Square
London SW1
222 1061

South Bank Free Foyer Music
921 0613

Wigmore Hall
36 Wigmore Street
London W1
935 2141

Rock, Folk, Jazz, Black Music

All major and most minor London music venues are listed in *City Limits* and *Time Out* as well as the national music press. Some record shops also have information on concerts and one or two of the larger ones (Tower, HMV, Virgin) sell tickets. There are hundreds of general and specialist music shops in London, far too many to list.

Black Music Association
146 Manor Park Road
London NW10
961 4857
Information and advice on all areas of black music.

English Folk Dance and Song Society
Cecil Sharp House

2 Regent's Park Road
London NW1 7AY
485 2206

Jazz Services
5 Dryden Street
London WC1
National information and touring organisation.

Early Music

Early Music Centre
Charles Clore House
17 Russell Square
London WC1B 5DR
580 8401/2

Promotes and coordinates the early music network in Britain; offers a public information service, educational expertise, workshops and publications.

Publications

British Music Yearbook (Rhinegold, £10.95), ed. Marianne Barton.
Covers offices and societies, professional services, performers, folk, jazz and light music, early music, festivals and competitions, trade, education, libraries, museums and music in places of worship.

Jazz and Improvised Music in Greater London (Greater London Arts, approx £3.50).
Covers rehearsal and recording studios, regional jazz administrations, funding, music industry and development agencies, agents, promoters and organisations, jazz shops, jazz and arts festivals, venues, education authority contacts, regional organisations and media contacts.

The Folk Directory (English Folk Dance and Song Society).

DANCE

British Ballet Organisation
Woolborough House
39 Lonsdale Road
London SW13 9PJ
748 1241

Dance Books (Bookshop)
9 Cecil Court
London WC2N 4EZ
836 2314

Laban Centre for Music and Dance
Laurie Grove
London SE14 6NH
692 4070

National Organisation for Dance and Mime
9 Rossdale Road
London SW15 1AD
788 6905

National Resource Centre for Dance
University of Surrey
Guildford GU2 5XH
0483 571281 (university switchboard)

Sadlers Wells
Rosebery Avenue
London EC1
278 8916
Royal Opera House, Royal Festival Hall, Purcell Room, ICA and others have regular shows. Listings magazines have more details and also information on dance classes.

Publications

Dance Handbook (Longman, £10.95), Allen Robertson/Donald
   Hutera.
*Covers the history of dance as well as providing extensive
information on ballet and modern dance, complete with useful
'databank'.*

Dance Yearbook (Dance Books).

MUSEUMS

British Museum
Great Russell Street
London WC1
636 1555

Museum of London
London Wall
London EC27 5HN
600 3699

Museum of Mankind
6 Burlington Gardens
London W1
437 2224

Museums Association
34 Bloomsbury Way
London WC1A 2SF
404 4767
Represents museums and art

*galleries and their staffs. Publishes
Museums Yearbook annually,
Museums Journal quarterly and
Museums Bulletin monthly.*

Natural History Museum
Cromwell Road
London SW7
589 6363

Science Museum
Exhibition Road
London SW7
589 3456

Victoria and Albert Museum
Cromwell Road
London SW7
589 6371

Publications

Museums Association Yearbook (Museums Association/
   Rhinegold), ed. Sheena Barbour.
*Includes a full directory of museums and galleries in the British
Isles.*

TELEVISION

Screenings

The ICA and the National Film Theatre often screen series of
influential television programmes.

Cable and Satellite

A number of cable TV stations are now in existence, including Premiere (recent movies), Superchannel (Old British programmes), MTV (music) and Bravo (classic films, mainly 1930s and 1940s).

Sky TV and BSB are currently the only two satellite stations in Britain. The initial sales of satellite dishes have been very low and the future of these services of questionable quality is in doubt.

BBC Television
Wood Lane
London W12
743 8000

Channel 4
60 Charlotte Street
London W1P 2AX
631 4444

London Weekend Television
South Bank TV Centre
London SE1 9LT
261 3434

Thames TV
306–316 Euston Road
London NW1 3RB
387 9494

TV AM
Breakfast TV Centre
Hawley Crescent
London NW1 8EF
267 4300

FILM AND VIDEO

Cinema listings are freely available especially in *Time Out* and *City Limits*. There are basically two kinds of cinema in London: chains and independents. The chains such as Cannon, ABC and Odeon tend to show the latest hits and blockbusters, while the independents have wider and more satisfying repertoires covering the whole of cinema history. Independents such as the NFT or the Everyman in Hampstead usually run excellent seasons of related films. The ICA also has an excellent record of screening non-mainstream films that would otherwise often remain unseen in London.

For people wishing to get involved in independent film-making, Greater London Arts (see above) have an information sheet on film and video workshops in Greater London, covering many organisations which offer equipment hire, training, advice and workshops. They also have a sheet covering independent film and video distributors.

British Film Institute and National Film Archive
21 Stephen Street
London W1P 1PL
255 1444

London Film-Makers Coop
42 Gloucester Avenue
London NW1
586 4806

London Video Access
23 Frith Street
London W1V 5TS
734 7410
Coordinates the network of independent video-making.

The Media Centre
Bracknell
Berkshire
0344 427272
Runs the only national Independent Video-makers Festival in Britain.

Museum of the Moving Image
South Bank
London SE1
401 2636

National Film Theatre
South Bank
London SE1
928 3232

Commercial Video

There are hundreds of commercial video shops in London, for both hire and purchase. The largest commercial video selection in London is to be found at:

The Video Palace
34–35 Berwick Street
London W1
434 4217

Publications

International Film and Video Festivals (British Council).
Black and Asian Film and Video List (British Film Institute).
Directions (British Film Institute).
A list of training courses in film and video.

Kemp's International Film and TV Yearbook (Kemp's, 1989, £9.95).

PHOTOGRAPHY

The National Portrait Gallery and ICA, as well as many local arts centres, regularly stage exhibitions of photography and there are a number of courses and workshops. Contact your local arts centre, local council or the Photographers Gallery.

Photographers Gallery
5 & 8 Great Newport Street
London WC2
831 1722

RADIO

With the forthcoming deregulation of the airwaves, there are likely to be many more stations available to Londoners and many of the wavelengths below might change.

Wavelengths

BBC Radio 1 275m/1089khz or 285m/1063khz (MW) 88–91mhz (FM)
BBC Radio 2 330m/909khz or 433m/693khz (MW) 88–91mhz (FM)
BBC Radio 3 247m/1215khz (MW) 90–92.5mhz (FM)
BBC Radio 4 1500m/200khz (LW) 417m/720khz (MW) 92–95mhz (FM)
BBC World Service 463m/648khz (MW)
GLR (Greater London Radio) 206m/1458khz (MW)
Capital Radio 194m/1548khz (MW)
CFM (Capital) 95.8mhz (FM)
Capital Gold 194m/1548khz (MW)
LBC News Radio 261m/1152khz (MW) 97.3mhz (FM)
Radio Luxembourg 208m/1440khz (MW)

Pirates

City Radio 94.4mhz
Fresh FM 103.3mhz
JBC 104.3mhz
Kiss FM 94mhz

LWR 92.5mhz
Passion FM 90.6mhz
Sky 91.6mhz

Addresses

BBC External Services
Bush House
The Strand
London WC2 4PH
240 3456

BBC Radio
Broadcasting House
Portland Place
London W1A 1AA
580 4468

Capital Radio
Euston Tower

Euston Road
London NW1
388 1288

GLR
35a Marylebone High Street
London W1A 4LG
224 2424

LBC
Communications House
Gough Square
London EC4 4LP
353 1010

Publications

Arts and Radio Resource Directory (Greater London Arts).
Blue Book of British Broadcasting (Tellex Monitors).

WRITING

Pen International
c/o Africa Centre
38 King Street
London WC2
379 7939
*International membership
organisation for writers and
journalists organising meetings and
other activities.*

Society of Authors
84 Drayton Gardens
London SW10 9SB
373 6642

Writers Guild
430 Edgware Road
London W2
723 8074
Union for writers.

Publications

Writers' & Artists' Yearbook (A. & C. Black).
Book Writers' Handbook (Alison & Busby).
Magazine Writers' Handbook (Alison & Busby).
Writers' Guild of Great Britain Yearbook (Writers Guild).
Poetry Groups and Workshops in and Around London (Poetry
   Library).
NUJ Freelance Directory (National Industrial Council).
Publishers' Handbook (Grosvenor Press International).

BOOKSHOPS

Diana Stephenson's *Bookshops of London* (Lascelles) is an
excellent guide to London's retail outlets for new and secondhand books. It lists around 1,000 bookshops with indexes by
subject and by name of shop. Also fascinating is *The Bookshops
of London* by Martha Redding Pease (Junction Books).

LIBRARIES

Local libraries are underused and underfunded. They are a mine
of information on what is happening locally and across London,
local organisations, health, education and much more, not to
mention books! Borough council arts and entertainment or
recreation departments will provide a list of libraries in your
borough.

FUNDRAISING

Funding for the arts in London and across the country is suffering as a result of government cutbacks on public spending. More and more bodies and individuals are having to go in for personal fundraising or risk closure of venues or cancellation of projects. The following directories are designed to help in the search.

Publications

Corporate Donors Handbook (Directory of Social Change).
Directory of Grant-making Trusts (Directory of Social Change).
Educational Grants Directory (Directory of Social Change).
Guide to Company Giving (Directory of Social Change).
Guide to Grants for Individuals in Need (Directory of Social Change).
Guide to Major Trusts (Directory of Social Change).
London Grants Guide (Directory of Social Change).
Major Companies and their Charitable Giving (Directory of Social Change).
Sponsorship Yearbook (Hobson).

SPORT

Borough councils usually run quite a range of sporting facilities from sports fields and pitches to indoor facilities, swimming pools, and so on. Obviously the availability and cost of facilities varies according to the borough and sport is suffering like everything else from enforced cuts in local government spending. However, if you contact the recreation department at your borough council they will usually provide you with a list of facilities in your area. Some boroughs offer discount schemes for regular users of those facilities that are not gratis. Women only and children only schemes are also quite common, and some councils run special facilities for people with disabilities.

For general information on sports facilities in the capital contact:

Sports Council
16 Upper Woburn Place
London WC1H 0QP
388 1277

or

Sportsline
222 8000

For information on sport for people with disabilities, see Chapter 11: People With Disabilities.

Books

Sports Pages
Cambridge Circus Shopping Centre
102 Charing Cross Road
London WC2 0JG
240 9604
*The best sports bookshop in
London.*

2

CHILDREN AND YOUNG PEOPLE

The following chapter gives a fairly detailed description of many of the services available to children and young people in London.

The process of growing up often seems to involve problems at home, at school or college, at work or with friends. At these times, many young people feel that there is nowhere to turn for someone to talk to and no one to give advice if needed. In my experience, it is very important for children and young people to be able to feel that they can gain access to someone who can be relied on, and, should the pressures get too great, who has the training to help them resolve their problems to best effect.

Inevitably, the following sections give a greater amount of space to organisations that deal with people's problems. Clearly, young readers or their families will not always be experiencing difficulties, but the enormous range of organisations which exist make for an interesting read in themselves. Most areas are covered, be they advice, information or leisure.

If you do need to contact any of the organisations listed here, you should feel free to ask as many questions as you like about what exactly the place does, to see if the way they work suits you. If the place doesn't feel right for you, the organisation should be able to give you details of other places that can help you.

Gerry McManamon
Project Worker, Portobello Project

GENERAL INFORMATION

Children and young people in London often suffer more than most from the pressures of city life. The number of young homeless is rising by the week and the number of young unemployed remains unacceptably high. The physical abuse of children, sexual or otherwise, is a problem that continues to shock and sicken. Despite more publicity, greater public awareness and more reported cases, abuse continues and is likely to do so. Children of low-income families inevitably suffer as a result of inadequate child benefit provision and the number of children in care is astounding, especially when it becomes apparent that in some cases children go into care for no other reason than the lack of availability of suitable accommodation for their family.

The picture appears bleak but there are many local and national bodies, statutory and voluntary, attempting to make life better for young people and children. Furthermore, there is a vast range of facilities for sport, the arts and many other leisure activities both on a local and on a London-wide scale. This chapter is meant to be a guide for both adults and children. It outlines some of the problems as well as some of the facilities available to help children and their parents whether they are in need of counselling, advice or simply information on where to go for leisure, play and education.

NB   A useful first point of call for children, parents and young people on all matters relating to facilities and opportunities for children and young people is the Area Youth Office in your borough, the address and phone number for which is listed under the name of your borough in the phone book. They can tell you about centres, clubs, youth projects, advice centres, statutory and voluntary organisations. In matters relating to abuse, the local Social Services Department, NSPCC or other voluntary agencies should be able to offer assistance or advice.

PRE-TEENAGE/EARLY TEENAGE CHILDREN

London offers a remarkable range of activities for children. A useful book is *Kids' London* by Elizabeth Holt and Molly Perham (Pan Books). In the light of the latter's excellent coverage of children's leisure activities, I do not intend to cover the same ground. However, a selection of particular points of interest appears below.

Adventure Playgrounds

Either of the following can direct you to your local adventure playgrounds.

The London Adventure Playground Association
22 Underwood Road
London E1
377 0314

National Playing Fields Association
25 Ovington Square
London SW3
584 6445

Animals and Birds

Young Crusaders Against All Cruelty to Animals
Humane Education Centre
Avenue Lodge
Bounds Green Road
London N22
889 1595

Busy Bees
People's Dispensary for Sick Animals (PDSA)
South Street
Dorking
Surrey
Dorking 888291

RSPCA Junior Section
Causeway
Horsham
Sussex
Horsham 64181

Young Ornithologists Club
RSPB
The Lodge
Sandy
Bedforshire
Sandy 80551

Young Zoologists Club
c/o London Zoo or Whipsnade Zoo

Libraries and Books

Most local libraries have a children's section as well as information on local activities for children. Contact the local council for details of local libraries.

There are many children's bookshops in London, most of which are listed in Diana Stevenson's *Bookshops of London* (Lascelles). This useful little book also lists bookshops catering for children from ethnic minorities as well as non-sexist, non-racist books.

Bedtime Stories
245 8000

Federation of Children's Book Groups
Aptonfields
Houndslow Green

Barston, Near Dunmow
Essex
0731 820024
*Local branches organise meetings
to encourage children and parents
to read more. Occasional meetings
with writers to discuss their work.*

Letterbox Library
8 Bradbury Street
London N16 8JN
254 1640
*Non-sexist and multicultural
children's books by post.*

Library Association
45 East Hill
London SW18
870 9055
*A permanent reference library of
children's books.*

**Play Matters/The National Toy
  Libraries Association**
68 Churchway
London NW1 1LT
387 9592
*Toy libraries offering toys to
children of all ages as well as those
with disabilities or special needs.
Play Matters also liaises with
teachers and therapists as well as
statutory bodies, giving information
on choice of toys and organising
conferences and courses.*

Tapeworm Children's Cassettes
10 Barley Mow Passage
London W4 4PH
994 6477
*Cassettes of stories and music for
all ages.*

Playgroups

Pre-school Playgroups Association
61–63 King's Cross Road
London WC1Y 9LL
833 0991

Playschemes

Most councils run local playschemes, especially during the summer holidays. Contact the borough council Social Services Department for details.

Arts, Cinema, Theatre

Many theatres put on special shows for children and they should be contacted individually for information. Information can also be found in the listings magazines. The list below is not exhaustive by any means but it does give a number of theatres specifically aimed at children and other theatres offering regular children's shows.

Battersea Arts Centre
Old Town Hall
Lavender Hill
London SW11

223 2223
*Offers a range of shows, classes
and films for children.*

The Beck Theatre
Grange Road
Hayes
Middlesex UB3 2UE
561 8371
*Every Saturday afternoon the
Captain Crumble show offers
games, guests and prizes.*

Half Moon Theatre
213 Mile End Road
London E1
790 4000
*Saturday morning children's shows.
Also runs the Half Moon Young
People's Theatre, offering training
in dramatic and technical skills.*

Hoxton Hall Community Theatre
130 Hoxton Street
London N1
739 5431
*Children's activities include junior
drama, youth and junior clubs and
workshops and playgroups.*

ICA Children's Cinema
The Mall
London SW1
930 0493
*Regular premieres and runs of films
for children, a club for young
members who receive a regular
newsletter.*

The Little Angel Marionette Theatre
14 Dagmar Passage
Cross Street
London N1
226 1787
*The famous puppet theatre giving
shows every weekend and every
day during school holidays.*

Millfield Theatre
Silver Street
London N18
807 6680
*Special children's shows throughout
the year.*

Polka Children's Theatre
240 The Broadway
Wimbledon
London SW19
543 4888/0363
Shows every day Tues–Sat.

Puppet Theatre Barge
Little Venice
Blomfield Road
London W9
249 6876
*Floating marionette theatre using
hand-carved marionettes, shadow
puppets, lighting and original
music.*

Questor's Theatre
Mattock Lane
London W5
567 0011
*Runs regular drama groups for all
ages starting at age 5. Covers all
aspects of work in the theatre.*

St George's Theatre
Tufnell Park Road
London N7
607 1128
*Shakespeare's plays and
complementary workshops for
school audience and the public. An
introduction to Shakespeare and the
theatre for children (8–13) and
children's shows Saturday
afternoons for 3–11 year olds.*

See Saw Children's Theatre
Christ Church Hall
Finchley High Road
London N12
446 4864
*Professional acts for children every
Saturday morning.*

Unicorn Theatre for Children
Great Newport Street
London WC2
379 3280
*The oldest theatre for children and
the only one solely for children in
the West End.*

Museums

Most museums have something of interest for children or young people but there are three that are likely to be of particular interest.

**Bethnal Green Museum of
  Childhood**
Cambridge Heath Road
London E2
981 1171/980 3204
*Games, toys, dolls' houses, teddies,
magic lanterns, models and
children's fashion.*

**The London Toy and Model
  Museum**
21 Craven Hill
London W2
262 7905/9450

*An indoor and outdoor museum
housing a collection of model trains,
cars, planes, dolls, bears and so on.
Working garden railway and
gardens with boating pond.*

Pollock's Toy Museum
1 Scala Street
London W1
636 3452
*Includes a collection of old toy
theatres, dolls, teddies and folk toys
from all over the world.*

General

The London magazines *Time Out* and *City Limits* have extensive listings including information on activities suitable for children. Particularly useful is the Capital Radio magazine *London for Kids*, available from most large newsagents and some bookshops.

Artsline
388 2227/8
*Information and advice on arts and
entertainment for the disabled as
well as details of crèches.*

Children's London
246 8007
*Phoneline with recorded
information on activities for children
in London.*

Kidsline
222 8070
*Phone-in service which gives
information on children's events in
London: 4pm–6pm schooldays,
9am–4pm school holidays.*

National Portage Association
4 Clifton Road
Winchester, Hants, SO22 5BN
0962 60148
*In some boroughs a service is
available to bring educational toys
to the home. The NPA has details of
local schemes.*

**We Welcome Small Children
  National Campaign**
93a Belsize Lane
London NW3 5AY
586 3453
*Promotes the provision of good
facilities in public places, shops, etc.
for carers with small children.*

CHILDREN'S WELFARE AND CHILD ABUSE

A 1984 US study showed that in reported cases of sexual abuse 82 per cent of those abused were female and 96 per cent of offenders were male, also that 80 per cent of offenders were known to the abused child. Research by Childline showed that 97 per cent of all cases of sexual abuse take place in the victim's family circle. In cases of both sexual and other physical abuse, the natural father is responsible for 50 per cent of the cases of abuse against girls and 37 per cent of the cases against boys. Other research in Britain showed that 12 per cent of girls and 8 per cent of boys have been sexually abused by the age of 16 years. No social group is immune from the abuse of children.

Abuse can take many forms: sexual abuse, physical abuse, emotional abuse and neglect. Such abuse may be the result of any one or a combination of many causes. Tension in the parents' relationship, financial problems, failure of parents to understand their child's needs, social conditions may all be factors, quite apart from straightforward violent behaviour by one parent, most often the male.

Physical Abuse

Physical abuse is usually said to have occurred when a child is physically hurt, injured or killed. Injuries might include bruising, cuts or burns. Physical abuse includes giving a child poisonous substances, inappropriate drugs or alcohol.

Sexual Abuse

Sexual abuse is said to have occurred where a child, male or female, is sexually abused by adults. This may be by sexual intercourse, fondling, masturbation, oral sex, anal intercourse or exposure to pornographic material.

Neglect

Neglect is said to have taken place when parents have failed to meet the basic and essential needs of their children like food, clothes, warmth and medical care. This includes leaving children alone and unsupervised. Refusing to give, or simply failing to recognise the need for love and affection is considered to be emotional neglect. Of course, neglect can result from several causes. It might be wilful neglect, the product of nothing less than unforgivably selfish behaviour, or it might be involuntary neglect resulting from insufficient understanding of physical and emotional needs.

On the other hand, it can also be the result of social conditions. Low income, insufficient social security benefits, poor health facilities, all contribute to the inevitable neglect of children's real needs. The number of children seen begging in London's streets and tube stations is increasing. The evidence of one's own eyes is far stronger than abstract statistics, however frightening those statistics may be. Changes in social security benefit rules and the changes in NHS health provision demanded by the government have only served to make life more difficult for those with the fewest resources to combat their problems.

Emotional Abuse

Constant lack of love or affection, threats, verbal abuse, taunts and shouting can all lead to loss of a child's confidence or self-esteem so that they become nervous or withdrawn. This is classified as emotional abuse. It is worth noting, too, that the emotional effect of abuse can persist long into adulthood, and that organisations exist to help adults with problems relating to abuse suffered in childhood.

Fears and Responsibilities

Parents fear that if abuse is suspected, their child will be taken away from them immediately. Many cases of abuse go unreported for this reason. In fact only a minority of cases require the removal of a child from its home, although a child may occasionally be removed to an immediate place of safety. If after thorough investigations it is decided that it is in a child's best interests to take him/her into care, the local authority or the NSPCC will apply to the Juvenile Court for a care order. Only if a care order is granted can a child be taken into care, which may last until the child is 18 or 19. The Children Bill currently before Parliament will change certain aspects of these complex laws.

Other worries relate to social workers and medical examinations. Social workers have no right of entry to a home without a warrant and police presence. In the case of examinations, if an investigating officer believes such action is necessary the permission of the parent or guardian and if possible of the child is sought. If this is refused, permission can be granted through the courts. Doctors might give emergency treatment in exceptional circumstances.

Experts place great emphasis on understanding children's needs and the NSPCC campaign 'Putting Children First' and its associated booklet is aimed primarily at parents and guardians. Parents cannot be expected to meet all their children's needs unaided. Governments and councils must accept their share of the responsibility for children's well being as well as professionals, voluntary organisations and the parents themselves.

Most importantly, if you know or suspect that a child is being abused contact the NSPCC, the Social Services Department or the police at once. Social workers, health visitors, family doctors, teachers, school nurses and religious leaders can all help if you suspect that abuse is taking place.

Obviously avoiding abuse is preferable to dealing with its consequences. The NSPCC suggests a code for parents to discuss with their children, covering such things as making a child feel she/he will be believed; making sure a child is not alone if she/he is not with an adult; not allowing a child to go into a public lavatory unaccompanied; thorough checking of babysitters; always getting children to tell you who they are going to be with, where they are going and when they are going to be home; allowing children to decide who they wish to kiss and cuddle and impressing on them the importance of not talking to strangers.

For parents it is important to learn to recognise the signs of abuse. It is extremely difficult to diagnose but such things as apparent personality changes, recurrent medical problems, bedwetting, nightmares, and so on may be the signal that something is wrong. These issues and many others are dealt with in a free NSPCC leaflet, 'Protect Your Child'.

Organisations Active in the Field of Child Abuse

NSPCC (National Society for the Prevention of Cruelty to Children)
67 Saffron Hill
London EC1N 8RS
242 1626

The major national charity dealing with the prevention of child abuse. Around 50,000 cases per year are dealt with by the NSPCC. The society has around 60 local Child Protection Teams which carry out investigations into allegations of abuse and provide assessment and treatment services. They work together with Social Services Departments, Health and Education authorities and local organisations. A number of the teams also have Family Centres which provide additional therapeutic and preventive services through which it integrates the different aspects of its work, drawing together experienced staff, local resources and contacts and other professionals.

The society also runs a number of Family Care Centres, playgroups, mother and baby centres and drop-in centres. NSPCC's staff are fully trained social workers.

NSPCC offers consultancy to other childcare organisations both nationally and locally. The society has powers to take legal proceedings under the Children and Young Persons Act 1969, and works in association with, not as an alternative to, other welfare organisations, both statutory and voluntary. It offers a 24-hour advice line for parents, professionals and child abuse referrals, develops therapeutic approaches to the treatment of child abuse, works directly with abused children, and publishes research into child abuse and its treatment.

Childline
Addle Hill Entrance
Faraday Building
Queen Victoria Street
London EC4V 4BU
236 2380
Advice Line 0800 1111

> Dear Childline, please give my thanks to the man who answered the phone late last night. He listened to my problem and gave some advice. I am very grateful. Please don't ever let Childline close.

The above are the words of a child who wrote to Childline, reproduced in its first annual report. Childline's primary aim is to listen to children in distress, to offer them sympathy and support and to offer help if a child is in danger. Childline operates a free advice line (0800 1111) for children who have been abused or who have some other problem they wish to talk about. Eight hundred calls a day are taken although many more simply cannot be answered due to insufficient resources. Many of the children who call, often anonymously, go on to tell somebody else, such as a social worker, teacher or friend about their ordeals, more confident that they will be believed as a result of Childline's reassurance and advice.

Although most calls relate to some form of physical or sexual abuse, no problem is too large or small and calls are received on a range of topics such as parental drunkenness, drugs or divorce. A team of experienced volunteers and qualified counsellors offer advice or refer children to appropriate agencies.

Eighty per cent of those who contact Childline are girls. Eighty per cent of those calling about sexual abuse and 92 per cent of those calling about physical abuse are under 15 years of age. Two-thirds of callers have been suffering for more than a year, usually without telling anyone at all. Adults call Childline, too, many to talk about abuse they suffered as children.

Kidscape
82 Brook Street
London W1Y 1YG
493 9845

Formed in 1986, Kidscape provides information on teaching children how to deal with potentially dangerous situations such as sexual abuse. The Kidscape Programme is based upon a two-year project involving parents, teachers and children in selected schools across Britain. Many primary schools have taken on the programme which teaches children to trust their own feelings in sensing dangerous situations, how to differentiate between good and bad touching, to break rules if necessary to protect themselves and always to seek adult help.

SCOSAC (Standing Committee on Sexually Abused Children)
2nd Floor
Crown House
London Road
Morden,
Surrey, SM4 5DX
545 3428/9

A London-wide scheme to coordinate and integrate resources for dealing with child sexual abuse. Aims to assist people working in the community with children and develop policies for intervention at agency level that are 'child-centred'. Provides consultation, liaison and training. SCOSAC is open to application for membership from any interested childcare worker in the field. SCOSAC also offers a resource bank of books, audio-visual material, reading lists and general information.

Criminal Injuries Compensation
  Board
Russell Square House
Russell Square
London EC4
636 9501

First Key
Hartley House
Green Walk
London SE1
378 7441
*An information and consultancy
service for voluntary and statutory
agencies and professionals as well
as those preparing to or having just
left care. Works to enable those
leaving care to live independently
by providing suitable
accommodation.*

**In Support of Sexually Abused
    Children (ISOSAC)**
PO Box 526
London NW6

Incest Crisis Line
PO Box 32
Northolt, Middx
422 5100

Incest Sisters in Survival (ISIS)
23 Tunstall Road
London SW2
274 0412

Rape Crisis Centre
PO Box 69
London WC1X 9NJ
278 3956 (office)/837 1600 (24
hours)

Samaritans
*Twenty-four-hour listening and
befriending service. Numbers to call
in your area in Chapter 7: Health*

SOCA (Survivors of Child Abuse)
c/o Viking Community Centre
Radcliffe Way
Northolt
Middx UB5 6HW
842 2333

Survivors
c/o 38 Mount Pleasant
London WC1
833 3737
*For victims of male rape and sexual
abuse.*

Tavistock Clinic
120 Belsize Lane
London NW3
435 7111
*Three departments: adult,
adolescent, and child and family.
Deals both with those who have
been abused and abusers.*

Victim Support Schemes
17 Electric Lane
London SW9 8LA
737 2010
*Helps victims of all kinds of crime
with support and advice.*

Voice for the Child in Care
60 Carysfort Road
London N8
348 2588
*Aims to arrange for children in care
to have access to an independent
person and to improve professional
standards.*

Women's Therapy Centre
6 Manor Gardens
London N7
263 6200

Children's Refuges
The Children's Society (see general
addresses, below) can provide
details of refuges under their
control.

YOUTH HOMELESSNESS

As explained in Chapter 8: Housing, the scale of youth
homelessness is very hard to estimate with any accuracy other
than to say that it is massive. A recent estimate by Centrepoint
showed a figure of 50,000 people between the ages of 16 and 19

sleeping rough, in squats or on people's floors. The reasons for this are manifold, but it is widely accepted that the failure of governments to recognise and act upon the massive number of young people on the streets is largely responsible.

The majority of young people who find their way to one of the organisations listed below are confused, distressed, hungry and tired. In many cases they are new to London and have been attracted by a false image of glamour, or of job availability, both of which soon prove to be far from the truth. As Alone In London make clear in their literature, it is not unusual for the combination of fear, confusion and the lack of a place to stay to quickly lead to other problems related to drugs, alcohol, gambling, or any number of associated problems. Prostitution is an increasingly common resort for young women and to a lesser degree young men in need of cash, with all the associated dangers of violence, VD and AIDS.

In any town or city, young people living alone for the first time are often unprepared for the rigours of independent life. Finding a home is not easy to begin with but for young people leaving a family home in London or coming to London for the first time, the problems are exacerbated by difficulties arising from financial hardship, social security benefit cuts and poor work prospects, not to mention the problems which might have forced them to leave home in the first place.

The changes in social security benefit rules are likely to contribute still further to the rising level of homelessness among young people in London. Changes in rules for housing benefit and the new Social Fund under which young people are not prioritised are likely to mean that even those who have previously been able to live in bed and breakfast hotels will be unable to keep up their payments and will be faced with the threat of living and sleeping on the streets. The further decline in availability of cheap rented housing as a result of the 1988 Housing Act will only make things worse.

Making up a particularly large and vulnerable group of young homeless people are the thousands leaving care every year. At the age of 18 teenagers in care are no longer the responsibility of the state. When Social Security Secretary John Moore decided in his wisdom that young people might use the benefits system to avoid employment or training schemes, he changed existing regulations so that school leavers could only claim reduced benefit – enough to pay for living expenses but not to cover board and lodging, which is supposedly the responsibility of the parents.

For young people living happily in the family home, that did not mean immediate homelessness, even if it did mean less money coming into the house. However, for those young people not living at home such as those coming out of care, the result of the new legislation was that many could simply no longer afford to pay their rent and have money to live on. In May 1989, Suzie Hayman in *The Guardian* quoted two examples of how the changes have affected individual young people.

John is 17 and in the first year of YTS. Up to now social services have topped up his YTS allowance so he could pay his landlady £55 a week for room and meals, leaving £10.30 a week for clothes, bus fares, entertainment and such luxuries as soap and toothpaste.

Michelle, 18, lives in a bed and breakfast hostel. She too is a YTS trainee and was left with £20.30 after paying her landlady, to buy lunch and evening meals and for other living expenses.

With a further set of changes just made, Michelle's money has gone down to £14.13 each week and John's to £2.65 – not even enough to pay his fares to and from work. For them there is no happy family – Michelle's stepfather has thrown her out and John has suffered abuse in his family.

Clearly, the future ability of these young people to pay rent is in doubt. To make matters worse, the government blocked attempts to amend the Children Bill to allow for such eventualities as those mentioned above. They said that such legislation came within the boundaries of a social security bill and yet when such a bill came up in April 1989, an amendment allowing anyone under 25 not able to live at home to receive full adult benefit was rejected by the government! See also Chapter 8: Housing.

Organisations Active in the Field of Youth Homelessness

Alone in London Service
West Lodge
190 Euston Road
London NW1
387 6184

Assists young single homeless by offering advice, counselling and accommodation. Runs an advice centre, drop-in service and telephone inquiry service for young

*people up to the age of 21.
Maintains a hostel and a shared
house. Works to help former ALS
residents find long-term
accommodation.*

Centrepoint Soho
33 Long Acre
London WC2
379 3466
*Aims to prevent youth
homelessness and counteract its
effects. Runs an emergency
nightshelter for under-19s and a
long-stay hostel. Lets flats and
bedsits at fair rents, works to
improve public awareness of the
problem of youth homelessness.*

Girls Alone Project
76 Oakley Square
Camden
London NW1
387 7801
*Runs a long-stay hostel for 16–19-
year-old single homeless women.
Women are referred by a social
work agency.*

Leaving Home Project
5 Egmont House
116 Shaftesbury Avenue
London W1
437 2068
Works to improve public awareness,

*especially among young people, of
the problems of housing and
homelessness and the process of
leaving home. Offers a library and
resource service for teachers, youth
workers, etc.*

Melting Pot Foundation
361 Clapham Road
London SW9
274 9566
*Runs a hostel for young black
people in the Clapham area and
gives support and advice on
housing problems.*

Message Home
799 7662
*A service advertised in tube stations
which contacts families of people
who have left home to let them
know they are all right, without
giving any information other than
that offered by the person who has
contacted them.*

Piccadilly Advice Centre
100 Shaftesbury Avenue
London W1
*Free confidential advice and
information service to young people
who are new to London or
homeless for some other reason.
Information, training and speakers
all available.*

EMPLOYMENT

It is not a good idea to come to London unless you know you
have somewhere to stay while you look for work. It is all too easy
to end up sleeping rough and fall into the vicious circle of not
having enough money to put a deposit on somewhere to live and
not being able to find a job if you have no home address, no
phone, no money, no food and hardly any clothes. The rise in
unemployment in the 1980s has affected young people in
particular. The national figure for unemployment among the
under-20s in 1988, before under-18s were removed from the
unemployment statistics, was more than 290,000, that is, 40,000
more than in 1977. This figure is despite the vast increase in

young people 'hidden' from the statistics by embarking on government training schemes or feeling compelled to continue in full-time education. Four hundred thousand were on YTS schemes in 1988.

Over the same period, benefit entitlements have decreased and opportunities for young people are likely to remain at a premium. In January 1989, the unemployment figure for under-25s in Greater London (not including 16 and 17 year olds) was 62,840.

Careers Advice

The local careers office can be traced either from the phone book (under the name of the borough) or through the local Job Centre or educational establishment. Unemployment projects can be found in most boroughs and can be contacted through your Area Youth Office. The Job Centre will inform you of official training schemes and information on jobs available in your area.

London Employment Training
224–236 Walworth Road
London SE17
701 6329

Youthaid
9 Poland Street
London W1
439 8523
Researches into youth unemployment and the associated problems. Campaigns for its alleviation and reduction and publishes material on the subject to increase awareness of its severity.

Voluntary Work

For information on volunteer work in your area, contact a Citizens Advice Bureau, Law Centre or other advice agency (see Appendix), or

Community Service Volunteers
237 Pentonville Road
London N1
278 6601
Places young people in full-time volunteer posts for up to a year in the social services, conservation and the local media. Board, lodging and pocket money is provided. Training courses are also arranged.

Volunteer Centre
29 Lower King's Road
Berkhamsted
Herts HP4 2AB
0442 73311

GENERAL ADVICE AND COUNSELLING
FOR YOUNG PEOPLE

As mentioned elsewhere in this book, general advice on all kinds of subjects can always be obtained from the local Citizens Advice Bureau, Law Centre or other independent advice centre (see Appendix). However, there are other advice agencies aimed specifically at young people's general problems and at providing a free and reliable counselling and advice service.

Acorn Youth Information Centre
55 High Street
Acton
London W3
992 8182
Drop-in centre offering counselling, information and advice on a wide range of matters for 12–25 year olds.

Apex Trust Wandsworth
168–170 Battersea Park Road
London SW11 4ND
627 3726/3882
Counselling and information, specialising in job-related advice and training for over 16s.

Basement Youth Project
227 Earls Court Road
London SW5
373 2335
Advice and counselling for 16–25 year olds, also has a well-women clinic and a needle exchange for advice on drug abuse and AIDS/HIV and provision of clean needles.

Brent Consultation Centre
Johnston House
51 Winchester Avenue
London NW6 7TT
328 0918
Advice and counselling on all emotional problems for 16–23 year olds.

Bromley Y
17 Ethelbert Road
Bromley,
Kent, BR1
464 9033/4
Individual counselling for young people (14–25) and parents. Also has evening group meetings.

Brook Advisory Centre
233 Tottenham Court Road
London W1P 9AE
323 1522
Free contraceptives and counselling for young people about sexual and emotional problems.

Capital Radio Helpline
PO Box 194, Euston Road
London NW1
388 7575
Open to all ages for advice and assistance on any subject.

Central Wandsworth Youth Advisory Service
97 East Hill
London SW18 2QD
870 5818/870 6574
Advice, counselling and information for 15–23 year olds. Also free pregnancy testing.

Chelsea Pastoral Foundation
155a Kings Road
London SW3
351 0839
Counselling for 18–25 year olds for individuals or, if appropriate, small groups.

Contact a Family
16 Strutton Ground
London SW1
222 2211
Telephone line and network of self-help groups for children with special needs.

Croydon Youth Counselling Service
132 Church Street
Croydon, CR0 1RF
680 0404
For 14–25 year olds. Individual and group counselling.

Friends of the Children Society
9 Priory Close
London E18 2QT
504 4644
An organisation dedicated to helping children in need of help or a friend. Works with poor and needy children, assesses needs, provides clothing, food, activities.

Just Ask
112 Great Russell Street
London WC1
636 4308
Counselling, information and advice. Works especially with young, unemployed or low-waged people. No age limit.

Kings Corner Project
92 Central Street
London EC1V 8AJ
253 6776
Counselling for 16–25 year olds on any personal problem.

Link
Fountains Mill
81–82 High Street
Uxbridge, Middx, UB8 1JR
0895 38884
Counselling, information and advice for young people in Hillingdon (14–25).

London Youth Advisory Centre
26 Prince of Wales Road
London NW5
267 4792
A counselling, therapy and information service for young people aged 12–25. Deals with all problems affecting young people, especially contraception and pregnancy, emotional, sexual and psychological problems.

Nafsiyat
278 Seven Sisters Road
Finsbury Park
London N4 2HY
263 4130
Therapeutic help for individuals, families and young people with psychiatric or emotional problems. Offers specialist help to people from ethnic and cultural minorities.

New Horizon
1 Macklin Street
London WC1
242 0010/242 2238
Daytime youth centre for the under 21s. Also an information centre for DSS and homelessness related issues.

Newham Young People's Counselling Service
252 Katherine Road
London E7
552 5171
For 14–25 year olds in Newham.

Off Centre – Hackney Young People's Counselling Service
25 Hackney Grove
London E8
985 8566/986 4016
Advice on any problem for 13–25 year olds.

Open Door – Hornsey Young People's Consultation Service
12 Middle Lane
Crouch End
London N8
348 5947/6235
Psychotherapeutic help for 13–25 year olds. Negotiable fee.

Portobello Project
49–51 Porchester Road
London W2
221 4413
Information and informal advice service for young people (16–25) on areas including education, work, training, social security, accommodation, etc. Also runs

short courses. Produces particularly useful booklets on counselling services and accommodation and runs a mobile information service.

Rainer Foundation
227–239 Tooley Street
London SE1
403 4434
Working with young people who suffer disadvantage and discrimination. Working through community and residential projects such as centres for young women at risk of reception into care, intermediate treatment projects for young men at risk of being taken into custody; housing, resettlement and employment training for young homeless people or young people leaving care or custody.

Samaritans (Central London)
47 Marshall Street
London W11
439 2224
Twenty-four-hour service for all ages providing help and support in crisis situations. See Chapter 7: Health, for London numbers.

Soho Project
142 Charing Cross Road
London WC2 0LB
836 8121/240 1569
Information, help and advice especially on accommodation, social security, legal and medical problems. For 16–25 year olds.

Streetwise Youth
c/o Flat 3b
Langham Mansions
Earl's Court Square
London SW5
373 8860
Aims to face the problem of prostitution as it affects young people and to create a support service. Liaises with and represents young people to the police, probation service, courts and parents.

Teenage Information Network
102 Harper Row
London SE1
403 2444
Information and advice especially on benefits and accommodation. Also counselling on personal problems (13–25s).

TWO-E
2E South Hall
Edmonton
London N9 0TN
807 0637
General advice centre for young people up to the age of 28.

Under-21
Chestnuts House
398 Hoe Street
Walthamstow
London E17
509 1219
Counselling information and help in all problems. Free pregnancy testing.

Unity Care
112 Palace Gardens Terrace
London W8 4R6
221 1316
Counselling and advice for all ages.

Upstairs Project
182 Hammersmith Road
London W6
741 3335
Counselling, advice and outings for young people up to 25.

Walk-In Centre
42 Turnpike Lane
London N8
888 3138
Counselling and general information for all young people.

Welcare (Westminster Branch)
22 Mozart Street
London W10
960 4654
Individual counselling and information for 14–25 year olds in the Westminster area.

Women's Therapy Centre
8 Manor Gardens
London N7 6LA
263 6200
*Advice and counselling for girls and
young women, mainly 16–21.
Special groups for young women,
single mothers, Asian girls, incest
survivors and lesbians.*

YMCA
640 Forest Road
London E17
520 5599
*Programmes include vocational
training, drug and alcohol
education, counselling, health and
fitness and recreation.*

Young People's Counselling Service
Tavistock Clinic
120 Belsize Lane
London NW3 5BA
435 7111 ext 337
*Counselling and advice for 16–30
year olds.*

Youth Aid – The Hearsay Centre
17 Brownhill Road
London SE6 2H6
697 2152/7435
*Information and counselling for
14–25 year olds. Specialises in
employment and benefit related
advice.*

CHILDREN'S AND YOUNG PEOPLE'S RIGHTS

Children's rights have moved more into the public domain in recent years as a result of such events as the Cleveland Child Abuse Inquiry, the introduction of the Children Bill in Parliament, changes in the social security system and the abolition of the ILEA. Legal rights are a minefield of complex rules and regulations, any of which can be discussed with one of the organisations mentioned below.

However, it makes interesting and sometimes amusing reading to look over the official age regulations for many of the day to day aspects of the lives of young people. A selection appears below (with thanks to the Children's Legal Centre).

At the age of 5, you are of 'compulsory school age', can see a 'U' or 'PG' film unaccompanied, must pay child's fares on public transport and can consume alcohol in private!

At 7 you can open a National Savings Bank or Trustee Savings Bank account.

At 10 you can be convicted of a criminal offence, be strip searched by police and have an attendance centre order placed on you if you commit an imprisonable offence.

At 12 you can buy a pet!

At 13 you can get a part-time job as long as you do not work more than two hours on a school day or Sunday.

At 14 you can go into a pub but cannot buy alcohol; possess a shotgun or air weapon; males can be convicted of rape, assault with intent to commit rape and unlawful sexual intercourse and sentenced to custody in a detention centre.

At 15 you can be given youth custody if you commit an imprisonable offence, and can see a '15' film.

At 16 you can probably leave home without parents' consent, a young woman can consent to sexual intercourse (there is no specific law making lesbianism illegal but if one partner is under 16 the other can technically be charged with indecent assault), can marry with parental consent, can in some cases be granted tenancy of a flat by a housing association or local authority, leave school, work full time, claim Income Support, get a National Insurance Number, join most trade unions, apply for your own passport, join the armed forces (boys only) with parental consent, buy cigarettes and tobacco, drink beer, cider or wine with a meal in a restaurant, buy liqueur chocolates, buy fireworks, must pay full fare on public transport and prescription charges unless exempt for some reason, can enter or live in a brothel and sell scrap metal.

At 17 you can be sent to prison, can no longer be governed by a care order, can buy any firearm, hold a licence to drive most vehicles apart from HGVs, can join the armed forces (women) with parental consent and can become a street trader.

At 18 you reach the age of majority and are an adult in the eyes of the law, you can vote, serve on a jury, sign contracts, open a bank account other than those mentioned earlier, change your name, make a will, see an '18' film, buy and drink alcohol in a bar, bet in a betting shop, be tattooed or take part in public demonstrations of hypnotism. You also have to pay for dental treatment unless in full-time education or are pregnant or are exempt for some other reason.

At 19 you cease to be automatically entitled to full-time education.

At 21 a man may consent to a homosexual act in private, men and women can become an MP or local councillor and apply for a licence to sell alcohol.

ADDRESSES

General

Children's Legal Centre
20 Compton Terrace
London N1
359 6251
*An independent organisation
aiming to clarify, develop and
improve the laws and policies
affecting children and young
people. Free advice for parents,
children and young people by
phone or letter, runs courses,
initiates research and responds to
all policies and proposals affecting*
*children. (The National Association
of Young People in Care is also
based at this address, tel. 226 7102.)*

Justice for Children
35 Wellington Street
London WC2 7BN
836 5917
*A group campaigning for a change
in the law relating to children in
England and Wales and pressing for
the creation of a family court to deal
with civil matters relating to
children and parents.*

Gay and Lesbian

Gay Teenage Group
Council for Voluntary Services
26 Bedford Square
London WC1B 3HU
636 4066
*Keeps lists of voluntary services on
a regional level. See Chapter 9:
Lesbians and Gay Men, for more
information.*

Lesbian and Gay Youth Movement
BM GYM
London WC1N 3XX
*Legal, housing and health advice,
penfriend scheme, campaigns,
telephone advice service, social
meetings and an annual festival.*

Lesbian Line
BM Box
1514
London WC1V 6XX
251 6911
*Advice and counselling for all
lesbians by phone.*

London Friend
86 Caledonian Road
London N1
837 3337 (gay men)
837 2782 (lesbians)
*Counselling and befriending service
for all gays and lesbians.*

**London Lesbian and Gay
  Switchboard**
BM Switchboard
London WC1N 3XX
837 7324

North London Line Project
c/o Old School Building
Highbury Station Road
London N1 1SE
359 2884
*One to one counselling for young
lesbians and gay men, a support
group for young gay men with AIDS
or HIV, a group for young gay men
who have been sexually abused and
the Incest Survivors Group for
young lesbian women.*

**Project for Advice Counselling and
  Education (PACE)**
c/o London Lesbian and Gay Centre
67–69 Cowcross Street
London EC1P 6BP
251 2689
*Counselling, information and advice
for young gay people.*

Youth Clubs

The abolition of the ILEA has left youth clubs in confusion with regard to future funding. With responsibility shifting to local authorities, themselves short of disposable funds, it would be no surprise if many youth clubs were forced out of existence purely as a result of a lack of money. The London Union of Youth Clubs, the major organising body for youth clubs in the Greater London area, is itself threatened by the ILEA's abolition. Fundraising will become a time-consuming priority for the LUYC as for many other voluntary groups.

The London Union of Youth Clubs
64 Camberwell Road
London SE5
701 6366

A London-wide association of more than 600 clubs, 5,000 workers and volunteers and 80,000 young Londoners. Primarily a mixed clubs/groups organisation with a particular commitment to work with girls and young women, and disadvantaged groups of young people. Provides field officers to visit and work with local groups, training and introduction to youth work, an arts bus visiting local groups to introduce young people to many forms of art and craft, a girls' work unit offering support and advice to youth workers in the field of working with young women, work on racial equality and work with young people with disabilities. LUYC also works with colleges to run London Employment Training, organising courses on everything from CV preparation and interview skills, to bookkeeping and massage.

Association of Combined Youth Clubs
579 Battersea Park Road
London SW11
228 9143

Supports, services, initiates and develops junior and youth groups within their neighbourhood.

Travel and Adventure

Children's Country Holidays Fund
1 York Street
Baker Street
London W1H 1PZ
935 8371/3/4

To give 5–13 year olds the opportunity of enjoying holidays they would otherwise not have access to.

Country Wings
Inter-Action Group
15 Wilkin Street
London NW5
267 9421
Helps organise groups to visit the countryside.

Drake Fellowship
Broomhouse Dock
Broomhouse Lane
London SW6
736 2015
Courses and trips for hill walking, camping, navigation, climbing, water skills and skiing.

Duke of Edinburgh Award Scheme
5 Prince of Wales Terrace
London W8
937 5205
Offers a programme of activities for 14–25 year olds with the prospect of obtaining an award. Operated in schools, youth organisations, firms and special centres.

Family Holiday Association
Hertford Lodge
East End Road
Finchley
London N3 3QE
349 4044

Provides holiday grants for those families unable to afford them, who have been recommended by social work agencies.

Forest School Camps
110 Burbage Road
London SE24
274 7566
Organises and runs standing camps and mobile activities for 6–17 year olds including those with physical or mental disability.

Student Travel Association (STA)
52 Grosvenor Gardens
London SW1
730 3402
Usually the best place to go for information on the cheapest way to travel in Britain, Europe and around the world for young people.

Youth Hostels Association
Trevelyan House
St Albans
Herts AL1 2DY
0727 55215
Also has a shop in Southampton Street, WC2 (Covent Garden) where you can join the YHA and buy its publications.

Miscellaneous

Association for Christian Youth Work
113 Loveday Road
London W13
567 7718

Association for Jewish Youth
50 Lindley Street
London E1
790 6407

Barnado's
Barkingside
Essex, IG6 1QG
550 8822
Providing residential and non-residential care and treatment

for all children in need but especially for the physically or mentally handicapped or emotionally disturbed. Runs day-care centres, homes and residential schools for children with special needs, community homes, hostels, playgroups, playbuses, fostering, adoption, intermediate treatment and holiday schemes.

British Youth Council
57 Chalton Street
London NW1
387 7559
A major forum for young people to

put their views to government, active in political education and many youth projects, both national and international.

Child Poverty Action Group (CPAG)
4th Floor, 1–5 Bath Street
London EC1V 9PY
253 3406
A campaigning organisation prominent in the fight against family poverty. Publicises availability of benefits, advises the advisors on changes in social security rules; draws attention to the needs of children in particular and the ways in which they are affected by poverty.

The Children's Society
Edward Rudolf House
Margery Street
London WC1
837 4299
Provides a range of projects to help children in need and publishes papers on related issues.

National Children's Bureau
8 Wakley Street
London EC1V 7QE
278 9441
An interdisciplinary organisation concerned with children's needs in all areas of society. Works with local

authorities, professional associations, voluntary bodies, universities and other educational institutions and individuals.

National Children's Home
85 Highbury Park
London N5 1UD
226 2033
A Christian-based voluntary child-care organisation working with local authorities and with responsibility for over 7,000 children in various forms of care. Also runs the Family Network, a free advice line for families. Phone the above number for details.

Opus (Organisations for Parents Under Stress)
106 Godstone Road
Whyteleafe
Surrey CR3 0EB
645 0469
An umbrella organisation of self-help groups for parents, e.g. Parents Anonymous, Parents Helpline, Parents Lifeline.

Save the Children Fund
Head Office
Mary Datchelor House
Grove Lane
London SE5 8RD
703 5400

Scouts, Guides and Boys Clubs

Boys Brigade
1 King's Terrace
Galena Road
London W12
741 4001

Girls Brigade
Girls Brigade House
Foxhall Road
Didcot
Oxon, OX11 7QB
0235 510 425

National Association of Boys Clubs
369 Kennington Lane
London SE11
793 0787

Scout Association
Baden-Powell House
Queen's Gate
London SW7
584 7030

Girl Guide Association
17–19 Buckingham Palace Road
London SW1W 0PT
834 6242

3

CITIZENS' RIGHTS

People who are unaware of their rights cannot claim them. This has two consequences: first, the unclaimed rights tend to be lost over a period of time; second, individuals suffer injustice.

It is particularly important in modern Britain to be aware of one's rights because they are in danger of being lost, not merely from unawareness on the part of individuals but also from a direct attack by government legislation. In the last ten years there has been a great increase in police powers, restrictions on TV and radio reporting of events in Northern Ireland, increased secrecy and censorship of the press in the name of national security, ever more interference in the internal affairs of trade unions, the creation of a climate of intolerance by legislation against lesbians and gay men, and the tightening of immigration laws and the right of asylum.

Further threats to our rights are on the horizon because of the privacy implications of the Poll Tax, the rights given to landlords under the Housing Act of 1988, electronic tagging of offenders and restrictions on the right to trial by jury.

The fundamental problem is that the government refuses to see that a tough law and order programme does not remove the difficulties it tries to cure. At best it might suppress some of the symptoms but, because the problems remain, there is an endless piling up of more and more repressive legislation. This tide can be reversed only by political campaigns but, while they are being conducted, the best defence for any individual is to have an outline of his or her rights and a knowledge of those organisations which can provide further advice and assistance. This chapter is not intended to be comprehensive; it is more a series of signposts; but it is hoped that it will point anyone who needs help in the right direction.

Malcolm Hurwitt
Chair of the Civil Liberties Trust;
Executive Member and Former Chair of the National Council
for Civil Liberties (Liberty)

DIMINISHING RIGHTS

Britain does not have a written constitution or modern Bill of Rights. British law is made up of statutes and common law created by judges and provides for very few positive rights.

Attacks upon citizens' rights and civil liberties in Britain and particularly in London have reached a new peak. The list of restricted freedoms is growing, seemingly by the week, and makes depressing reading, symbolising as it does the general atmosphere of authoritarian centralisation that has been the hallmark of Thatcherism since 1979: restrictions on TV and radio freedom such as the ban on interviews with those defined by the government as terrorists and their supporters in Northern Ireland; greater public secrecy and censorship in the name of national security, such as the *Spycatcher* affair; reduced freedom of information after the introduction of the new Official Secrets Act; increased provision for detention without charge; reductions in the right to trial by jury; longer prison sentences and fewer alternatives to prison for minor offences; internal detention without trial under the Prevention of Terrorism Act, the introduction of 'Clause 28', restricting the right of lesbians and gay men to promote their culture; discrimination against immigrants and tightening of immigration laws and the right to asylum; wider police powers at demonstrations in the wake of the recent Public Order Act; restrictions on trade unions' rights to strike, not to mention continuing discrimination against a whole range of minority groups.

The threat to the right of women to choose when and whether to have an abortion was beaten back only after massive opposition to the Alton Bill, and an amendment to the Embryo Research Bill threatens once again to reduce abortion time limits.

In a whole range of other areas, too, rights have been threatened. The introduction of the Poll Tax implies a number of potential infringements of privacy and other rights. There are also potential infringements of privacy in relation to the right of potential landlords to inspect housing records under the 1988 Housing Act. The right to a free education has been diminished as a result of changes in grant funding for students and the initiation of student loans, not to mention the abolition of the ILEA, following in the wake of the disappearance of the GLC, meaning that for all its deficiencies, there is no longer an elected London-wide body to coordinate education policy and arrangements. Threats to the NHS pose a danger to the right of every individual to free medical treatment.

The rights of Londoners have gradually diminished over the last ten years to a point where they no longer have any real say in the way their community is run. At least, they have no statutory say; local voluntary and self-help groups abound, although funding is scarce, but even these organisations are constrained by an ever more complex system of rules and regulations.

Borough Councils, too, are having previous powers removed. The higher spending councils who had tried to develop services under the GLC, especially services aimed at minority groups, tend to be the ones who are rate-capped by central government.

The abolition of the GLC and ILEA has left a confusing range of bodies with little or no public accountability. Borough Councils have had to take on many responsibilities they can ill afford, especially with resources from central government being restricted. There are London-wide voluntary committees such as the London Boroughs Joint Ecology Committee, but local authorities are not obliged to take part. Control is moving more and more towards central government. Lines of communication and responsibility are at best blurred and at worst non-existent.

The lack of an elected London-wide body to coordinate policy is clearly missed in areas such as transport (see also Chapter 14: Transport and Chapter 6: Green London). There is often a clear lack of coordination between boroughs, despite, or perhaps because of, the existence of alternative associations for Labour and Tory boroughs (the Association of London Authorities and the London Boroughs Association respectively).

This has a knock-on effect, too. Namely that the quality of life in London is degenerating at the same time as the network for protecting rights and conditions of life is falling apart. Means testing as a form of limiting rights to services is itself becoming a threat to individual well-being. (The rights of children and young people, women, ethnic minorities, people with disabilities, and elderly people are dealt with in the relevant chapters.)

In most cases, the National Council for Civil Liberties (NCCL) or an advice agency such as a Citizens Advice Bureau (CAB) or Law Centre (see Appendix) – who are themselves threatened by drastic cuts if the Local Government and Housing Bill goes ahead in its present form – can offer advice on rights and civil liberty. Clause 28 of the bill will change the way in which total allowable expenditure by local councils is calculated. In London alone advice centres like the CAB could have their funding cut by as much as 60 per cent.

National Council for Civil Liberties (Liberty)
21 Tabard Street
London SE1 6BP
403 3888

THE POLICE

Being fully aware of your rights and being able to state them calmly may prevent their abuse. The following information draws on a booklet published by the London Borough of Brent.

If you are stopped by the police it is best to be polite. Swearing, shouting or threatening might be considered an offence for which you could be arrested. It is best to answer questions like 'What is your name?' and 'Where do you live?' Never give a false name or address. You do not have to answer questions. You can go on your way unless the police want to search or arrest you. If the police keep asking questions you are within your rights to say, 'I'm not saying any more until I've had legal advice.'

The police can search you if they have reasonable grounds to suspect you are in possession of stolen goods, an offensive weapon or things which might be used for a burglary or another crime. Ask why the police want to search you. They must tell you before searching you.

The police can search you in the street but can only ask you to take off your jacket, coat and gloves. You do not have to take off other clothing unless they take you out of public view and unless the police officer doing the search is the same sex as you. The police must make a written record of any search. They have to give you a copy if you ask, so do ask for one. They do not have to give it on the spot.

If the police ask you to 'accompany them to the station' ask if you are being arrested, and if so, what for.

The police are allowed to use reasonable force if necessary if they are arresting you and taking you to the police station. Note the number of the officer making the arrest, so that a check can be made if and when evidence is given in court. Identification numbers are worn on the shoulders. You do not have to go to the station unless you are under arrest. Otherwise you may go if you wish and leave voluntarily at any time. If you are not under arrest you cannot be strip searched, photographed, fingerprinted or interfered with in any way without your consent.

Even if arrested you do not have to answer questions or write or sign a statement.

If you are taken to a police station the police may search you and take your possessions if they have good reason. Ask what the reason is and ask to keep your watch and a pen and paper to note numbers of officers involved and any other details of what happens to you.

You have the right to contact a solicitor and phone your family or a friend. You cannot be detained for more than twenty-four hours at a time unless the offence is very serious such as murder or rape. If they wish to continue holding you after twenty-four hours you must be taken before a court. In certain circumstances you can be held for longer if you have been charged with an offence.

The police can fingerprint you without your consent if you have been arrested, and may use force. They can photograph you too but cannot use force to do this.

Police have the right to strip search you for concealed objects which could be used to cause injury or to escape, or for things which may be evidence of an offence. If they want to carry out a strip search, ask why. You may only be strip searched by an officer of the same sex as you. (Strip searching has frequently been abused by police as a method of intimidation, for example against women peace protesters.)

Your mouth, anus, vagina, nose and ears may be searched either for class A drugs (heroin, cocaine, LSD but not cannabis) or anything which could be used to cause injury. A body search for drugs must be carried out by a doctor or nurse. A body search for other items can be carried out by an officer of the same sex as you if no doctor or nurse is available.

Samples of blood or semen can only be taken by a doctor or nurse and only with your written consent.

You have a right to see a solicitor, so ask to see one. Access can only be delayed in certain special circumstances. If you do not have your own solicitor, ask for the Duty Solicitor, a free service which will provide you with a solicitor at any time. The police have to keep ringing until contact is made.

On release, write down everything that has happened as soon as possible. Write down when, where, how, and why you were arrested and who arrested you. Write down all details of searches, questioning, fingerprinting, access to a solicitor and the times and identification numbers of officers involved.

Note for people under the age of 17: if you are under 17 you can only be interviewed at school if it is unavoidable. Tell police and teachers you want legal advice before being interviewed and ask them to contact your parent or guardian or social worker. Never admit guilt or accept a caution without legal advice. The police cannot interview a pupil at school unless the headteacher is also present.

At a police station, if you are under 17 you cannot be interviewed or asked for a written statement unless a parent, guardian or social worker is present.

If you are under 17 the police may want to issue a caution – a formal warning which is supposed to be given in the presence of a parent or guardian. Do not accept a caution as an easy way out, as this will be taken as admission of guilt.

Making a Complaint Against the Police

If you wish to make a complaint against the police, such as for assault, abuse, unfair treatment, etc., you can make an official police complaint, which will usually be taken up by the official Police Complaints Authority. In certain cases, a civil case may be brought by an individual against the police or an individual police officer.

If you wish to make a complaint, try to have all the following information, as recommended in the NCCL's book, *Civil Liberty* (Penguin).

1 The identity of the officers concerned, their numbers and the registration number of any vehicle concerned.
2 Date, time and place of the incident.
3 Witnesses' names and addresses.
4 Your own record of what happened, written as soon as possible afterwards.
5 If any injury occurred, obtain a medical examination as soon as possible, and photographs if the injury is visible.

You may wish to get legal advice from a CAB, Law Centre or other independent advice centre in your area before starting a complaints procedure (see Appendix).

Release
169 Commercial Road
London E1 6BW
693 8654
Twenty-four-hour legal and drugs advice. Produces a useful 'Rights of Arrest' card, available on request.

THE COURTS

Depending on income or savings, it may be possible for an individual wishing to take someone to court to receive free legal advice under the 'green form scheme' from a solicitor. Advice should always be sought before starting proceedings. You may also be eligible for Legal Aid to cover legal representation in court. Some solicitors operate a £5 fixed fee interview which gives you a one-off thirty-minute consultation to get advice about your problem.

Law Centres, CABs or other independent advice centres in your area may also be able to help. These people will also tell you whether your particular case will be heard by a county court, magistrates court or other tribunal such as an industrial tribunal which deals with discrimination in employment.

THE RIGHTS OF PRISONERS

Prisoners have two basic rights: access to the courts and respect for bodily integrity (i.e. not to be assaulted or medically treated against one's will). Certain rights to food, clothing and exercise also exist under the Prison Act 1952 and Prison Rules. Complaints can be made through the prison governor, or using an outside organisation, although letters from prisoners can be censored.

NACRO (National Association for the Care and Resettlement of Offenders)
169 Clapham Road
London SW9
582 6500
Advice, information, support, research.

Howard League for Penal Reform
322 Kennington Park Road
London SE11 4PP
735 3317

Inquest
Ground Floor
Alexandra House
330 Seven Sisters Road
London N4 2PJ
802 7430
Monitors deaths in custody.

Prison Department
Home Office
Eccleston Square
London SW1H 9AT
273 3000

Prison Reform Trust
59 Caledonian Road
London N1 9BU
278 9815

Prisoners' Wives and Families Society
254 Caledonian Road
London N1 0NJ
278 3981

Prisoners' Wives Service
51 Borough High Street
London SE1 1NB
403 4091

PROP (National Prisoners' Movement)
c/o BM PROP
London WC1N 3XX
542 3744

Women in Prison
25t Horsell Road
London N5 1XL
607 3353

Women Prisoners' Resource Centre
1 Thorpe Close
London W10
968 3121
Advice and information for women in prison or after release.

LEGAL AID

If you have a legal problem, a solicitor can advise you and if you are entitled to Legal Aid, this need not be expensive. With Legal Aid, the government pays part or all of your solicitor's bill. Over 50 per cent of those on Legal Aid do not pay anything at all.

There are three kinds of Legal Aid:

1 Legal Advice and Assistance ('the Green Form Scheme'). Covers any sort of help you may need from a solicitor and may include representation in some courts under 'Assistance by way of Representation'.
2 Civil Legal Aid – covers representation in civil cases.
3 Criminal Legal Cases – covers representation in criminal cases.

Qualification for Legal Aid

(Information supplied by Legal Aid Head Office)

If you receive income support (IS), you are entitled to free legal help. If you do not receive IS, your income and savings must be below certain levels. If you are living with a spouse and s/he is not your opponent, his/her income will be counted along with your own. This will be worked out either by your solicitor, if you apply for help under Legal Aid and Assistance, or by the Department of Social Security if you apply for Civil Legal Aid.

Income Limits: The limits for Legal Advice and Assistance are lower than those for Civil Legal Aid. If your income is higher than the basic limits, you may still be able to get help, so do inquire. Citizens Advice Bureaux, Legal Aid offices and Law Centres (see Appendix) can give information on exact income and savings limits.

To get legal help, go to a solicitor who takes Legal Aid cases, whom you will find by going to a CAB, Law Centre or other independent advice agency; consulting the Solicitors' Regional Directory in Town Halls, Courts or Legal Aid Offices; asking anywhere you see the Legal Aid logo, or asking a trade union official.

For a copy of the Legal Aid Guide or any other information, including information in, for example, Gujarati, Hindi, Punjabi, Bengali and Urdu, contact:

Legal Aid Head Office
Newspaper House
8–16 Great New Street
London EC4A 3BN.
353 7411

THE RIGHT TO DEMONSTRATE

No specific law gives a legal right to demonstrate, although such a right is obviously assumed to exist, since laws have been passed to restrict the right to assemble, march or demonstrate.

The Public Order Act 1986 increased the power of the police to impose conditions on demonstrations. In effect, it became the job of the police to balance the right to protest against the right of traffic to pass along a road, the right of street traders to sell their wares and the rights of individuals to use shops.

In many cases, seven days' notice of demonstrations must be given to the police. In certain circumstances, demonstrations may be banned by the police.

THE RIGHT TO FREE EXPRESSION

In 1688, the English Parliament passed a Bill of Rights. This law applied only to MPs, for whom it guaranteed freedom of speech. At no time has there been a British equivalent to the US First Amendment guaranteeing freedom of expression for all. The following organisations can provide information and advice about freedom of expression.

CITIZENS' RIGHTS **53**

**Campaign for Freedom of
Information**
3 Endsleigh Street
London WC1H 0DD
278 9686

**Campaign for Press and
Broadcasting Freedom**
9 Poland Street
London W1V 3DG
437 2795

National Union of Journalists
314 Gray's Inn Road
London WC1X 8PD
278 7916

Newspaper Society
Bloomsbury House
74–77 Great Russell Street
London WC1 3DA
636 7014

THE RIGHT TO PRIVACY

No general right to privacy is recognised in English law.
Information about you can be gathered by the police or the press
without your permission or knowledge. Certain provisions do
exist to prevent acts which most people would consider as
intrusions of privacy. The Data Protection Act 1984 contains
provisions on computer data about 'identifiable living individuals'. It does not apply to handwritten data which might apply
to education or medical records, employment or housing records.
(Although prospective landlords under the new Housing Act
have the right to inspect your housing records without asking
your permission.) If you believe computer data about you has
been misused you may complain to:

The Office of the Data Protection Registrar
Springfield House
Water Lane
Wilmslow
SK9 5AX
0625 535777
*Other information can be obtained from Law Centres, CABs, or independent
advice centres (see Appendix).*

THE RIGHTS OF MINORITIES

The Minority Rights Group
379 Brixton Road
London SW9 7OE
978 9498
*'An international human rights
educational charity and information
centre.' Investigates discrimination
and prejudice around the world. A
list of special reports is available
from the MRG's London office. MRG*

*also has local groups, a newsletter
and educational resources.*

Survival International
310 Edgware Road
London W2 1DY
723 5535
*Campaigning on behalf of tribal
people's land rights, through
lobbying, education and
publications.*

THE RIGHTS OF IMMIGRANTS, REFUGEES, AND ASYLUM SEEKERS

The laws on immigration currently in effect are the Immigration Act 1971 and the Immigration Act 1988. Immigration officers are directed on how to apply regulations by the Home Office. Immigration law does not give any specific rights to refugees.

The British Nationality Act 1981 defines how people may become British citizens.

For more information on these topics, see section on immigration in Chapter 5: Ethnic Minorities.

British Refugee Council
Bondway House
3–9 Bondway
London SW8 1SJ
582 6922

Joint Council for the Welfare of Immigrants
115 Old Street
London EC1V 9JR
251 8706

National Union of Students
461 Holloway Road
London N7 6LJ
272 8900

Refugee Forum
99 Chalton Street
London NW1
837 9293

UK Council for Overseas Students Affairs
60 Westbourne Grove
London W2 5FG
229 9268

UK Immigrants Advisory Service
County House
190 Great Dover Street
London SE1 4YB
357 6917

United Nations High Commission for Refugees
36 Westminster Palace Gardens
Artillery Row
London SW1P 1RR
222 3065

HUMAN RIGHTS

The UK is bound by a number of international treaties on human rights. Perhaps the best known is the European Convention for the Protection of Human Rights and Fundamental Freedoms. This treaty gives the possibility of redress if civil liberties are infringed and satisfaction is not obtained through the British courts or government. Cases may be taken up by the European Commission and Court of Human Rights. Complaints may be about law, acts of governmental bodies or court decisions.

Secretary of the Commission of Human Rights
Council of Europe
BP 431 R6

67006 Strasbourg Cedex
France

Amnesty International
99–119 Rosebery Avenue
London EC1R 4RE
278 6000
The world's leading organisation *dealing with prisoners of conscience, publishes reports of its investigations and carries out campaigning and lobbying activities.*

THE RIGHT TO COMPLAIN

Individuals or groups of people have the right to complain about public services including government departments, health, gas, electricity, water, communications, police, courts, media, transport, compensation for crimes, etc.

The Local Ombudsman
21 Queen Anne's Gate
London SW1H 9BU
222 5622
Independent organisation dealing with complaints against local authorities (except town or parish councils), water authorities, police authorities, Urban Development Corporations and certain other bodies.

The Parliamentary Ombudsman
Church House
Great Smith Street
London SW1P 3BW
276 2130

Consumers' Association
2 Marylebone Road
London NW1
486 5544

Amenities

Electricity Consumers' Council
Brook House
2–16 Torrington Place
London WC1E 7LL
636 5703

Water Authorities Association
1 Queen Anne's Gate
London SW1H 9BT
222 8111

Water Companies Association
14 Great College Street
London SW1P 3RX
222 0644

Gas
In the first instance, contact the local Gas Board. If you are not satisfied, contact the local Gas Consumers' Council. (Numbers in phone book.)

Communications

Post Office Users' National Council
Waterloo Bridge House
Waterloo Road
London SE1 8UA
928 9458

Office of Telecommunications
Atlantic House
Holborn Viaduct
London EC1N 2HQ
822 1650

Transport

London Buses Public Relations
55 Broadway
London SW1H 0BD
222 5600

London Regional Passengers Committee
Golden Cross House
8 Duncannon Street
London WC2 8JF
839 1898

Association of British Travel Agents (ABTA)
55–57 Newman Street
London W1P 4AH
637 2444

Air Transport Users' Committee
129 Kingsway
London WC2B 6NN
242 3882

Police

Police Complaints Authority
10 Great George Street
London SW1P 3AE
273 6450

Health

The Health Service Ombudsman
Church House
Great Smith Street
London SW1P 3BW
276 2035

General Medical Council
44 Hallam Street
London W1N 6AE
580 7642

UK Central Council for Nursing, Midwifery and Health Visiting
23 Portland Place
London W1N 3AF
637 7181

Dental Council
37 Wimpole Street
London W1M 8DQ
486 2171

Pharmaceutical Society
1 Lambeth High Street
London SE1 7JN
735 9141

Association of Optometrists
Bridge House
233–234 Blackfriars Road
London SE1 8NW
261 9661

Legal

Solicitors Complaints Bureau
Portland House
Stag Place
London SW1E 5BL
834 2288

The Lay Observer
Royal Courts of Justice
Strand

London WC2A 2LL
936 6000

Senate of the Inns of Court and the Bar
11 South Square
Gray's Inn Road
London WC1R 5EL
242 0082

**Criminal Injuries Compensation
Board**
10–12 Russell Square
London WC1E 7LG
636 2812 or 636 4201

Motor Insurers Bureau
New Garden House
Hatton Garden
London EC1N 8JZ
242 0033

Interights
46 Kingsway
London WC2B 6EN
242 5581
*Promotes the observance of
international human rights law.*

Justice
95a Chancery Lane
London WC2A 1DT
405 6019
*All-party law reform group which
investigates miscarriages of justice.*

Finance

Banking Ombudsman
Citadel House
5–11 Fetter Lane
London EC4R 1BR
583 1395

Media

Press Council
1 Salisbury Square
London EC4Y 8AF
353 1248

Director General BBC
Broadcasting House
Portland Place
London W1A 1AA
580 4468

**Broadcasting Complaints
Commission**
Grosvenor Gardens House
35 Grosvenor Gardens
London SW1
630 1966

**Independent Broadcasting
Authority**
70 Brompton Road
London SW3 1EY
584 7011

WORKERS' RIGHTS

There has been a gradual decline in the rights of trade unions and
individual workers since 1979, under the Employment Acts of
1980, 1982, 1988 and 1989; the Trade Union Act 1984, the Wages
Act 1986, the Social Security Act 1986 and several Department of
Employment codes of practice.

Trade Union Congress (TUC)
Congress House
Great Russell Street
London WC1B 3LS
636 4030

**Commissioner for the Rights of
    Trade Union Members**
Sunley Building
Piccadilly Plaza
Manchester M60 7JS
061 832 9111

Health and Safety Commission
1 Baynards House
1 Chepstow Place
London W2 4TF
221 0870

DISCRIMINATION

The chapters on young people, older people, people with disabilities, ethnic minorities, women, and lesbians and gay men all include information on rights and liberties.

Advertising Standards Authority
15–17 Ridgmount Street
London WC1E 7AW
580 5555

Campaign for Homosexual Equality
Room 221
38 Mount Pleasant
London WC1X 0AP
833 3912

**Citizens' Rights Office,
    Child Poverty Action Group**
1 Bath Street
London EC1V 9PY
253 3406

Commission for Racial Equality
10–12 Allington Street
London SW1E 5EH
828 7022

Equal Opportunities Commission
Overseas House
Quay Street
Manchester M3 3HN
061 833 9244

Gay and Lesbian Legal Advice
BM GLAD
London WC1N 3XX
253 2043

Gay Rights at Work
c/o Pickwick Court
London SE9 4SA

**LAGER (Lesbian and Gay
    Employment Rights)**
Room 205
Southbank House

Black Prince Road
London SE1 7SJ
587 1643 (Gay Men)/587 1636
(Lesbians)

Law Centres Federation
Duchess House
18–19 Warren Street
London W1P 5DB
387 8540

**London Lesbian and Gay
    Switchboard**
BM Switchboard
London WC1X 3XX
837 7324

Mental After-Care Association
Bainsbridge House
Bainsbridge Road
London WC1A 1HP
436 6194

**MIND (National Association for
    Mental Health)**
22 Harley Street
London W1N 2ED
637 0741

**Organisation for Lesbian and Gay
    Action (OLGA)**
PO Box 147
London WC2H 0BB
833 3860

Rights of Women
52–54 Featherstone Street
London EC1Y 8ET
251 6577

Runnymede Trust
62 Chandos Place
London WC2N 4HG
836 3266

Terrence Higgins Trust
BM AIDS
London WC1N 3XX
242 1010

THE RIGHTS OF CHILDREN AND YOUNG PEOPLE

British Agencies for Adoption and Fostering
11 Southwark Street
London SE1 1RQ
407 8800

Brook Advisory Service
233 Tottenham Court Road
London W1P 9AE
323 1522

Children's Legal Centre
20 Compton Terrace
London N1 2UN
359 6251

Lesbian and Gay Youth Movement
BM LGYM
London W1
317 9690

London Youth Advisory Centre
26 Prince of Wales Road
London NW5 3LG
267 4792

National Association of Young People in Care
20 Compton Terrace
London N1 2UN
226 7102

THE RIGHTS OF TRAVELLERS

The Romany Guild
50–56 Temple Mills Lane
London E15
555 7214

THE POLL TAX

The Poll Tax or 'Community Charge' is a system of local taxation due to replace domestic rates charged by local authorities on 1 April 1990. Most people over 18 will be obliged to pay the charge. The tax is dealt with in more detail in Chapter 13: Social Services, Benefits and Taxation, including its potential breaches of civil liberties.

4

EDUCATION

There can be no doubt that the education service is going through a period of change such as it has not seen since the 1944 Education Act. It has been a decade of major Acts: 1980, 1981, 1983, 1986, 1987 and 1988; each one an important Act. Hardly anything has been left untouched; composition and powers of governing bodies of schools and colleges, special education, teachers' pay and conditions, new kinds of secondary schools, the introduction of a National Curriculum with associated national testing systems, the removal of the polytechnics and many other colleges from local education authority control, the funding systems for schools, colleges, polytechnics and universities are simply the main changes. There were many, many smaller ones as well.

For inner London, there is the abolition of the Inner London Education Authority and the creation of thirteen new LEAs as the inner London boroughs and the City of London, for the first time ever, assume responsibility for the education service. Inner London has had a unified service for 120 years; starting with the London School Board, then the London County Council and, finally, ILEA. There have always been those who were opposed to a unified service but until the 1988 Education Reform Act, their arguments had always been rejected. Indeed, in the first draft of the Education Reform Bill the proposal was to allow boroughs who wished to do so to opt out, thus leaving a smaller area (though unstable because each year the other boroughs had to decide whether to remain in) but an amendment moved by two former ministers decreed that all boroughs, whether they wanted to or not, would become LEAs. The amendment was passed.

The chapter which follows sketches the changes which are

working their way through. Some have been welcomed, by and large, others have united a broad spectrum against them. Some changes were necessary, some were not. Whether they are popular or necessary is no longer of much importance; change is happening fast. Things will never be the same again.

David Mallen
Education Officer (ILEA)

THE EDUCATION REFORM ACT 1988

The Baker Education Reforms have caused the greatest upheaval in education in Britain since the 1944 Education Act, meeting with a barrage of criticism from teachers, governors, parents and students.

In recent years, education spending has been greatly reduced. Local authorities which planned our schools system have had their powers severely reduced; the taxes which funded them are to be discontinued and the legal framework that enclosed them has been replaced. The future success of schools will depend on their ability to compete for custom with other schools in their area. Worse still, the change has passed through Parliament and on to the statute books at a breathtaking speed. Indeed, most people have scarcely had time to understand the implications of Mr Baker's reforms, let alone decide whether they agree with them.

In effect, Mr Baker has created a market system for education. Secondary and large primary schools are to be self-governing. A body made up of parents, teachers and nominees from the Local Education Authority and local business will take responsibility for the budget, staff appointments and school affairs, as well as competing for parental custom with other schools.

Whilst the 1944 Education Act attempted to remove schools from the influence of the market, the 1988 Education Act is intended to reintroduce market principles into the provision of state schools while the Local Government Finance Act of 1988 changes the whole basis of local authority finance.

The immediate objectives of the 1988 Education Act can be summarised as follows:

1 To break the power of the local authorities traditionally responsible for the running of their own systems of education (easily their largest responsibility).
2 To erect a hierarchical system of schooling subject to market forces and yet more directly under state control in terms of curriculum, testing and underlying ideology.

The provisions of the Act can be divided into the following areas:

Devolution of Financial Responsibility

All secondary schools and all primary schools of more than 200 pupils will take responsibility for their own finances through their boards of governors and heads. Local authorities will no longer be able to plan and coordinate spending on education.

Open Enrolment

Schools will be allowed to enrol as many pupils as they like up to their maximum capacity – there will be no quotas. The government has said that this will allow greater parent choice. However, popular schools with responsibility for their own finances will soon begin to differentiate themselves from less popular establishments. This will end up as the springboard for the next step – opting out (see below).

Moreover, open enrolment will put some schools at risk. Brian Simon, in his book *Bending the Rules* (Lawrence & Wishart, 1989), described what might happen. Imagine three schools in a particular area, each with a capacity of 1,000, but with only 2,300 pupils to be enrolled in that area. If two of the schools recruit the maximum 1,000, the third less popular school, possibly on a council estate, will be left with only 300. This school will therefore get fewer teachers, less money and fewer subject options unless the local authority commits extra resources to it. It may even be forced into closure, thus reducing choice rather than increasing it as the government claims.

Less popular schools will have to resort more and more to fundraising. School buildings, books and equipment, the number of teachers available and hence the size of the classes will gradually correspond to the income of the community, just like shops, restaurants and other commercial facilities.

Fees for Extras

The charging of fees for certain activities previously offered free, such as school outings or music lessons, will be legitimised. Less popular and therefore poorer schools will no longer be able to afford such extra-curricular services. The new regulations do not distinguish between mainstream schools and special schools such as those catering for children with disabilities.

Opting Out

All secondary schools and primary schools with 300 or more pupils will be able to opt out of local authority control. A school's governing body at a single meeting may resolve to opt out and apply for grant maintained status, providing a simple majority is obtained in a vote of 50 per cent of the school's parents. No school may opt back until ten years after the initial decision. A school that opts out will be maintained by a grant paid directly from central government.

There are many anomalies in this ruling, not least the fact that parents with children transferring to a school considering opting out in the next year or two have no vote while those of children about to leave do. Furthermore, first governors of opted out schools would hold office for five to seven years; governors elected later would only hold the post for four years and members of the governing body of ex-Local Education Authority schools would be chosen by that governing body itself, i.e. it would become self-perpetuating.

Ultimately, Mrs Thatcher and Mr Baker want to create a new stratum of schools to fill the gap between the independent (public and private) schools for the wealthy and the 'popular' schools for the masses left with the local authorities. This stratum, independent of LEAs, will be financed by the state, but partially subject to market forces, and aimed primarily at the children of middle-class families.

Among other objections are that the coherent and comprehensive planning of education provision in an LEA area will be undermined, and that it is unfair that schools should be able to pick and choose the best pupils and leave the rest to the responsibility of the local authority.

The government also planned to establish twenty or so City Technology Colleges (CTCs), relying on funds extracted from industry. These colleges were to concentrate on scientific subjects and mathematics, and have longer hours and different terms from other schools. Some have already been established but after much opposition it seems likely that the development of further CTCs will be stopped at an early stage.

Opted out schools and CTCs will form a confused system, subject to market forces. Below them will be what is left of today's LEA systems, consisting principally of a set of financially devolved schools run by governing bodies, continuously threatened by further opting out.

The National Curriculum and Testing

There is now to be a national curriculum for all pupils in maintained schools between the ages of 5 and 16 and tests in all subjects at 7, 11, 14 and 16.

There is a broad consensus that a common core of subjects is desirable but that there should be guidelines, not legislation. It is also widely believed that these guidelines should be established by full discussion with all those involved, especially teachers. Many of those involved in the legislation are not even educationalists.

The curriculum's foundation subjects are English, Maths, Science, Technology, a modern foreign language, History/Geography, Art/Music/Drama/Design, PE and Religious Education.

However, the curriculum shows a singular lack of consideration both of recent successful multicultural approaches to education and of special educational needs.

Perhaps even more worrying is the fact that there is a serious lack of qualified teachers to implement the national curriculum. At the start of the 1989–90 school year, hundreds of pupils had to be sent home because there were no teachers to teach them. Around 1,000 ILEA posts were unfilled at the beginning of the 1989–90 school year.

Further and Higher Education

Polytechnics and other larger FE institutions have been removed from local authority control and established as semi-independent corporations financed by central government through a new funding body, the Polytechnics and Colleges Funding Council (PCFC), which has replaced the National Advisory Body.

The fundamental aim is the transformation of further education into a feeder system for the local business world.

In the case of adult and community education, the delegation of full financial control to institutions whose prime intention is the provision of a different kind of education is likely to marginalise it and hinder its success. Indeed, most colleges have a wide range of courses, some of recreational or personal interest. The proposed composition of governing bodies is likely to distort the balance in favour of employment interests and disregard wider community interests.

There has also been an assault on the relative autonomy of universities and their independence. Higher education is for the first time directly under state control in a manner which will threaten its character, its freedom and its quality.

There are two main strands to this:

1 The abolition of the University Grants Commission, traditionally a buffer between state and universities, but whose degree of independence has been eroded. It has been replaced by the University Funding Council, with fifteen members appointed by the Secretary of State, six to nine from higher education and the rest from 'other backgrounds'. It will no longer have the important function of advising the government on the level of funding required. Its job is to act as a conveyor belt for government decisions – to administer the funds provided by the Secretary of State.

2 The abolition of tenure in university posts, long held to be the guarantee of freedom of thought and expression among university teachers.

The Abolition of ILEA

London has had a unitary education system for 120 years. Under the Greater London Council (GLC) the Inner London Education Authority (ILEA) was set up as a directly elected educational authority – the only one in the country – with full responsibility for all aspects of publicly provided educational facilities in inner London. ILEA covers thirteen boroughs: Hammersmith and Fulham, Kensington and Chelsea, Camden, City of London, City of Westminster, Hackney, Islington, Tower Hamlets, Greenwich, Lewisham, Southwark, Lambeth and Wandsworth. It has no responsibility for the outer boroughs.

London parents were outraged by the amendment to Baker's Bill allowing the abolition of ILEA. An intensive ballot was organised for Londoners with children in ILEA schools – supervised by the Electoral Reform Society. Ninety-four per cent of those voting (137,000) rejected the proposition, 8,000 accepted it. There was a 55 per cent turn out, higher than in local elections, but no attention was paid to the results by the government.

Conclusion

The Education Act is inspired by an ideology that places the mechanics of the market place and competition above all other considerations. Local financial management, open enrolment, grant maintained schools and CTCs are all justified with the argument that the resulting competition for customers between schools will inevitably lead to a general improvement of educational practice and standards. 'Good' schools will drive out 'bad'. Popular schools will expand, increase their prestige, flourish and perhaps become independent, while unpopular schools, mostly in inner cities, will go into a spiral of decline, low morale and eventually, ceasing to be viable, will close.

The market place philosophy cannot, of course, lead to equality of provision and does not seek to. Competition is bound to lead to a hierarchy. That is its intention. To achieve this, schools must be taken out of the supposedly evil hands of local authorities. It is now parents (as governors) who are to run the schools. Parents are set up in opposition to the local authorities.

Schools are set to become semi-independent small businesses which must compete with each other in order to remain viable at a time when rolls are falling rapidly in most areas.

There are a number of books on the subject of the Baker reforms. I particularly acknowledge Frances Morrell's *Children of the Future* (Hogarth Press) and Brian Simon's *Bending The Rules* (Lawrence & Wishart). Also useful are Ken Jones's *Right Turn* (Radius) and Julian Haviland's *Take Care, Mr Baker* (Fourth Estate).

EDUCATION IN LONDON AFTER ILEA

At the time of going to press, none of the inner London boroughs was clear as to the exact form and organisation of their education systems after April 1990. However, each one has produced an Education Development Plan describing in some detail the way in which they see education moving in each borough. These can be obtained along with any other information you require on education in your borough from the Borough Education Department (see end of chapter).

A further problem is that it is not yet clear what financial resources are to be available to each authority. Inner London will suffer particularly badly from the implementation of the Poll Tax and will receive a smaller amount of business money as a result of the new Uniform Business Rate. The difference should be made up from grants from central government which are worked out according to each borough's 'needs'.

Preliminary figures show quite a difference between what ILEA spends on certain boroughs now and what the government says they should be spending. If they spend according to government assessments, about 25 per cent of the education bill will be footed by poll tax payers. However, if more is spent, it must be paid for entirely from the community charge. In simple terms, this means that the choice may have to be made between huge poll tax bills for local residents or huge cuts in education spending. Outer London boroughs vary in their opinions with regard to possible knock-on effects of ILEA abolition.

NURSERY AND PRE-SCHOOL EDUCATION

Under Section 24 of the Education Act 1980, LEAs have the power rather than the duty to provide nursery education. ILEA maintained nursery schools will be transferred to the successor authority.

A child can usually attend a nursery school or nursery class at a local primary school at the beginning of the term following his/her third birthday.

There are always waiting lists for nurseries and it is wise to put down your child's name as soon as possible if you wish him or her to attend a nursery school. There are no fixed catchment areas and parents can apply to a school of their choice. However, priority may be given to children who already have a brother or sister at the school, where medical or family circumstances influence the child's needs, where there are special educational needs including the need to learn English as a second language, or where the school is the nearest one to the child's home. Most children attend nursery schools on a part-time basis.

Financial pressures have forced some closures. Hackney, for example, is badly affected and under-5s are likely to suffer from social services cuts. Hackney's lists are increasing at seventy-five per month and there are around 2,000 on their waiting lists.

The abolition of ILEA and the rules concerning opting out might create problems for nursery schools. For a start, comprehensive planning will be difficult. There is already often poor communication between pre-school and primary school planning departments and if primary schools usually fed by particular nursery schools choose to opt out, there may be difficulties in direct movement from nursery schools and classes to primary schools.

Nursery provision varies considerably from one borough to the next. For instance, in Greenwich 50 per cent of children have nursery places, in Barnet 60 per cent and in Lewisham 41 per cent. In all cases, demand exceeds supply and there is little indication that changes in local education funding will improve matters, although attempts have been made under ILEA to expand provision and are likely to continue under the boroughs' auspices. Between 1972 and 1987 ILEA figures had increased from 32 nursery schools and 241 nursery classes to 49 schools and 506 classes.

Boroughs usually have a range of educational provision for under-5s. There are nursery classes within primary schools. There are also sometimes voluntarily run toddlers clubs, playgroups, day care services run by social services' departments, private day care provision and childminders. Contact the local social services department to find what is available. The local education department will provide information on all local nursery schools and classes.

British Association for Early Childhood Education
Studio 3.2
140 Tabernacle Street
London EC2A 4SD
250 1768
Assists in the establishment of nursery schools and classes and offers specialist help to local authorities and others in the field.

National Campaign for Nursery Education
33 Hugh Street
London SW1V 1QJ

Campaigns for increased facilities for pre-school children. Provides support to local campaigners, lobbies press and government.

Pre-school Playgroups Association
61–63 King's Cross Road
London WC1Y 9LL
833 0991
Encourages the formation of playgroups and mother and toddler groups for the under-5s. Has many local branches.

PRIMARY EDUCATION

Children reach statutory school age at the beginning of the term following their fifth birthday, although some boroughs have an admissions policy allowing earlier entry if required. If children have attended a nursery class at a local primary school they will usually move up to the infants class at that school, although this is not compulsory. Entry is not automatic, though, and parents still have to apply to the headteacher for a place. There are no fixed catchment areas but every school has a maximum entry figure in any particular area.

Primary schools may consist of separate infants and junior schools, or a single school with infant and junior classes. Parents can apply directly to schools for their own information booklets.

In the majority of cases parents will be able to send their children to the school of their choice. In a few instances if a popular school has reached its maximum capacity, you may be offered a place at your second choice school. You are also allowed to apply for admission to a school outside your borough and will be accepted if there are spaces, although priority will be given to pupils living in the borough.

If you are unsuccessful in obtaining a place for your child at the school of your choice, you have the right of appeal. Appeals should be addressed to the Director of Education in that borough. In the case of voluntary schools the initial appeal must be made to the school governors.

Pupils who attend an infant school will transfer to a junior school in the September following their seventh birthday. If the child is transferring from an infants department to a junior department of the same school or to a 'paired' junior school, no application form is necessary. However, if a child is going to transfer to a different school altogether, application must be made to the headteacher of the school of your choice by 28 February in the year of transfer.

Voluntary aided schools including church schools may have slightly different criteria for entry but the basic procedure is the same.

The degree to which a primary school is affected by the education reforms depends partly on its size. Schools with 200 or fewer pupils will not take full financial responsibility, unlike larger primary schools and all secondary schools. As a rule, the new LEAs created by the 1989 Education Act will also support voluntary aided church schools in their boroughs.

Transfers

Parents wishing to transfer their child to another primary school should approach the Head of the school the child is currently attending and advise him/her of their intention. They should then send a written request to the Director of Education. If the reason for a transfer is simply that you are moving house, you should advise both the Head of your child's current school and the Head of the school to which you wish the child to be transferred. Requests for transfers to voluntary aided schools will be considered by that school's governors.

Transport

Under the 1944 Education Act, there is no obligation for the local authority to pay travelling expenses unless the distance to the nearest suitable maintained school is two or more miles for under-8s and three or more miles for over-11s. The ILEA has often been more generous, however, and the new LEAs have not yet defined their policies, so it is wise to apply in any case if you are unsure of your entitlement. Applications should be made to the Director of Education in your borough.

Meals

Multichoice meals are available at most primary schools. Parents on Income Support qualify for free school meals for their children. Applications should be sent to the Director of Education. Schools also provide space for children bringing packed lunches.

SECONDARY EDUCATION

In their last year at primary school, children may take the '11 plus' exam in order to gain entry to a grammar school if they so wish, although there are no grammar schools in the vast majority of London boroughs. Most children attend a local comprehensive school, but it is possible to apply for a place at a school outside your borough. Parents are usually asked to name first, second and third preference schools and the local education authority attempts to meet these requests according to available places. Priority may be given to pupils with a member of their family already at a school, who have special medical or family circumstances or who live nearby and would have a longer journey to an alternative school. Criteria for establishing priority admissions have to be published by the school or LEA.

Secondary schools in London have faced considerable problems in recent years. The lower birth rate has reduced the number of secondary school pupils by about 40 per cent, leading to many amalgamations across the capital. Also shortages in staff have affected many schools, though not to the same extent as primary schools.

All ILEA schools and educational establishments of secondary age now run the London Record of Achievement for over 15s.

Full lists of secondary schools in a particular borough can be obtained from the local education department. In addition there are usually booklets giving brief descriptions of each school.

FURTHER AND HIGHER EDUCATION

Colleges and polytechnics are maintained by local authorities. Twenty-four colleges are currently under ILEA control and there are many more in the outer boroughs. Lists can be obtained from the boroughs in question. Apart from post-school courses, colleges can offer an alternative for pupils aged 16 and over as a place to take A-levels and alternative courses.

The University of London and City University are mainly funded by the new University Funding Council; Polytechnics by the Polytechnics and Colleges Funding Council.

Grants

A major problem both for existing students and for A-Level students now considering further or higher education is the question of grants. The government has consistently failed to increase student grants in line with inflation and to ensure a satisfactory minimum grant for all students. The proposed introduction of a loan system, whereby students will have to borrow thousands of pounds to be paid back at a later date, will put off many potential students and hang a financial millstone around the neck of thousands more. The government has said that it wishes to increase the number of students in higher education. However, the reaction of the universities has been to point out that if this is to be the case and the government will not provide substantially increased funding, then students themselves will have to pay part, if not all, of their tuition fees, hitherto the responsibility of the LEA.

As the National Union of Students (NUS) has pointed out, this could saddle even an ordinary arts or science student with a three-year bill of £15–20,000, and a trainee doctor on a five-year course, up to £50,000. If such proposals ever come into effect, post A-Level education will become ever more the preserve of the wealthier classes and turn it into a privilege rather than a right based on academic capability.

Information on grants can be obtained from your local education authority. Information about courses and entrance requirements for particular establishments can be obtained directly from the college, polytechnic or university.

Students' Unions

All colleges, polytechnics and universities have a union of some kind, but the main bodies are ULU, NUS and NUS London.

NUS London/University of London Union (ULU)
Malet Street
London WC1G 1HY
631 3541/637 1181

NUS Central Office
Nelson Mandela House
461 Holloway Road
London N7 6LJ
272 8900
Represents UK students locally, nationally and internationally. Disseminates information to students on educational and social issues.

Other Student Organisations

International Students Trust
International Students House
229 Great Portland Street
London W1N 5HD
631 3223
Residence and centre for both British and overseas students with restaurant, bar and other facilities and activities.

Overseas Students Trust
177 Vauxhall Bridge Road
London SW1V 1ER
834 4466
Promotes the education in the UK of overseas students. Research and information.

Thomas Wall Trust
1 York Street
Baker Street
London W1H 1PZ
939 3994
Provides supplementary grants or loans to students in need of financial assistance. Restricted to students seeking a first qualification.

UK Council for Overseas Student Affairs
60 Westbourne Grove
London W2 5SH
229 9268/9
Aims to look after the needs and

promote the interests of overseas students studying in the UK. Five hundred organisations are members of UKCOSA, including academic and professional bodies, voluntary, regional and student organisations. Offers advice, training and resources.

World University Service
20–21 Compton Terrace
London N1 2UN
226 6747
Aims to highlight the importance of education in world development. Assists refugees and victims of oppression through educational programmes.

ADULT EDUCATION

There are many opportunities for adult education in London, especially in the inner boroughs. ILEA's provision of both examination and leisure courses has been second to none for some time. Its annual directory, *Floodlight*, has offered hundreds of courses in many adult education institutes across the capital. It is to be hoped, but is by no means guaranteed, that newly formed borough education authorities will continue to provide this service.

After the demise of the ILEA, four adult-education centres, wholly or partially funded by the ILEA, will become part of a trust and will receive grants initially from the London Residuary Body and later from central government, though it seems very likely that they will be expected to raise a much higher proportion of their costs from non-governmental sources. The four centres are the Working Men's College, Mary Ward College, the City Lit and Morley College (all listed below).

The outer boroughs, too, have a wide range of day and evening courses available, at a variety of lengths and prices. Contact your borough education department for full details of courses and institutions in your area.

The Workers Educational Association
Temple House
9 Upper Berkeley Street
London WH 8BY
402 5608

Founded in 1903. Courses are open to all adults. There are no other entrance requirements and no exams to sit. A wide range of both day and evening courses of varying lengths are available. There are also day-release courses, one day and weekend schools, residential summer schools both at home and abroad.

Syllabuses are worked out jointly by tutor and students. Courses cost around £2 per student per class.

WEA has a particular concern for educationally disadvantaged groups: ethnic minorities, people in areas of urban deprivation or retired people. Information on courses being held in your local area can be found in libraries, local newspapers or by contacting the central London office which covers all of Greater London as well as Surrey, Middlesex, part of Essex and part of Hertfordshire.

Working Men's College
Crowndale Road
London NW1 1TR
387 2037/8208

Founded in 1854 and the oldest adult education institute in the country. Fees payable for exam or non-exam courses. Close association with the Francis Martin Women's College, the University of London Extra-Mural Department and the Workers Educational Association.

Birkbeck College
University of London
Malet Street
London WC1E 7HX
580 6622

City Lit
Stukeley Street
Drury Lane
London WC2B 5LJ
242 9872

City University
Extra-Mural Studies
Northampton Square
London EC1V 0HB
253 4399 ext 3268/3252/3277

Mary Ward Centre
42 Queen Street

London WC1N 3AQ
831 7711

Morley College
61 Westminster Bridge Road
London SE1 7HT
928 8501

Open University
Walton Hall
Milton Keynes
MK7 6AA

University of London
Department of Extra-Mural Studies
Goldsmiths College
Lewisham Way
London SE14 6NW
692 7171 ext 8000
692 4398 (after 5pm)

Part-time courses are also run by the London polytechnics, namely the Polytechnic of North London, City Polytechnic, Thames Polytechnic, Polytechnic of the South Bank, Polytechnic of Central London and Polytechnic of East London.

Adult Literacy and Basic Skills Unit
Kingsbourne House
229–231 High Holborn
London WC1V 7DA
405 4017
The central focus for adult literacy and basic skills work in England and Wales. Publishes books and packs for tutors involved in the area.

Age Concern England, Education and Leisure Officer
60 Pitcairn Road
Mitcham
Surrey CR4 3ll
A clearing house for information on education for older people. Organises conferences and undertakes consultancy work.

Third Age Trust
6 Parkside Gardens
London SW19 5EY
Promotes self-help educational activities among retired people of all ages.

PEOPLE WITH SPECIAL NEEDS

There are fears that the new education reforms will hit special needs provision, especially as schools move towards opting out and pay less attention to special needs and more to creating an élite image.

The Warnock Report estimated that one pupil in five has special educational needs at some time or other during their education. In London, this figure is higher still. ILEA had 104 special schools and all boroughs have some degree of special provision. Contact your local education department for details.

KIDS
80 Waynflete Square
London W10 6UD
969 2817
A personal service for families with children with developmental or learning difficulties, or who are diagnosed as handicapped. Organises home visits by trained visitors to help parents with direct teaching techniques.

National Bureau for Handicapped Students
336 Brixton Road
London SW9 7AA
274 0565
Information and advice on all aspects of education and at all levels of handicap. Regional and local support groups.

Parents in Partnership
The Portakabin, Clare House
St George's Hospital
Blackshaw Road
London SW17
767 3211
Promotes the educational requirements of people with special needs and provides an advice and support network for parents.

Voluntary Council for Handicapped Children
c/o 8 Wakely Street
London E1V 7PE
278 9441

CAREERS ADVICE AND TRAINING

Local careers offices are usually attached to borough council offices. Schools, colleges, universities and polytechnics often have careers advisers, too.

Training in practical and management skills is available from a variety of sources such as day or evening courses run at local colleges.

Manpower Services Commission
236 Gray's Inn Road
London WC1X 8HL
278 0363
*Runs a number of public
employment and training courses.*

Rural Development Commission
141 Castle Street
Salisbury
Wiltshire, SP1 3TP
0722 336255

Business in the Community
227a City Road
London EC1V 1JU
253 3716

Cooperative Development Agency
Broadmead House
21 Panton House
London SW1Y 4DR
839 2988

Government Schemes

(a) Youth Training Scheme

The YTS is aimed at 16- or 17-year-old school leavers. It provides training and work experience for up to two years, sometimes leading to qualifications. People on YTS receive a very small weekly allowance. Unfortunately, the YTS scheme is frequently abused by employers who take on a YTS employee for a limited period with the prospect of long-term employment after the period of training, only to replace the trainee at the end of the set period with another trainee, because of benefits offered by the government to employers who take on YTS trainees.

(b) Employment Training Schemes

Employment Training (ET) is aimed at unemployed people aged 18 and over to improve their chances of finding employment. It provides work experience and off-the-job training. It usually lasts for six months. ET trainees receive a weekly allowance equal to the amount of benefit they were receiving previously, plus a premium of £10.

People may be placed on an ET scheme after the compulsory

'Restart' interview they receive after six months of unemployment. (See also Chapter 13: Social Services, Benefits and Taxation.)

Both YTS and ET have been criticised as a government ploy to cut unemployment figures.

COMMUNITY EDUCATION

Most boroughs have some form of community education scheme. Community education projects provide opportunities for training or leisure activities within the community while at the same time providing the opportunity for people of all ages and cultures to meet and learn together. Borough education departments will give details of local projects.

Streetwork
c/o Notting Dale Urban Studies Centre
189 Freston Road
London W10 6TH
Promotes urban and local study through research and support to local initiatives.

ALTERNATIVES TO MAINSTREAM EDUCATION

Rudolf Steiner Education

There are three kinds of Rudolf Steiner Schools: Waldorf Schools, Homes/Schools/Adult Centres for disabled people, Schools/Adult Centres for the maladjusted.

The first Waldorf School was established in 1919 in Stuttgart, West Germany. There are around twenty in the British Isles. Each school is independent but there are certain common links. Waldorf Schools are divided into three phases: Kindergarten (ages 4 to 6), Lower School (ages 6 to 14) and Upper School (ages 14 to 18). There is a balance between practical, artistic and intellectual subjects throughout the child's education and new subjects are introduced at different stages of the child's development.

Steiner schools are co-educational and run by a group of senior teachers with no headteacher. There are no internal examinations. Some pupils are prepared for external examinations but pupils are not automatically prepared for GCSEs or A-Levels.

Steiner schools are not part of the state education system and fees are payable, although these are usually set according to parents' ability to pay.

To quote from the organisation's own literature:

> Education in a Rudolf Steiner School recognises the inner development of the child and seeks to nourish it with appropriate experiences at each stage, through a wide-ranging curriculum ... treats all subjects as inter-dependent, so that science, art and craft weave a meaning-ful whole with the human being as the focus; emphasises the human relationships of the child and teacher in unstreamed, mixed classes of diverse backgrounds and abilities; nurtures all the faculties of the child – artistic and practical as well as intellectual – as complementary aspects of a spiritual whole. Teachers in a Rudolf Steiner school work out of a holistic view of life based on Rudolf Steiner's philosophy of Anthroposophy which has its roots in Christianity.

Homes and schools for people with disabilities are closely linked with medical professionals and include such techniques as Curative Eurythmy, the therapeutic application of an art of movement that is part of the curriculum in all Steiner schools.

Schools for maladjusted children are for those unable to learn and develop within an ordinary school environment. There are also provisions for emotionally disturbed school leavers and adults.

Steiner Schools Fellowship
c/o Elmfield School
Stourbridge
West Midlands DY8 2EA

The Secretary
Delrow College
Aldenham
Watford, Herts, WD2 8DJ
For information on schools and homes for children with disabilities.

Rudolf Steiner Bookshops
35 Park Road
London NW1

and
38 Museum Street
London WC1

North London Rudolf Steiner School
PO Box 280
London N8 7HT
348 5050

Waldorf School of South-West London
12 Balham Park Road
London SW12 8DR
675 4443

Montessori Education

The Montessori Society runs schools based on the teaching methods of educationalist Maria Montessori. The society stresses respect for the child as an individual and the development of learning skills as opposed to imparting knowledge for its own sake.

At school children undertake tasks carefully chosen to match their stage of development, using materials designed to allow the child to correct his/her own mistakes. Fundamental to the Montessori approach is the recognition of the influence of environments on the development of children. A Montessori school attempts to provide children with a supportive yet challenging environment in which they may gain experience through activities and movement. Children are also encouraged to see themselves as part of a group.

Montessori schools currently cater only for children up to the age of 6 years, although this may eventually be extended to age 12. Fees are payable.

Montessori Society
26 Lyndhurst Gardens
London NW3
435 3646

Maria Montessori Training Organisation AMI
Address as above.

The international training centre for teachers learning the Montessori approach to education.

Montessori School
Lower Road
Harrow on the Hill
London
864 8097

Education at Home

Education Otherwise
25 Common Lane
Hemingford Abbots
Cambs PE18 9AN (for general information)
0983 78680

London Contacts: North
Jeffrey Benge
17 Nelson Mandela Close

Coppetts Road
London N10 1LA
883 7906

London Contacts: South
Mike and Margaret Gilbert
45 Burntwood Lane
London SW17 0JY
947 7706

Formed by a small group of parents in 1977. A self-help organisation with seventy local groups offering support, advice, and information to families practising or contemplating home-based education as an alternative to conventional schooling.

The name is taken from the Education Act which says that parents are responsible for their children's education, 'either by regular attendance at school or otherwise'.

Activities include workshops for children, residential weekends, conferences and seminars and public meetings. Education Otherwise does not promote a particular form of education, but encourages parents to find the kind of education most suitable for their children. Produces a bi-monthly newsletter, booklets and a contact list for members.

The organisation emphasises that it does not wish to work in conflict with schools or the education authorities and supports the concept of an education system which provides a resource to all members of the community whatever their age. If a parent decides to take his/her child out of the education system, for whatever reason, s/he is likely to encounter a good number of problems. For example, it is unlikely that they will receive any help from the local authority with learning materials, meal costs and so on, even though they would be paying them if they were at school. Sometimes, arrangements can be made for children to sit exams in schools.

Membership costs £12.50 p.a. for which members receive six fifty-page newsletters (available to non-members for £2.50).

'Public' and Private Schools

'Public' and private schools represent a distasteful form of selection that is based on money, class and ideology, not on a belief that all children should have equal access and choice in education.

Private schools are an unfair drain on highly qualified staff because of their ability to offer higher wages and better working conditions. They offer unfair and undemocratic access to better facilities based on no more than an ability to pay for them.

EDUCATION AND DISCRIMINATION

Race

It is illegal for any educational body to discriminate on the grounds of race in the following ways:

1 Terms on which a child or adult is admitted.
2 Refusal to admit.
3 Provision of more facilities or better facilities for particular racial groups.
4 Expulsion or in any other way putting someone at a disadvantage.

5   Acting in any other way which involves race discrimination.

Contact the Commission for Racial Equality for information on how to proceed. See also Chapter 5: Ethnic Minorities.

Commission for Racial Equality
Elliot House
10/12 Allington Street
London SW1E 5EH
878 7022

Afro-Caribbean Education Resource Centre
Wyvil School
Wyvil Road
London SW28 2TJ
627 2662
Develops resources for use in primary schools with the aim of ensuring that cultural diversity is reflected in the curriculum.

National Anti-racist Movement in Education
PO Box 9
Walsall
West Midlands
WS1 3SF
0922 720824 ext 300

Promotes introduction of anti-racist perspectives in education through representations to teachers, unions, government, etc.

National Convention of Black Teachers
PO Box 30
Pinner
Middlesex HA5 5EU
866 1682
Aims to fight discrimination, racism and fascism in all areas of education and to present the point of view of black pupils and teachers.

Tamarind Education Products
PO Box 296
Camberley
Surrey GU15 1QW
0276 683979
Teaching materials for children of all races, piloted in schools by teachers.

Sex

The Sex Discrimination Act makes it illegal to discriminate on the grounds of sex in the following ways.

1   Admissions policies.
2   Access to classes, courses or other benefits, facilities or services provided by the school or college.
3   Any other unfavourable treatment.

Contact the Equal Opportunities Commission for information on how to proceed. See also Chapter 15: Women.

Equal Opportunities Commission
Overseas House
Quay Street
Manchester M3 3HN
061 833 9244

CISSY (Campaign to Impede Sex Stereotyping in the Young)
c/o 177 Gleneldon Road
London SW16 2BX
677 2411
Concerned with avoiding the sexual stereotyping of children. Publishes resource lists covering useful addresses and publications.

Sexual Orientation

Section 28 of the 1988 Local Government Act made illegal the 'intentional promotion of homosexuality' by local authorities and made teaching about homosexuality in schools more difficult.

There have been instances of local authorities banning:

1   The publication of a list of advice agencies for young people because one or two of the addresses amongst hundreds were lesbian or gay organisations.
2   The performance of a play by a 'theatre in education' group because of a scene involving homosexuals.
3   The confirmation by a gay teacher of his sexuality when his class asked him about it.

For more information contact the Campaign for Homosexual Equality. See also Chapter 9: Lesbians and Gay Men.

Campaign for Homosexual Equality
Room 221
38 Mount Pleasant
London WC1X 0AP
833 3912

ADDRESSES

General

Advisory Centre for Education
18 Victoria Park Square
London E2 9PB
980 4596
Research, information and advice service campaigning for positive changes in state schools.

Association for Science Education
College Lane
Hatfield
Herts AL10 9AA
07072 67411

Forum and services for science teachers.

British Council
10 Spring Gardens
London SW1A 2BN
389 4938

Campaign for the Advancement of State Education
25 Leybourne Park
Kew Gardens, Richmond
Surrey, TW9 3HB
669 5929

Central Bureau for Educational Visits and Exchanges
Seymour Mews House
Seymour Mews
London W1H 9PE
486 5101

Children's Legal Centre
20 Compton Terrace
London N1 2UN
395 9392

National Association for Gifted Children
1 South Audley Street
London W1Y 5DQ
499 1188

Brings together parents, teachers and others interested in the education of 'gifted children'. Organises support for families and hopes to improve provision in schools.

National Confederation of Parent Teacher Associations
43 Stonebridge Road
Northfleet
Gravesend
Kent DA11 9DS
0474 60618

ILEA Offices

ILEA Information Centre
Room 77, County Hall
London SE1 7PB
633 1066

Hammersmith and Fulham/ Kensington and Chelsea Divisional Office
50 Brook Green
London W6 7BJ
603 3388

Camden/City of Westminster Divisional Office
3 Picton Place
London W1M 5OD
486 0190

Islington Divisional Office
Northstar House
556–564 Holloway Road
London N7 6JW
272 7727

Hackney Divisional Office
41 Stamford Hill
London N16 5SR
802 3177

City of London/Tower Hamlets
Harford Street
Mile End Road
London E1 4PY
790 1288

Greenwich Divisional Office
Riverside House East
Beresford Street
London SE18 6DF
855 3161

Lewisham Divisional Office
Capital House
47 Rushey Green
London SE6 4AT

Southwark Divisional Office
2 Camden Square
London SE15 5LE
703 0855

Lambeth Divisional Office
50 Acre Lane
London SW2 5SS
274 6288

Wandsworth Divisional Office
Amies Street
London SW11 2SW
924 3434

Inner London Borough Education Departments

Peter Mitchell
Education Development Team
Room 225, Camden Town Hall
Judd Street
London NW1 2RU

Reg Hartles
Town Clerk's Office
Guildhall
London EC2P 2EJ

Neil McClelland
Education Policy and Planning Unit
29–37 Wellington Street
London SE18 6PW

Gus John
Education Planning Office
Hackney Town Hall
Mare Street
London E8 1EA

Christine Whatford
Director of Education
London Borough of Hammersmith
  and Fulham
Town Hall
London W6 9JU

Chris Webb
Chief Education Officer
Islington Town Hall
London N1 2UD

Michael Stoten
Chief Education Officer
Town Hall

Hornton Street
London W8 7NX

Bebb Burchell
Chief Education Officer
Lambeth Town Hall
Brixton Hill
London SW2

Leisha Fullick
Education Team
Room 404, Lewisham Town Hall
Catford
London SE6 4RU

Gordon Mott
Education Action Team
Southwark Town Hall
Peckham Road
London SE5 8UB

Anne Sofer
Public Relations Office
Tower Hamlets Town Hall
Patriot Square
London E2 9LD

Donald Naismith
Education Transfer Office
Wandsworth Town Hall
Wandsworth High Street
London SW18 2PU

Gwyn Robins
Education Officer
13th Floor, Westminster City Hall
London SW1

Outer London Education Departments

Chief Education Officer
Barking and Dagenham Borough
  Council
Barking Town Hall
Barking
Essex IG11 7LU
592 4500

Education Department
Barnet Borough Council
Town Hall
Friern Barnet
London N11 3DL
368 1255

Director of Education
Bexley Borough Council
Town Hall
Crayford DA1 4EN
303 7777

Education Department
Brent Borough Council
PO Box No 1
Chesterfield House
9 Park Lane
Wembley, Middlesex HA9 7RW
904 1244

Director of Education
Bromley Borough Council
Sunnymead
Bromley Lane
Chislehurst BR7 6LH
467 5561

Director of Education
Croydon Borough Council
Taberner House
Park Lane
Croydon
Surrey CR9 3JS
686 4433

Chief Education Officer
Ealing Borough Council
Hadley House
79/81 Uxbridge Road
London W5 5SU
579 2424

Chief Education Officer
Enfield Borough Council
Civic Centre
Silver Street
Enfield
Middlesex EN1 3XA
366 6565

Education Offices
Haringey Borough Council
48 Station Road
London N22 4TY
975 9700

Director of Education
Harrow Borough Council
PO Box 22
Civic Centre
Harrow
Middlesex HA1 2UW
863 5611

Director of Educational Services
Havering Borough Council
Mercury House
Mercury Gardens
Romford RM1 3DR
Romford 70 66999

Director of Education
Hillingdon Borough Council
Civic Centre
Uxbridge
Middlesex UB8 1BW
0895 50111

Director of Education
Hounslow Borough Council
Civic Centre
Lampton Road
Hounslow
Middlesex TW3 4DN
570 7728

Directorate of Education
Kingston-upon-Thames Borough
   Council
Guildhall
Kingston-upon-Thames
Surrey KT1 1EU
546 2121

Director of Education
Merton Borough Council
Station House
London Road
Merton SM4 5DX
542 8101

Director of Education
Newham Borough Council
379–383 High Street
Stratford E15 4RD
534 4545 ext. 30159

Director of Educational Services
Redbridge Borough Council
Lynton House
255–259 High Road
Ilford
Essex IG1 1NN
478 3020

Directorate of Education
Richmond-upon-Thames Borough
  Council
Regal House
London Road
Twickenham TW1 3QB
891 1433

Director of Education
Sutton Borough Council
The Grove
Carshalton SM5 3AL
661 5000

Chief Education Officer
Waltham Forest Borough Council
Municipal Offices
London E10 5QJ
539 3650

5

ETHNIC MINORITIES

A very important phenomenon of human behaviour, as compared to animals, is the ability to act purposefully, intentionally and decisively. We behave not instinctively or as if subjected to governing forces, but with a consciousness of what we are doing. We are for the most part goal-directed and we guide the way we act towards specific targets and objectives. To have such objectives, we need knowledge about them and how they might be achieved; we can then act on the basis of such knowledge.

This chapter is concerned with providing basic knowledge about London's ethnic minorities, and the social legislation which affects them. The 1976 Act is the third Race Relations Act since 1964. One of the factors prompting the 1976 Act has been the government's aim to 'harmonise the powers and procedures for dealing with sex and race discrimination so as to secure genuine equality of opportunity in both fields'. Behind the immediate causes for the change in the law, there can be detected deeper causes for concern which have been equally important spurs to government actions. In nearly every speech made in support of earlier race relations legislation, it was stressed that these laws were necessary in order to prevent the kind of civil disorders seen in the USA.

But the law is not the only means necessary for effective progress towards equality of opportunity. The law is capable of dealing not only with individual discriminatory practices, but also with patterns of discrimination which may no longer involve explicit acts of discrimination. In addition to the law, the policies, practices and attitudes of central and local government are of critical importance. But all this rests upon the assumption that the enforcement of the 1976 Act will be effective and that the body set up to carry out the Act, the Commission for Racial Equality, has both the resources and central government's support to carry out its functions.

How effective can it seriously be if the most subversive influence on its success is the existence of the quite contradictory assumptions of the immigration laws and the kind of racist propaganda which is associated with them? A race relations law assumes that the black minorities are part of the community and are here to stay. An immigration law assumes they are here on sufferance and that if things get bad, they should go. A race relations law assumes that the threat of law comes from denying black people the protection of the law. The immigration laws assume that the black minority are a threat to law and order by simply being here.

This chapter deals with these important aspects of our life; the complexities of modern living, the movement of people and their rights and responsibilities. It is an easy compendium of facts and information. Information, as a politician once said, is like a volcano. It erupts and spews. But what you use from the lava depends on you and the lava left.

Lionel Morrison
Principal Information Officer
Commission for Racial Equality

GENERAL INFORMATION

The impact of the Thatcher years on Britain's ethnic minority populations has been staggering. True, the Race Relations Act is still intact, but the issue of racism has been largely ignored by society in general. A cultural and social climate has developed in which racial discrimination has become almost respectable. All post-war British governments have passed their share of racist laws but the present one takes the biscuit for its marginalisation of our ethnic communities.

Withdrawal of central government funding to local councils and the abolition of the GLC has had the knock-on effect of cutting funding to local and community groups of all kinds, with ethnic minority groups being particularly badly hit. The Commission for Racial Equality (CRE) has had its funding from the government cut to such an extent that it is being forced to turn away cases of discrimination that come to its notice and to reduce support funding to community organisations. The total funding given by the government to the CRE is less than the Ministry of Defence's budget for publicity alone. In such an atmosphere it is indeed remarkable that so many groups continue to exist and to provide invaluable services, and that all the cultures represented in London continue to develop their identities and mark their valuable presence in the capital in so many ways.

THE RACE RELATIONS ACT AND RACIAL DISCRIMINATION

The Race Relations Act was passed in 1976 to strengthen the law against racial discrimination. The Act is supposed to protect individuals against discrimination on the grounds of race as a job applicant, employee, contract worker, house buyer, tenant or prospective tenant, customer or client of any organisation or person concerned with the provision of goods, facilities or services, school pupil, student or trainee, member or prospective member of a club and many other situations.

Legal action may be taken if you think you have been discriminated against. The Act gives legal protection against victimisation for any action you may take. The Commission for Racial Equality will help you and give free advice in such matters.

Commission for Racial Equality
Elliot House
10–12 Allington Street
London SW1E 5EH
828 7022

Employment

When the Conservatives came to power in 1979 there were 44,465 black people registered as unemployed or 3.6 per cent of the total unemployed. By 1984 this had risen to 212,645 or 7.3 per cent of all unemployed. By 1985, 41 per cent of Afro-Caribbean men under 25 and 26 per cent of Asian men of the same age were out of work.

Discrimination by employers is extensive despite the law. In many cases it is hard to prove, especially if it takes place at an early stage, even pre-interview.

It is possible to act against discrimination at work under the terms of the Race Relations Act. If a person feels that they have suffered from one of the following, the CRE will try to help.

Types of Discrimination at Work

(a)   Direct discrimination
Treating a person less favourably than others are or would be in the same circumstances. This may apply to offers or terms of employment, for example.

(b)   Indirect discrimination
Applying a condition which, whether intentionally or not, adversely affects a particular racial group. The way in which a job is advertised may fall into this category.

(c)   Discrimination by means of victimisation
Treating a person less favourably than others are or would be in the same circumstances because that person has made a complaint or allegation of discrimination, or has acted as witness or informant in connection with proceedings under the Act.

Employers, employment agencies, training organisations, trade unions and qualifying bodies are all covered by the Act.

NB   There are some exceptions to the Act. An employer or training body may provide training for a specific racial group if the purpose is to enable them to work in a field where that group is currently under-represented. Trade unions may encourage members from a particular racial group to join them if that group is under-represented.

In certain cases, membership of a particular racial group can be a genuine occupational qualification, such as in acting, modelling or providing services to a particular racial group to promote their welfare, when the services can be most effectively provided by a member of the same group. The Act does not apply to employment in domestic households. There are other specific exceptions relating to employment overseas.

What to Do About Discrimination at Work

If discriminated against, a person may make a complaint to an industrial tribunal. The Commission for Racial Equality can advise you on possible courses of action and likely outcomes. The CRE also publishes a code of practice for employment which might be useful to both employers and employees as well as trade unions. If for any reason you cannot or do not wish to contact the CRE directly, a trade union representative or one of the organisations listed at the end of the chapter will help you.

Housing

It is unlawful for anyone selling property or letting rented accommodation to discriminate on grounds of race against a would-be buyer or tenant, either in respect of the actual refusal to sell or let a property or in respect of the terms on which the property is offered, including being put on a waiting list. The Act covers estate agents and accommodation agencies as well as individuals and councils.

The only exceptions are in the case of someone selling property when the seller is owner or part owner, wholly occupies the property and is selling privately without advertising or using an estate agent. Also in the case of letting rented accommodation where the landlord or a close relative lives on the premises and shares facilities with the tenants, and there is room for only one or two households or up to six individual occupants in addition to the landlady's/lord's or her/his relatives' household.

A new code of conduct for private landlords and tenants has recently been introduced. It is too soon to conclude whether or not it has had an effect. If you feel you have been discriminated against, contact the CRE.

For historical and sociological reasons, ethnic groups tend to be concentrated in the inner cities. Discrimination and low income combine to make poorer accommodation more likely among ethnic minorities.

A 1979 survey of national dwelling patterns gave the following results, which seem to have changed very little since that time.

	W. Indian	Asians	White
Owner-occupied	34%	61%	45%
Local authority	53%	17%	35%
Private rented	13%	22%	20%
Overcrowding	18%	27%	6%
Lacking at least one amenity	14%	30%	12%

Other surveys have shown that ethnic minorities are more likely to take longer to house and to have poorer accommodation.

The Commission for Racial Equality (CRE) claims that many estate agents and private accommodation agencies discriminate against ethnic minorities. Often this is as a direct result of pressure from white residents' groups. Such discrimination may be a policy decision made by the agency or they may have been instructed not to accept people of certain races by the landlords/ladies on their books. The Race Relations Act in fact states that this is illegal. Afro-Caribbean, Asian and Irish people in particular have suffered from this kind of discrimination.

Racism in B&B hotels and hostels is a big problem. The Act does cover temporary accommodation, so if you feel you have been discriminated against contact the agency from whom you heard of the accommodation, then report it to the CRE or your local Community Relations Council (see list below).

Harassment of council tenants is a common problem all too often ignored or not treated seriously either by councils or by the police. If you are being harassed contact the council, the Community Relations Council or the Federation of Black Housing Associations.

Federation of Black Housing Associations (FBHO)
374 Gray's Inn Road
London WC1X 8BB
Campaigning on black people's housing needs and promotes housing initiatives. Information and advice.

Education

According to the Race Relations Act, schools, colleges or universities must not discriminate by openly refusing to admit an applicant, admitting an applicant on different terms or providing different benefits, facilities, or services. Discrimination may be allowed in relation to the education or training of persons normally resident overseas, or in steps to meet the special needs of particular racial groups.

Despite these laws, breach of which should be reported to the CRE, discrimination in education persists at all levels. Discrimination in college and university admissions, for example, is widespread and in some cases clearly intentional discrimination by those concerned. In others, it may be unintentional discrimination by someone making a discriminatory decision due to the racist attitudes of predecessors.

Such a case occurred in 1988 at St George's Hospital Medical School. In the words of a CRE report:

> In February 1988, the Commission published its report of the investigation . . . The investigation found that the school had discriminated on racial grounds against undergraduate applicants since at least 1982. The discrimination took the form of a computer program which gave lower scores to 'non caucasian' applicants as compared with similarly qualified white applicants. The program had been devised to mimic the decisions of selectors and was an accurate replication of their preferences and prejudices. It is estimated that over 60 candidates a year were discriminated against.

Recommendations and reports, even when commissioned by government offices have been ignored and local authorities in London have been ridiculed for attempting to implement anti-racist education policies. Former Tory Party Chair, Norman Tebbit, accused ILEA of driving pupils to truancy by 'anti-sexist, anti-racist, gay, lesbian, CND rubbish'. The announcement of ILEA's abolition was partly, according to Mrs Thatcher, as a result of 'political indoctrination' of pupils. Clearly, the local authorities will have their work cut out to cater for their ethnic population's education after ILEA's abolition.

Afro-Caribbean Education Resource
    Centre
Wyvil School
Wyvil Road
London SW28 2TJ
627 2662

Promotes the development of learning materials to ensure adequate representation in the curriculum.

All-London Teachers Against Racism and Fascism
Room 216
Panther House
Mount Pleasant
London WC1

Centre for Information on Language Teaching and Research
Inner Circle
Regent's Park
London NW1

Centre for Multiracial Education
University of London Institute of Education
Bedford Way
London WC1
636 8000

National Convention of Black Teachers
PO Box 30
Pinner
Middx, HA5 5HF
866 1682
Fighting discrimination, racism and fascism in all its forms in education; support and advice to individuals, seminars, etc.

National Committee on Racism in Children's Books
5 Cornwall Crescent (The Basement)
London W11 1PH
221 1353
Research, resource and information centre.

Pubs, Shops, Restaurants etc.

It is unlawful for anyone who provides entertainment, food, drink or accommodation to the public to discriminate on the grounds of race.

Other Goods, Facilities or Services

As above. This applies to insurance companies, building societies, car hire firms, government departments, doctors, services provided by local authorities, etc.

Private Clubs

Any club or association with more than twenty-five members must not discriminate in admitting members or in providing bar service to members. The only exception is for clubs whose purpose is to provide benefits to members of a particular racial group, for example, a sports club whose members must be of a particular national origin.

Advertising

It is normally unlawful to publish or display adverts which indicate an intention to discriminate. Exceptions might be educational facilities for overseas students or organisations attempting to meet the special needs of a particular group.

Instructions, Pressure or Aid to Discriminate

It is unlawful to direct a person over whom one has authority to instruct or induce discrimination, such as instructing an estate agent to discriminate or pressurising a neighbour with respect to the sale of a house.

Loopholes

Clearly, there are a number of loopholes in the Act and certain racist or discriminatory actions remain possible. For example, an educational establishment could discriminate against a particular racial group without doing so openly. Tacit discrimination is considered by many to be a feature of the university system and statistics are used to support this (see above, re St George's Medical School).

Racist attitudes cannot be legislated against; they must be confronted, educated and campaigned against.

RACIAL HARASSMENT, VIOLENCE AND THE POLICE

Stories of racial harassment by individuals, racist organisations or the police abound in London. A CRE report in 1987 said that racist attacks were widespread and common and that racial harassment was growing. Even Metropolitan Police figures for racist attacks, considered by many to be a considerable underestimate, showed a doubling between 1983 and 1988. In August 1989, police and community organisations reported that the number of serious racial assaults in London was 60 per cent higher in the first six months of the year than in the same period in 1988. The total number of reported attacks rose from 1,117 to 1,290 and serious attacks (those meriting a GBH charge) rose from 120 to 190.

Moreover, these are only the reported cases. In the words of a CRE report, entitled 'Racial Attacks':

In the metropolitan area, the number of recorded incidents in 1985 rose by more than 400 over the previous year, to a total of 1937, of which 349 were serious assaults. Yet there were many unrecorded incidents. In Tower Hamlets, for example, 277 were reported to the police, but the local police monitoring group dealt with 495. Further indications of under-reporting were given in a poll conducted by London Weekend Television's 'London Programme'. This found that 1 in 4 Asians in the boroughs of Redbridge, Waltham Forest, Tower Hamlets and Newham had been racially attacked, 1 in 10 of them seriously . . . Community organisations are adamant that under-reporting is entirely a reflection of lack of faith in the police. Without an independent and reliable method of verification it is difficult to ascertain the balance of truth. It is clear, however, that problems over the definition of a racial attack persist, and that many victims prefer to report incidents to community organisations rather than to the police.

A study carried out in Newham, in 1986, found that 1 in 4 of Newham's black residents had been victims of some form of racial harassment in the previous twelve months. Two out of every three victims had been victims more than once, and 116 victims reported 1,550 incidents of racial harassment which included 774 cases of insulting behaviour, 188 cases of attempted damage to property, 175 cases of attempted theft, 174 cases of threats of damage or violence, 153 cases of physical assault and 40 cases of damage to property. Many of these cases would have gone unreported to the police.

Racial attacks are against the law. This includes physical assault, verbal abuse or harassment such as graffiti, letters or damage to property. *The Voice* newspaper has quoted examples of attacks involving objects being pushed through letterboxes, such as dirty nappies, condoms, rubbish, lighted matches and excrement. In parts of London people are afraid to leave their homes for fear of racial harassment, and indications are that the police have so far failed to improve their image of not bothering to answer many calls complaining of racial attacks or harassment. Nevertheless, reports of harassment should still be made and perhaps a record kept by the victim of what happens.

Racial Attacks in Education

A Commission for Racial Equality report entitled, 'Learning in Terror: A Survey of Racial Harassment in Schools and Colleges', concludes:

> The problem of racial harassment extends right through the education system from nursery and infants schools to colleges and universities and affects pupils, students, parents and staff. Incidents of harassment do not occur in isolation: they spill over between the school, the street, the housing estate and the football terrace. Abuse, graffiti and violence as both threat and actuality serve as a constant reminder of the intolerance of white society and the vulnerability of ethnic minority people.
>
> The Scottish Ethnic Minority Research Unit carried out a survey of racial harassment of school children in South Glasgow in 1986. There is little reason to believe that its findings would have been very different if the survey had been carried out in certain parts of London. Within the sample, 25% had suffered damage to property, 37% had experienced personal racial attacks and 100% had been subjected to racial abuse.

The Police

In January 1989, a 65-year-old woman from Notting Hill complained that she was pushed over by a policeman who was trying to arrest her grandson. As often happens it will be 'thoroughly investigated' and probably get lost in the complaints procedure. Such was the case with the death of Blair Peach during a demonstration in Southall in 1979. Despite the fact that it was established that Peach was killed by a blow from a policeman, and that illegal weapons were being carried by the police, no police officer was ever brought to justice and no settlement was made by the Metropolitan Police regarding Peach's death for nearly ten years. The report of internal investigations was never made public.

A Policy Studies Institute report on the Metropolitan Police commissioned by the Met themselves found that racialism and racial prejudice were pervasive. An Institute of Race Relations report in 1987 showed that similar attitudes actually played a part in shaping police policy and strategy. Inner city areas with high proportions of black people were chosen for a new kind of 'public order policing'. The Broadwater Farm estate has suffered more than most from repressive police tactics as the Gifford Report showed.

The Metropolitan Police have recently made a good deal of noise about cleaning up their act on racial harassment, not that they ever actually admitted its existence. However, in February 1989, their publication of a booklet for individuals and organisations entitled *London Racial Harassment Action Guide,* in Greek, Chinese, Vietnamese, Turkish, Arabic, Portuguese, Filipino, five Asian languages and English was at least a step in the right direction and contained some useful practical information.

Nevertheless, simplistic 'advice' like 'If you do get attacked, shout or scream as loudly as you can, it may frighten your attacker(s) and attract help' seems patronising, and unhelpful to say the least. What if the only people around are members of the group attacking you and any excessive noise from you might incite further attacks to keep you quiet? The booklet is available from libraries or police stations.

IMMIGRATION, NATIONALITY AND REFUGEES

Nowhere is racism clearer than in Britain's Nationality Act. Indeed, it was largely through the immigration laws of the 1960s and 1970s that racism was institutionalised in Britain.

The infamous statement by Mrs Thatcher in the lead-up to her 1979 election victory, implying that it is perfectly natural to feel animosity towards people with a different culture, has become an unspoken but accepted fact: 'People are really rather afraid that this country might be rather swamped by people with a different culture and . . . if there is any fear that it might be swamped people are going to react and be rather hostile to those coming in. So if you want good race relations you have got to allay people's fears on numbers.'

Over the last ten years immigration rights have been gradually withdrawn. For example, it has been estimated that it is around thirty times harder for a Nigerian to enter Britain than for a Canadian. Furthermore, male Commonwealth citizens settled in Britain before the 1971 Immigration Act came into force in 1973 had an automatic right to be joined here by their wives and dependent children. (Even so between 1977 and 1983 British emigration posts in the Indian subcontinent refused 21.1 per cent of applications from women seeking to join their husbands and 38.5 per cent from children seeking to join their parents. In the vast majority of these cases, the ground for refusal would be that the entry clearance officer was 'not satisfied' that the applicant was related as claimed to the sponsor.) The 1988 Immigration Act abolished this right. It is now necessary for an individual to prove that s/he can maintain relatives without recourse to public funds. Also rights of parents, grandparents and children over 18 to join relatives have been severely limited.

These are just the tip of a growing iceberg. Refusal of refuge, deportation and repatriation are all on the increase and it is more difficult (and more expensive) to obtain citizenship or nationality.

It should also be noted with some cynicism, perhaps, that any apparently progressive race relations legislation is always followed swiftly by new laws on immigration and nationality.

African Refugee Housing Action Group Ltd
2nd Floor
St Margaret's
25 Leighton Road
London NW5 2QD
482 3829
Resettles refugees in short-life and permanent accommodation and offers help and support in all aspects of settling in Britain. Also runs refugee and immigration rights campaigns. The African Refugee Women's Group can be contacted c/o this address.

British Council for Aid to Refugees (British Refugee Council)
Bondway House
3–9 Bondway
London SW8 1SJ
582 6922

Immigration Appeals
Thanet House
Strand
London WC2
353 8060

Joint Council for the Welfare of Immigrants (JCWI)
115 Old Street
London EC1V 9JR
251 8706

Campaigning on immigration and nationality. Advice and information for groups and individuals and training for advice agencies. Helps families who have been split up because immigration authorities do not believe they are related, alleged illegal entrants, people refused entry at airports or threatened with return to their country of origin, and so on.

Migrant Services Unit
c/o LVSC
68 Chalton Street
London NW1 1JR
388 0241
Working with migrant workers (and some refugees and asylum seekers) bringing their needs to the attention of policy-makers and service providers. Organises training for migrants and for those wishing to work with migrants.

Minority Rights Group
379 Brixton Road
London SW9 7OE
978 9498
Have produced reports on immigration and nationality as well as the wider rights of minorities.

Refugee Forum
99 Chalton Street
London NW1
837 9293

**United Kingdom Council for
 Overseas Student Affairs
 (UKCOSA)**
60 Westbourne Grove
London W2 5SH
229 9268/9
*Looking after and promoting the
needs of overseas students in
Britain.*

UK Immigrants Advisory Service
County House
190 Great Dover Street
London SE1
*Advice and assistance to anyone
with rights to appeal under the 1971
Immigration Act. Help for asylum
seekers and alleged illegal entrants.*

**United Nations High Commission
 for Refugees**
36 Westminster Palace Gardens
Artillery Row
London SW1P 1RR
222 3065

Arts

Information on local and community ethnic arts projects,
including theatre, film, painting, etc. can be obtained from the
Minority Arts Advisory Service and from local Community
Relations Councils (see list at end of chapter).

**Minority Arts Advisory Service
 (MAAS)**
28 Shacklewell Lane
London E8 2EZ
254 7295
*Promotes black and third world arts,
publishes* Artrage *magazine,* MAAS
Register, *a directory of Black and
Third World artists in Britain,* MAAS
Training Bulletin, *and* Black Arts In
London *magazine.*

**Organisation for Black Arts
 Advancement and Learning
 Activities (OBAALA)**
Obaala House
225 Seven Sisters Road
London N4 2DA
263 1918
*Runs the Black Art Gallery, Black Art
Bookshop, Obaala Poetry Theatre,
Obaala Summer Arts School and an
annual project for 11–16-year-old
Afro-Caribbean children. Advice and
information.*

ETHNIC GROUPS AND ORGANISATIONS

Guide To Ethnic London (Michael Haag), available from
bookshops and libraries, is a useful resource, particularly on the
historical background of ethnic populations in London. *The
South London Guide* (Stockwell Press) also has a number of local
addresses. As a rule, information on local ethnic organisations
can be found at the local Community Relations Centre (addresses
at end of this chapter).

Information on religious centres and places of worship can be found in Chapter 12: Religious and Spiritual Belief.

In many cases, information can be obtained from embassies which can be found in the telephone directory.

Asia and Indo-China

Asian Action Group
30 Willoughby Road
Hornsey
London N8 0JG
341 3802/340 8054
Asian youth and community resource centre.

Asian Centre
8 Caxton Road
London N22
889 6938

Asian Women's Forum
Wood Green Shopping City (2nd Floor)
Nursery Premises
50 Mayes Road
London N22
888 2446

Asian Women's Network
52–54 Featherstone Street
London EC1Y 8TR
251 9276
Library and information service.

Asian Women's Resource Centre
134 Minet Avenue
London NW10
961 5701
General advice on all matters affecting Asian women in London.

Asian Women's Resource Centre (ASHA)
27 Santley Street
London SW4
737 5901/274 8854 (24 Hour)

Asian Youth Association
15 Vineyard Hill Road
Wimbledon
London SW19 7JL
946 8129
or 640 3838 (Oz Khan)

A progressive youth project, addressing issues around racism and access within youth provision. Women's group, dance, music, drama, discos, etc.

Bangladesh Association
5 Fordham Street
London E1 1HS
247 3733

Bangladesh Centre
24 Pembridge Gardens
London W2 4DX
229 9404

Bangladesh Women's Association
91 Highbury Hills
London N5 1SX
359 5836
Advice and counselling on all aspects of life in London.

Britain–Vietnam Association
244 Ellerdine Road
Hounslow
Middlesex TW3 2PY

Camden Chinese Community Centre
173 Arlington Road
London NW1 7EY
267 3019
Educational, cultural and other opportunities.

Chinese Information and Advice Centre
68 Shaftesbury Avenue
London W1
836 8291

Confederation of Indian Organisations
5–5a Westminster Bridge Road
London SE1 7XW
928 9889

Coordinates and services Indian organisations across the country.

Festival of Chinese Arts
PO Box 892
London NW1 0NF
359 9843
A forum for the presentation of popular Chinese arts by Chinese people in London.

India Welfare Society
11 Middle Row
London W10 5AT
969 9493
Counselling, advice, classes and events.

Indian Workers Association
112A The Green
Southall
Middx UB2 4BQ
574 6019/7283
Provides for the welfare of immigrants through advice, social and cultural activities.

Institute of Indian Culture
4a Castletown Road
London W4
381 3086/4608

Millan Asian Centre
59 Trinity Road
London SW17 7SD
767 8620/767 8710
Advice and counselling, childcare, support for elderly people, language classes, legal advice and other services for the Asian community, primarily in Wandsworth.

Muslim Women's Welfare Association
200 Capworth Street
London E10
539 7478

National Association for Asian Youth
46 High Street
Southall
Middx, UB1 3DB
574 1325/5900 (fax)

Umbrella organisation providing specialist services in training and development in youth work.

Pakistan Centre
41 Station Parade
London NW2
450 9428

Pakistan Welfare Association
181 Haydons Road
London SW19 8TB
542 6176
Advice on all aspects of social welfare, education, plus classes, translating and liaising with official bodies.

Pakistan Women's Welfare Association
20 Blackstock Road
London N4 2DW
226 4427

Philippines Resource Centre
1 Grange Way
London NW6
624 0270

Philippine Women's Support Committee
BM Box 758
London WC1 3XX
603 1873

Ramgarhia (Sikh) Community Development Project
Mason's Hill
London SE18
317 9701

Society for Anglo-Chinese Understanding
152 Camden High Street
London NW1
485 8236

South London Brahmin Samaj
294 Franciscan Road
London SW17
672 1918
Social and cultural group for the Brahmin community including prayer sessions, sport, etc.

Tibet Society and Tibet Relief Fund of the UK
Olympia Bridge Quay
70 Russell Road
London W14
603 7764
Assisting Tibetans who fled their country and became refugees after the Chinese invasion. Newsletter available.

Vietnamese Refugees Community in London
Community Hall
North Peckham Estate
Hordle Promenade East
London SE15 6JB
703 0036
Advice services for Vietnamese refugees, press and information work, supports individual cases especially of family reunion.

Africa and the Caribbean

The Africa Centre
38 King Street
Covent Garden
London WC2E 8JT
836 1973
Cultural centre, bookshop, crafts, bar, food, discos, live music, films, exhibitions, etc.

African National Congress
28 Panton Street
London N1
837 1930
For a free South Africa and an end to apartheid.

Afro-Caribbean Library Association
Hornsey Library
Haringey Park
London N8 7JA
348 3351

Anglo-Ivorian Society
60 Worship Street
London EC2A 2DJ
377 9134
Fosters social, cultural and commercial exchanges between the UK and the Cote d'Ivoire.

Anti-Apartheid Movement
13 Mandela Street
London NW1 0DW
387 7966

Black Cultural Archives
Wyvil School
Wyvil Lane
London SW8
627 2662

British Moroccan Society
c/o SPANA
15 Buckingham Gate
London SW1E 6LB
828 0997

British Tunisian Society
38 Morinson Road
London SW11 1BP

Caribbean Community Centre
416 Seven Sisters Road
London N4 2LX
802 0550
Recreational, cultural, educational, social and religious facilities. Housing help and counselling for homeless young black people.

City of London Anti-Apartheid Group
BM City AA
London WC1N 3XX
837 6050

Commonwealth Institute
Kensington High Street
London W8
603 4535

East African Asian Association
889 3685

Eritrean Relief Association
96 White Lion Street
London N1 9PF

Ghana Welfare Association
Greater London House
547–551 High Road
London E11 4PB
558 9311

Informs and educates Ghanaians about all welfare rights and benefits, runs programmes for children, women's development, culture, people with disabilities and recreational events.

Museum of Mankind
6 Burlington Gardens
London W1
437 2224

Moroccan Information Centre
61 Goldborne Road
London W10 5NR

Mozambique Angola Committee
PO Box 839
London NW1 7EF
733 0518 (evenings)

Mozambique Information Office
7a Caledonian Road
London N1
278 8691

Namibia Refugee Project
22 Coleman Fields
London N1
359 4362

Namibia Support Committee
PO Box 16
London NW5 2LW
267 1941/2

Society for Libyan Studies
c/o Institute for Archeology
31–34 Gordon Square
London WC1H 0PY
387 7050

Somali London Community and Cultural Association
17 Victoria Park Square
Bethnal Green
London E2

Standing Conference of West Indian Organisations in GB
5 Westminster Bridge Road
London SE1 7XW
928 7861/2
Information relevant to the West Indian community, legal advice, counselling. Campaigns on behalf of groups or individuals where injustices occur.

SWAPO of Namibia
96 Gillespie Road
London N5
359 9116/7

Ujamaa Centre and Bookshop
14 Brixton Road
London SW9
820 1855
Self-help and cultural centre.

West Indian Concern
Caribbean House
Bridport Place
London N1
739 0840
Wide-ranging advice and information centre.

West Indian Women's Association
71 Pound Lane
Willesden
London NW10 2HU
451 4827
Runs a women's meeting group, advice on housing and welfare, etc., runs an after-school junior club for 8–15 year olds and a pensioners group. Organises sport, dance and other activities.

Western Sahara Campaign
180 Brixton Road
London SW9 6AT

Jewish

Anglo-Israel Association
9 Bentick Street
London W1M 5RP
486 2300

Anglo-Jewish Association
5th Floor, Woburn House
Upper Woburn Place
London WC1H 0EP
387 5937/8

Association for Jewish Youth
50 Lindley Street
London E1 3AX
790 6407

**Association of Jewish Refugees in
  Great Britain**
8 Fairfax Mansions
London NW3 6JY
*A social work service including
sheltered accommodation for
refugees from Nazi oppression.*

Board of Deputies of British Jews
Woburn House
Upper Woburn Place
London WC1
387 4044

**Committee for the Welfare of
  Iranian Jews in Great Britain**
17 Arden Road
London N3 3AB
346 3121

Israel Information
2 Palace Green
London W8 4QB
937 8050

Jewish Welfare Board
221 Golders Green Road
London NW11 9DW
458 3282

League of Jewish Women
Woburn House
Upper Woburn Place
London WC1

MAMAM – for a Progressive Israel
Hashomere House
37a Broadhurst Gardens
London NW6 3BN
328 5451

Union of Jewish Students
1 Endsleigh Street
London WC1 0DS
387 4646/380 0111

Europe

Albania

Albanian Society
26 Cambridge Road
Ilford
Essex IG3 8LV
*Meetings, videos, films, concerts, all aimed at promoting good relations
between British and Albanian people.*

Cyprus, Greece, Turkey

Anglo-Turkish Society
43 Montrose Place
London SW1
235 8148

**Committee for the Defence of
  Democratic Rights in Turkey**
84 Balls Pond Road
London N1 4AJ
254 0387

Cypriot Community Centre
26 Crownsdale Road
London NW1
387 6617

Cypriot Women's League
96 Palmerston Road
London N22

Greek Cypriot Brotherhood
4 Porchester Terrace
London W2 3TL
723 4001/402 8904

*Social, cultural and educational
events, promoting Cypriot culture
and interests in Britain.*

**National Federation of Cypriots in
  Great Britain**
Address as above
*Promoting cultural and other links
between members of the Greek
Cypriot community.*

Turkish Cypriot Cultural Association
14 Graham Road
London E8 1BZ
249 7410
*Exhibitions, meetings, lectures,
classes, seminars and training.
Social and welfare work with the
elderly, counselling for women and
single parents.*

Union of Turkish Women in Britain
110 Clarence Road
London E5
986 1358
*Advice, translation and
interpretation service with emphasis
on women's problems. Dancing,
folk singing, and other social
activities as well as support for
human rights in Turkey.*

Union of Turkish Workers
Union Chapel, Compton Terrace
Upper Street
London N1
985 4072/986 1358
*English language and other
educational courses, sport, cultural
and social activities, advice on
welfare rights, etc.*

Ireland

**Action Group (for Irish Youth and
  Irish Commission for Culture and
  Education)**
82 Salusbury Road
London NW6 6NY
328 9029

The Irish Centre
52 Camden Square
London NW1
485 0051
*A mine of information about Irish
activities in London; will provide
information on all kinds of subjects
including the annual London Irish
Festival, held in July in Roundwood
Park, Willesden.*

**Irish In Britain Representation
  Group**
Branches in Camden 482 0824
              Haringey 348 3354
              Lambeth 326 4740

Irish Youth Project
c/o Kilburn Irish Youth Action Group
St George's Annexe
Linstead Street
London NW6
624 0915

London Irish Women's Centre
59 Stoke Newington Church Street
London N16 0AR
249 7318
*Women-only drop-in centre, support
and advice on abortion,
contraception, violence, welfare,
health and legal rights; library, Irish
books, records and musical
instruments, educational,
recreational and cultural focal point,
and a base for Irish women's
groups around London.*

St Gabriel's Endeavour Project
722 Holloway Road
London N19
263 3288
*Young Irish people meet Tuesday
evenings 7.00–9.30pm for
discussions, social evenings,
welfare advice, sports and games,
training courses.*

**South London Irish Welfare
  Association**
138–140 Hartfield Road
London SW19
540 0759 (Welfare)
543 0608 (Centre)

Italy

The Italian Institute
39 Belgrave Square
London SW1
235 1461
*Compiles a list of exhibitions, concerts, cinema, opera, drama, radio
programmes and lectures in Britain that are of Italian interest.*

Poland

Polish Cultural Institute
34 Portland Place
London W1
636 6032/3
*Run by the Polish Embassy. Holds
exhibitions of Polish art, shows
Polish films.*

**Polish Social and Cultural Centre
(POSK)**
238–246 King Street
London W6
741 1940

*Includes bookshop, cafe, restaurant,
auditorium (for Polish classical and
folk music, opera, dance and drama,
films) social club, youth club and
library.*

Solidarnosc Information Office
Park House
North Side
Wandsworth Common
London SW18
874 8635

Portugal

Portuguese Community Centre
7 Thorpe Close
London W10
969 3890

Soviet Union

British–Soviet Friendship Society
36 St John's Square
London EC1 4JH
253 4161
*Building friendship between the two countries, assistance and advice to
organisations and individuals, organises tours, penfriends, talks and
cultural activities.*

Spain

Federation of Spanish Associations in the UK
116 Ladbroke Grove
London W1 5NE
221 2007

Information and advice on all aspects of life in Britain, meetings for Spanish women and for young people; coordinates Spanish organisations in Britain.

Switzerland

Anglo-Swiss Society
Rose Cottage
Hastingleigh
Ashford
Kent, TN25 5HW
023 375 233
Meetings, dinners, lectures, etc.

Latin America

Brazilian Centre
15 Berkeley Street
London W1
499 0877

Britain–Cuba Resource Centre
c/o CARILA (see below)

Chile Solidarity Campaign
129 Seven Sisters Road
London N7 7OG
272 4298

Colombia Solidarity Committee
Priory House
Kingsgate Place
London NW6 4TA

El Salvador and Guatemala Committee for Human Rights
88 Margaret Street
London N1
631 4200/4203

Latin American Advisory Committee
Beauchamp Lodge
2 Warwick Crescent
London W2

Latin American Bureau
1 Arnwell Street
London EC1R 1UL
278 2829
Disseminates information on social, economic, political and human rights issues in Latin America and the Caribbean.

Latin American Women's Group/CARILA
29 Islington Park Street
London N1
359 2270

Latin American Women's Rights Service
Priory House
Kingsgate Place
London NW6 4AT
372 6408
Advice and information on social and health issues. Classes and activities for Latin American women in Greater London.

Nicaragua Solidarity Campaign
23 Bevenden Street
London N1
608 0414

Middle East

Anglo-Jordanian Society
144 Southwark Street
London SE1

**Arab Advice and Information
 Bureau**
634 Linen Hall
162–168 Regent Street
London W1R
734 7335

Arab Club of Britain
PO Box 2101
London W13 8BT
997 0541

Arab Research Centre
5 Belgrave Square
London SW1X 8PH
235 7642

Arab Student Aid International
BM Box 4942
London WC1

Arab Women's Council
8 Redcliffe Square
London SW10
373 0688

Bahrain Society
c/o Inchcape plc
40 St Mary Axe
London EC3A 8EU
321 0110

British Lebanese Society
34 Grosvenor Street
London W1X 9FE

**Council for the Advancement of
 Arab British Understanding
 (CAABU)/Anglo-Arab
 Association/Arab British Centre**
21 Collingham Road
London SW5 0NU
373 8414

Iranian Women's Support Group
c/o Spare Rib
27 Clerkenwell Close
London EC1

Iranian Centre
465a Green Lanes
London N4
341 5005/348 9115

Iraqi Cultural Centre
177–178 Tottenham Court Road
London W8 9LF

**Islamic Cultural and Education
 Centre**
75 Falcon Road
London SW11
228 4267 (day)
223 1867 (evening)

Jordan Information Centre
Jordan House
47 Brunswick Place
London N1 6EE
253 3030

Kurdish Cultural Centre
13–15 Stockwell Road
London SW9 9AU
274 6251
*Social and cultural activities; advice
and information on social and
welfare issues; campaigning and
development work.*

Kurdish Refugee Support Group
489 Kingsland Road
London E8
249 6930

**League of Arab States Mission in
 London**
52 Green Street
London W1Y 3RH
629 0732

**Lebanon Information Processing
 Service**
c/o British Refugee Council
Bondway House
London SW8 1SJ
582 6922

London Friends of Palestine
21 Collingham Road
London SW5 0NU

Medical Aid for Palestine
29 Enford Street
London W1H 1DG
723 7766

Muslim Information Service
233 Seven Sisters Road
London N4
272 5170/263 3071

Palestine Liberation Organisation
4 Clareville Grove
London SW7
409 2865

Palestine Solidarity Campaign
BMPSA
London WC1N 3XX

Saudi British Society
21 Collingham Road
London SW5 0NU
373 8414

Saudi Information Office
Cavendish House
18 Cavendish Square
London W1
629 8803

Syrian Arab Association
4 Gordon Square
London W1R 3AE

Yemen Society
Tricontinental House
18 Linver Road
London SW6 3RB
736 0752

Australia and New Zealand

A number of free magazines with news from Australia and New Zealand, classified advertisements for jobs, accommodation, etc., are widely available on street stands, usually outside tube stations. The main ones are *London Australasian Weekly* (LAW); *Southern Cross, TNT and New Zealand News UK.*

Aboriginal Land Rights Support Group
Black Australian Information Centre
52a Acre Lane
London SW2 1RW
221 4585
Campaigning organisation offering research and information and acting as a focal point for aboriginal visitors to the UK.

New Zealand News UK
New Zealand House
80 Haymarket
London SW1Y

Romany and Other Travellers

Advisory Committee for the Education of Romany and Other Travellers
Mary Ward Centre
42 Queen Square
London WC1N 3AJ
831 7079
Works with travellers and others to achieve effective access to community services such as health and education.

London Roadside Travellers Group
Box 18
Kingsland High Street
London E8 2NS

The Romany Guild
50–56 Temple Mills Lane
Stratford
London E15
555 7214

COMMUNITY RELATIONS COUNCILS

National Association of CRCs
8–16 Coronet Street
London N1 6HD
739 6658

Committee for Community Relations
39 Eccleston Square
London SW1V 1PD
834 9692

Barking and Dagenham Council for Racial Equality
Methodist Church
London Road
Barking
Essex IG11 8AL
594 2773

Barnet Community Relations Council
1 Friern Park Road
North Finchley
London N12 9DE
445 6051

Bexley Council for Racial Equality
Riverside Baths
3 Walnut Tree Road
Erith, Kent
0322 340316

Brent Community Relations Council
194 High Road
Willesden
London NW10
451 4499/4490

Bromley Community Relations Council
c/o 13 Valan Leas
Cumberland Road
Bromley BR2 0PE

Camden Committee for Community Relations
58 Hampstead Road
London NW1 2PY
387 1125

Croydon Council for Community Relations
70 Park Lane
Croydon
CR0 1JE
686 8014/8524

Ealing Community Relations Council
2 The Green
High Street
Ealing
London W5 5DA
579 3861

Enfield Community Relations Council
Enfield Highway Library
258 Hertford Road
Enfield EN3 5BN
805 6121

Greenwich Council for Racial Equality
115–123 Powis Street (2nd Floor)
Woolwich
London SE18
855 7191/2/3/4

Hackney Council for Racial Equality
1 Crossway
London N16 8LA
241 0097

Hammersmith and Fulham Council for Racial Equality
241 King Street
London W6 9LP
741 5715

Haringey Community Relations Council
14a Turnpike Lane
London N8 0PT
889 6871/4

Harrow Community Relations Council
64 Pinner Road
Harrow, Middlesex HA1 4HZ
427 6504

Hillingdon Community Relations Council
Darren House
65 High Street
Uxbridge
Middlesex UB8 1JP
0895 56536

Hounslow Community Relations Council
45 Treaty Centre
Hounslow
Middlesex TW3 1ES
570 1168

Kensington and Chelsea Community Relations Office
Westway Information Centre
140 Ladbroke Grove
London W10 5ND
969 2433 ext 285

Kingston Group for Racial Understanding
107 Whitton Road
Hounslow TW3 2EJ

Lewisham Council for Community Relations
48 Lewisham High Street
London SE13 5JH
852 9808

Merton Community Relations Council
36 High Street
Colliers Wood
London SW19 2AB
540 7386

Newham Council for Racial Equality
175 Upton Lane
London E7
471 4621

Redbridge Community Relations Council
Methodist Church Hall
Ilford Lane
Ilford
Essex IG1 2JZ
514 0688

Southwark Council for Community Relations
125 Camberwell Road
London SE5
252 7033

Sutton Community Relations Council (Three-Borough Project)
Hill Rise
Bishopsford Road
Morden
London SW4 6BL
640 7652

Tower Hamlets Association for Racial Equality
347–349 Cambridge Heath Road
London E2 9RA
729 5775

Waltham Forest Community Relations Council
25 Church Hill
Walthamstow
London E17 3AB
521 8851/2/3

Westminster Community Relations Council
472 Harrow Road
London W9 3RU
289 2277/8

OTHER ADDRESSES

Black Rights UK
221 Seven Sisters Road
London N4 2DA
281 2340

Campaign Against Racist Laws (CARL)
56 Edithna Street
London SW9 9JP
733 8508

Campaigning against current laws on immigration, nationality and passport controls.

Centre for Research in Ethnic Relations
Arts Building
University of Warwick
Coventry CV4 7AI

Greater London Action for Race Equality (GLARE)
Room 312
Southbank House
Black Prince Road
London SE1
587 0740
Umbrella group for community and race equality organisations.

Home Office Research and Planning Unit
50 Queen Anne's Gate
London SW1H 9AT
213 3000

Institute of Race Relations
2–6 Leeke Street
King's Cross Road
London WC1X 9HS
837 0041
Produces materials which can be used as a basis of education and training on racism. A quarterly journal, Race and Class, *is available from IRR and good bookshops.*

Kala Ujamaa Ltd
Southbank House
Black Prince Road
London SE1 7SJ
582 9116/587 0243/582 9424
A central source of information on black cooperatives in a number of languages.

London Interpreting Project
245a Coldharbour Lane
London SW9 8RR

National Ethnic Minority Advisory Council
2nd and 3rd Floors
13 Macclesfield Street
London W1V 7HL
349 8765
Advice and assistance to ethnic minorities in matters relating to immigration, housing, translation, interpretation, social services, etc.

Policy Studies Institute
100 Park Village East
London NW1
387 2171

Race Today
165 Railton Road
London SE24

Runnymede Trust
11 Princelet Street
London E1 6QH
375 1496
Research and information on race issues.

Searchlight
37b New Cavendish Street
London W1
Anti-racist, anti-fascist magazine.

Standing Conference of Ethnic Minority Senior Citizens
5–5a Westminster Bridge Road
London SE1
928 8108

United Nations Association
3 Whitehall Court
London SW1A 2EL
930 2931

War On Want
37–39 Great Guildford Street
London SE1 0ES
620 1111

Ethnic Minority Press

The Commission for Racial Equality has a list of publications available (and mostly published) in Britain, and their contact addresses. The list includes publications in the following languages: Bengali, Chinese, Gujarati, Greek, Hindi, Punjabi, Tamil, Telugu, Turkish, Urdu and English.

Those published in English are aimed mainly at the various Asian, African and Caribbean nationalities represented in this country.

6

GREEN LONDON

Born in the Marylebone Road, I spent my childhood in and on the outskirts of London. It was wartime and travel into the surrounding countryside was difficult if not impossible.

Yet my childhood memory banks are full of tiddlers in jam jars, tadpoles and toad spawn, primroses, cowslips and bluebells and the annual picking of a bunch of real wild flowers for my Mum's birthday. Back in those days it did no harm, there were plenty to go round.

Thanks to the work of dedicated people like Octavia Hill and Robert Hunter, founders of the National Trust, places like Wimbledon Common, Epping Forest, Dartford Heath, Belmont Common and many more had remained unenclosed and un-developed. Likewise, thanks to their campaigning, our cities had public gardens for recreation and laughter in addition to cemeteries for tombstones and mourning.

Back in those not too far off days, there was also plenty of other green space, forgotten corners, end-of-the-street back lots, old brick pits, disused railway sidings and thanks to Adolf Hitler, an increasing number of bombed sites which became havens for wildlife, wild flowers and VE Day parties.

So it was that the London of my youth was interleaved with greenspace corridors and oases, both official and unofficial, in which wild London held its breath in anticipation of the war of development to come. So, too, I was able to cut my botanical teeth using De Crespigny's *New London Flora*, published in 1877, and find that much that he recorded was still in place; like the first entry, '*Acer Campestre* – Woods and Hedgerows frequent'. Yes, at the tail end of the war there were woods still coppiced and hedges still laid as part of the economy of our countryside. So, too, when between 1965 and 1976 the members and friends of the London Natural History Society surveyed the flowering plants and ferns found growing wild within twenty miles of St Paul's Cathedral, an amazing wealth of plants was still found. Yet as shown by the survey's first record (*Lycopodium Innundatum*; a plant of bare wet peat, was last seen near London in 1930 in Keston Bog, if one ignores the piece planted in Epping Forest in 1952, which did not survive long. One would like to know what place was robbed for the sake of this folly) the losses are many.

With the new appalling spate of infill and redevelopment in progress, we can hold our breath and hope, or, like the campaigners of the past, join the members of the London Wildlife Trust and work towards a greener living city – the only truly sustainable market place for all our futures.

London: A Living Guide – Read all about it !

PS   If you live or work in London and are not members of an organisation like the London Natural History Society or London Wildlife Trust, then you should be ashamed of yourself! Please join.

David Bellamy (TV Botanist)
Conservation Foundation

GENERAL INFORMATION

It may come as a surprise that more than a hundred species of birds nest regularly in Greater London and that the same number again can be spotted at different times of the year. Around 2,000 species of plant are known to grow wild within 20 miles of St Paul's. Wild creatures from foxes to badgers and from squirrels to kestrels are far from rare.

The rapid urbanisation process of the last 150 years has destroyed much of London's original rural land, but fortunately some remains. Ancient woods and commons are home to a vast range of trees, plants, animals and insects; heaths, marshes and ponds are still to be seen in many parts of London, with the beautiful countryside of Kent only a short train or bus ride away.

Unfortunately, much of what remains is under threat either from development, or from the twin evils of pollution and neglect. The disposal of London's waste is an increasing problem and the failure to recycle vast amounts of reclaimable material results in huge financial wastage, not to mention pollution. Fumes from factories and traffic are a potential health hazard, as is the capital's water supply.

This chapter aims to provide a brief outline of the major environmental problems facing London, while at the same time showing the impressive range of ecologically important areas that exist in the capital. It also attempts to provide a fairly comprehensive list of the major groups and organisations active in the London area. Small local campaigns are not mentioned but most can be contacted through the larger organisations.

POLLUTION

Air

London's air is seriously polluted. Polluted air can and does cause illness, kill animals, plants and trees and generally make London an unpleasant place in which to live. The burning of fuel produces gases and smoke. In winter, these discharges combine with fog to form a poisonous 'smog'. Discharges such as sulphur dioxide from power stations, exhaust fumes containing carbon monoxide, nitrogen oxides and lead all contribute to London's unhealthy environment.

It is now proven that lead in petrol can cause brain damage in young children but Britain is way behind many other countries in combating pollution from exhaust fumes. Nevertheless, a great deal of progress is being made in persuading people to use lead-free petrol. Having a car converted for lead-free petrol is not expensive and most new cars are already able to use it. (Contact CLEAR (Campaign for Lead-free Air) for information on leaded and unleaded petrol, where to get it and which cars it suits.)

Unfortunately, in the landslide of publicity about lead-free fuel, it has often been overlooked that carbon monoxide, nitrogen oxides and hydrocarbons, all present in petrol, also cause problems especially for heart and lung complaints. Sufferers of conditions such as asthma, of which there are 200,000 in Greater London, are among the worst affected.

Hydrocarbons can cause cancer and along with nitrogen oxide can lead to respiratory infection. Every year since 1972 when World Health Organisation monitoring of the ozone layer began, the London figures have exceeded WHO's recommended limits. LBC Radio has recently begun to give ozone alerts, years after this began in the USA.

Nitrogen oxides and sulphur dioxide also react with water and other substances in the air to form acids. The resulting acid rain can cause serious damage to lakes, forests and other green areas. A recent study showed all soil within a six mile radius of Marble Arch to be lead-contaminated.

Pollution is also a threat to buildings, both ancient and modern. Acid rain has dissolved more of the dome of St Paul's Cathedral in the last ten years than all that was thrown at it in the previous 300. Many buildings in London are smothered with black residues from exhaust fumes. Even treasures kept indoors in museums and archives have to be protected.

Is there a solution? Undoubtedly the answer is yes, but it is no easy job persuading individuals to change their habits, and companies to pay attention to proper safety standards much stricter than those allowed by the present government. More stringent car exhaust standards, including the introduction of catalytic converters to filter out pollutants such as exist in the USA, would be one step that could be implemented very rapidly. EEC limits on exhausts are three times weaker than their US counterparts. Better diesel engines, better maintenance, better quality fuel and better policing of limits are all necessary if there is to be any major change.

Cleaner power stations and stricter restrictions on factory

waste disposal are equally essential. An inspector of factory waste disposal in France told me he could not believe, on the one hand, the lenient government limits on the regulation of waste from factories and power stations in Britain and, on the other, the failure of many factories to adhere even to those weak limits. At present, there are no plans to reduce the pollution from sulphur dioxide from the seven power stations on the Thames Estuary.

Campaign for Lead-free Air (CLEAR)
3 Endsleigh Street
London WC1H 0DD
278 9686

Clean Air Council
Becket House
Lambeth Palace Road
London SE1

Water

1. Drinking Water

Your drinking water is probably not as healthy as you think. A good deal of research has been done on nitrates and pesticides in water, much of it with worrying results. If you have any doubts about the quality of your tap water or would like to know more about your water supply, write to the local Water Authority or water company. Address the letter to the Head of Tap Water Quality. If possible quote a map reference. Ask if the water comes from surface or underground sources. Ask for a list of pesticides tested in your area and the results of the tests. State any time when your supply has been suspect. Send copies of your letters and replies to Friends of the Earth, who have done a considerable amount of research themselves.

Changes which you may notice in your water supply include discoloration, perhaps resulting from poorly maintained mains or high levels of aluminium. There may also be variations in taste or odour. These problems can be caused by contamination of water supplies with aluminium, nitrates, pesticides, nitrites, ammonium, trihalomethanes, cadmium, lead, industrial solvents, and polycyclic aromatic hydrocarbons and bacteria.

FoE or the Environmental Health Authority can tell you about 'Maximum Admissible Concentrations' of substances in your water. They will also interpret any information you are sent in response to inquiries about your water supply.

2. Rivers

The Thames in particular is affected by pollution from factory discharges and emissions from the heavy river traffic. But many rivers in Greater London suffer from pollution resulting from acid rain, untreated sewage (resulting either from ancient decaying sewage pipes or from pipes connected wrongly by 'cowboy' plumbers), chemicals and litter. The destruction of plant and animal life in rivers and streams is horrifying.

Institute of Water Pollution Control
Ledson House
53 London Road
Maidstone
Kent ME16 8JH

International Association on Water Pollution Research and Control
1 Queen Anne's Gate
London SW1
222 3848

Research and conferences on water pollution.

National Water Council
1 Queen Anne's Gate
London SW1H 9BT

Pure Rivers Society
74 Dagenham Avenue
Essex RM9 6LM

Land

Land pollution covers discarded paper and bottles, pets' mess, rubbish dumps, dumped chemicals and abandoned cars. Much land pollution consists of substances or items that could have been recycled or at least disposed of safely. For information on recycling see below. For general information on litter or waste disposal contact the Tidy Britain Group, Keep Britain Tidy, Council Cleaning Departments or the London Waste Regulation Authority (see below).

Lead

Lead is present in food, water, petrol, industrial discharges, paint and consumer goods. It is poisonous to humans and can cause anaemia, high blood pressure and damage to the nervous system. It interferes with children's production of Vitamin D and can cause brain damage. For adults, the main sources are food, air, water, some paints, ink, earthenware glaze and eye cosmetics. For children the problem is more acute as their bodies are smaller but they inhale the same amounts. Contact Friends of the Earth for more details.

Noise

The single most common complaint to Environmental Health Officers is neighbour noise and the number of complaints is rising fast. Traffic and aircraft noise can also be a serious problem.

**British Association for the Control
   of Aircraft Noise**
30 Fleet Street
London EC4

Noise Abatement Society
PO Box No. 8
Bromley
Kent BR2 0UH

What To Do About Pollution

1. Complaining

In the first place, report any instance of pollution to your Borough Environmental Health Department at the main council offices (see appendix for list of all Borough Council addresses). It is always worthwhile sending a copy of any letters you write or receive to a local environmental group such as Friends of the Earth, who may already be working on similar examples.

2. Personal Action

For the individual, there are certain obvious measures: using private transport less, except bicycles, and public transport more; converting cars to lead-free petrol; disposing properly of litter and waste; writing to the relevant authorities; and most important, joining or supporting organisations, be they political parties or pressure groups, which campaign for the protection of the environment.

Health and Safety Executive
Baynards House
1 Chepstow Grove
London W2
229 3456 x6721

**Her Majesty's Inspectorate on
   Pollution**
Department of the Environment
Romney House
43 Marsham Street
London SW1
212 8981

RECYCLING

It has been calculated that if you put the waste swept from Greater London's streets, in one year, in Trafalgar Square, it would cover Nelson's Column (170ft) five times over.

In 1985, the following amounts of waste were produced in London (LWRA figures):

Inert wastes	8,150,000 tonnes
Commercial and industrial waste	3,040,000 tonnes
Household wastes/CA sites	2,420,000 tonnes
Total	13,610,000 tonnes

Availability of land for waste disposal within Greater London is declining. Counties outside London already receive more than 70 per cent of London's waste. A particular problem whose urgency is increasing by the week is that most of London's landfill dumping sites will soon be filled. The current plan of some local planning authorities is that more 'waste hills' will be built, to be covered by grass at a later date.

For general information on recycling and a resource list, write to the Recycling Department at Friends of the Earth London Unit. Alternatively contact:

Waste Watch
26 Bedford Square
London WC1
636 4066
A national campaign to promote recycling.

What Can Be Recycled?

Failure to recycle or properly dispose of waste is damaging or destroying many important habitats in London, as elsewhere. Recycling can encourage conservation and is a smaller consumer of energy than processing virgin materials, not to mention the fact that natural resources from rainforests to mineral deposits are running out at an alarming rate.

Charities often benefit from recycling schemes, quite apart from the savings in time, money and energy used in the disposal of waste that can be put to better use elsewhere. Of course, a further benefit is that recycling schemes are likely to create local employment.

Around 70 per cent of domestic waste consists of packaging material. Some of this is not recyclable and much is used purely for the purpose of making a product look attractive. We pay the bill. Milk bottles are returned an average of twenty times; cartons, on the other hand, cannot be reused or recycled.

Expanded plastics containing CFCs, which are not recyclable, are helping to destroy the ozone layer, yet there are alternatives (bottles, cans, paper). Nowadays manufacturers regularly use the absence of additives as a selling point. Why not make recyclable packaging equally attractive to the consumer?

Paper

We import far too much of the raw material for paper and board manufacture and do not recycle anything like enough of what is produced – only 29 per cent. However, the value of waste paper fluctuates wildly which is why most areas do not have a paper collection service.

Recycled paper is NOT all dreary grey, with the texture of toilet paper. It is becoming much more popular and more widely available. Several large organisations such as Virgin, Body Shop, World Wildlife Fund, and Southwark and Richmond councils are now committed to using recycled paper.

FoE Recycling Unit
26–28 Underwood Street
London N1
490 1555

Books for a Change
52 Charing Cross Road
London WC2
836 2315
Stocks a wide range of writing, copier, duplicator and computer paper and envelopes.

City Papers
7 Curtain Road
London EC2 3LP
377 5112

Bulk orders for A3 and A4 copier paper only.

Conservation Papers
Freepost
Reading, RG6 1BR
0734 668611
Coloured stationery and wrapping paper by mail.

Paperback Limited
Bow Triangle Business Centre
Unit 2
2 Eleanor Street
London E3 4NP
980 2233
Suppliers of recycled paper in bulk.

Oil

A total of 1.25 million tonnes of waste oil enters the ocean every year. Much more is trapped in river banks, sewage systems and the ground. Only 270,000 tonnes out of the 830,000 used every year is reclaimed. A million gallons of waste oil is unaccounted for in London every year. Where does it go? Remember that a gallon of oil in water covers an area equivalent to two football pitches.

Remember also that while it is preferable to burn waste oil in some form of boiler, for example in a garage, rather than dump it illegally, some oil such as sump oil contains lead and burning it releases pollutants. As a rule, local authorities have facilities for the disposal of waste oil, as do some garages (contact FoE or London Waste Regulation Authority).

There are many good reasons for disposing of waste oil properly. Unfortunately, strict, enforceable laws are not yet one of them.

Nevertheless, local authorities do have some control over oil burning. The same regulations apply to burning waste oil as to burning it as part of an industrial process under the terms of the Health and Safety at Work Act and the Clean Air Act, and it is only permissible to burn certain types of oil on certain sites.

However, oil is still dumped illegally in London's rivers. It can quickly ruin the water supply and kill wildlife, and can also kill the bacteria that break down effluent in sewage systems if it leaks into them.

Oil can be a health hazard in other ways, too. For instance, the additives in lubricating oil have made it into a carcinogenic substance.

Glass

Discarded or dumped waste glass can be a serious danger to humans and animals for obvious reasons. Furthermore, because it is large it tends to clog landfill sites.

At present, 14 per cent of waste glass is already recycled for further use. There is a 25 per cent energy saving in producing glass from cullet, every tonne of which used saves 30 gallons of oil.

Bottle banks were introduced in 1977 by the Glass Manufacturers Federation. These are often situated in supermarket car parks and the glass collected saves glass manufacturers time and money. However, a wider system of returnable bottles, allowing bottles to be used several times, would be preferable.

When returning bottles remove tops and caps. Rinse the bottles and sort them out into different colours.

Glass Manufacturers Association
19 Portland Place
London W1N 4BH
580 6952

Textiles

Textiles account for 3 per cent of our waste, a very small amount of which is reclaimed – and 70 per cent of that is exported. Giving to jumble sales or charity shops is an easy way of ensuring clothes are reused. Apart from that, woollens can be respun and cloth rags can be used for flock in bedding, industrial wiper cloths or roofing felt. Some local authorities have a rag skip in their civic amenity sites and there are many rag merchants and charity shops.

Cans

There is a 95 per cent energy saving when aluminium is recycled rather than smelted from bauxite. The problem is that it is often mixed up with other materials. In 1979 the Can Makers Federation set up Save-A-Can. The scheme is similar to bottle banks and the number of disposal banks is increasing. Scrap merchants pay around 30p per kilo (fifty cans) for aluminium cans from voluntary groups.

**Aluminium Can Recycling
  Association**
Suite 308
I-Mex House
52 Blucher Street
Birmingham B1 1QU
021 633 4656

**Can Makers Recycling Information
  Service**
36 Grosvenor Gardens
London SW1 0ED
629 9621

Save-A-Can
Elm House
19 Elmshott Lane
Cippenham
Slough, Berkshire
06286 66658
*Information on can banks in
London.*

Plastics

A total of 36 per cent of all plastics used in Britain are accounted for by packaging. A major problem for recycling campaigns is that there are thirty different kinds of plastic in common household use in Britain. Some are reusable such as PET (used to make the bomb-shaped bottles with black bottoms). It is more expensive to collect than glass but saves oil in the long run.

Most plastics that are dumped do not biodegrade at all. So-called biodegradable plastics do break down partly but still remain in the ground in small pieces. Plastics could feasibly be burned for fuel but they contain toxins. However, proper incineration is both possible and desirable.

British Plastics Federation
5 Belgrave Square
London
SW1X 8PH
235 9483

Waste Recycling Centres and Civic Amenity Waste Disposal Sites

Barking and Dagenham: 592 4324
Bexley: Dartford 76692
Bromley: 658 3747/464 3994
Croydon: 688 7003/660 9337
Enfield: 886 7185/366 4455
Haringey: 801 5592
Havering: Upminster 25723
Hounslow: 890 0917
Kingston upon Thames: 549 6373
Merton: 337 9979/947 2656
Redbridge: 504 5808
Sutton: 644 7297
Waltham Forest: 521 4079/
  529 4831

Barnet: 452 3918/368 8083
Brent: 998 3747
Camden: 485 1553
Ealing: 578 5674
Greenwich: 311 5229
Harrow: 907 8936
Hillingdon: 841 4546/561 4783
Kensington and Chelsea: 352 9402
Lambeth: 670 2048
Newham: 591 3834
Richmond upon Thames: 876 3281
Tower Hamlets: 987 3077
Wandsworth: 871 2788/9

Flytipping

The dumping of waste, mostly builders' rubble, on areas of open land not intended for rubbish dumping, is a serious problem. Around a million tons of such rubble is dumped on open ground in the Greater London area every year, often on an organised scale. The London Waste Regulation Authority tries to regulate such dumping and catch those guilty of spoiling many open spaces but it is a very big job that relies on public vigilance as much as the goodwill of builders. The LWRA has a flytipping hotline open twenty-four hours a day to take information on any dumping seen taking place by the public. Call 928 9988.

ENERGY

Nobody has provided detailed information on energy in London since the demise of LEAN. Some councils provide some information otherwise no one offers advice on the subject. Three or four nuclear waste trains travel through London every week on their way to Sellafield. Much concern remains over the possibility of leakage and accidents, despite government assurances to the contrary.

ALARM
52 Acre Lane
London SW2
737 4144
Campaigns against the transport of irradiated fuel.

Campaign for Nuclear Disarmament
22–24 Underwood Street
London N1 7JG
250 4010

Consumers Against Nuclear Energy (CANE)
PO Box 697
London NW1

London Nuclear Information Unit
Room 326a
Camden Town Hall
Euston Road
London NW1 2LL
860 5747

PLANNING AND BUILDINGS

Friends of the Earth's booklet 'Capital Schemes' looks in some detail at the Department of Transport and road schemes in London. See also Chapter 14: Transport.

Planning Aid for London
100 Minories
London EC3N 1JY
702 0051
An advice agency for people with all kinds of planning problems.
Produces a newsletter in association with the Open Spaces Society (25a Bell Street, Henley-on-Thames, Oxon, RG9 2BA. 0491 573535) and Friends of the Earth London Unit.

Professional Institutions Council for Conservation
12 Great George Street
Parliament Square
London W1
222 7000
Encourages greater liaison between those involved in the planning, management and development of natural resources and those concerned with the built environment.

RIBA Community Architecture
66 Portland Place
London W1N 4AD
580 5533 ext 4033

SAVE Britain's Heritage
68 Battersea High Street
London SW11 3HX
228 3336
Concerned with saving important buildings from demolition and showing how they can be converted for alternative use.

Society for the Protection of Ancient Buildings
37 Spital Square
London E1 6DY
377 1644
Advisory service, courses for architects, involved in conservation of architectural heritage.

Town and Country Planning Association
17 Carlton House Terrace
London SW1
930 8903/4/5

PARKS AND OPEN SPACES

Threats to Sites

More than eighty sites in Greater London are likely to be built on in the next five years, forty of which are of great ecological importance. Among the better known sites under threat are:

Oxleas Wood, Greenwich

Oxleas Wood is an 8,000-year-old woodland in Greenwich. It is soon to have a four-lane highway driven through it linking the South Circular Road to the planned East London River Crossing. The neighbouring Shepherdleas Wood will also be affected.

The two woods have been classified by the Nature Conservancy Council as a Site of Special Scientific Interest. They also constitute a London Heritage Site and an Area of Special Character of Metropolitan Importance.

The woods are enjoyed by thousands of people but this has not prevented the government from approving a plan to build the highway, despite the fact that at the public inquiry in 1986, 8,300 representations were heard opposing the plan as against only ninety-nine in favour.

Originally, the inquiry inspector recommended that the road should be cut through the wood then covered with a tunnel. This would still seriously affect the wood's water table and disturb its complex ecology. But even this small glimmer of hope has all but disappeared. The Department of Transport has claimed that a 'cut and cover' solution is not possible as it would be too expensive – even though the same project will be allowed to pass under a section of Ealing Common that has only been in its current state for forty years, at a cost of £15–20 million. The Oxleas cut and cover would cost only £10 million.

There is still some hope that the scheme can be delayed and a new public inquiry held as ministers have decided to change the design of the bridge due to be built near to the wood.

Camley Street Natural Park

12 Camley Street
London NW1 0NX
833 2311

Camley Street Natural Park is a real oasis of plant and animal life situated behind King's Cross station and flanked by the Regent's Canal. It is managed by London Wildlife Trust with support from Camden Council and local volunteers. The 2½-acre site has facilities for school and adult groups, though booking is advisable if a large number of people is visiting in a group. Otherwise, individuals can drop in any time between 10am and 5pm.

However, this unique site is now threatened by the plans to build a terminus for the Channel Tunnel Rail Link and to redevelop the King's Cross area. The entire site with its many species of plants, birds and insects, often the only chance local schoolchildren have had to see such species in the wild, will disappear under concrete.

London Wildlife Trust and its many supporters are not convinced that there is no alternative to bulldozing the site, as developers claim.

Local Sites

All London's boroughs have parks and open spaces to offer, some more than others. The following list is by no means exhaustive and concentrates on areas of natural or ecological interest rather than those used purely as sport or play areas. The Recreation Department of the Borough Council will provide details of all parks and gardens and other open spaces in its area. Most councils publish a range of leaflets on specific parks, woods or walks (see Appendix for council addresses). Two fascinating books are David Goode's *Wild In London* (Michael Joseph) and Bob Smyth's *City Wildspace* (Hilary Shipman), both of which I acknowledge for filling in gaps in my available information.

Barking and Dagenham

Barking has a number of open spaces, mostly recreational, such as Barking Park, Mayesbrook Park and Parsloes Park. A quieter green space can be found surrounding the remains of Barking Abbey and St Margaret's church. There are plans to create a nature reserve in the Dagenham Corridor in the Dagenham Road area of the borough near the Beam river. However, another part of the borough, Barking Reach, is under threat from the developers.

Barnet

Two streams which join to form the Brent, Silk Stream and Dollis Brook, pass through Barnet. Both are in danger of serious pollution from untreated sewage as a result of inefficient plumbing. Pymmes Brook and Marshall's Brook also flow through the borough providing a habitat for waterside wildlife. The Welsh Harp (see Brent) is also partly in Barnet. Rowley Green in Arkley, with its woodland, ponds, bog and grassland; Totteridge Fields in the Dollis Brook valley; Darlands Lake on Totteridge Common; Copthall Railway Walk and Burnt Oak Walk (across the valley of Dean's

Brook), Coppets Wood with its ancient coppiced areas of oak and hazel and Glebelands with its many wetland plant species are all areas of particular natural interest, making Barnet an especially rich borough in sites of natural importance.

Moat Mount and Scratchwood Countryside Park

Close to the residential areas of Mill Hill and Edgware. Shown on maps since the sixteenth century. Rich in woodland, flora and fauna. Nature trail available from the council.

Bexley

Bexley, like Bromley, includes a portion of Kent countryside. Three areas are of special interest.

Crayford Marshes, Erith

At the mouth of the River Darenth, consisting of a network of water-filled ditches and serving as a feeding and nesting ground for a range of birds such as heron and redshank.

Lesnes Abbey Wood

An important wood containing oak and sweet chestnut, hornbeam and wild cherry. Part of the wood overlooks the abbey ruins. Famous for its spring daffodils.

North Cray Woods, Sidcup

An area of ancient oak and ash currently managed by London Wildlife Trust.

Brent

Paddington Old Cemetery

Built in 1855, the cemetery has survived the urban development that swallowed Willesden into London. A haven of wildlife in the midst of a creeping urban sprawl.

Gladstone Park

The only remnant of the fields that once surrounded Willesden and Dollis Hill. Bought by the local authority in 1898 and preserved as an open space. Squirrels, ducks and other birds are common in the park; hazel and hawthorn trees have been planted to enhance the existing wildlife.

Welsh Harp

Also known as Brent Reservoir, the Welsh Harp is an oasis of water and marine life in an area flanked by the North Circular and the Edgware Road. Opened in 1835, the reservoir offers tranquil walks, picnic areas and peaceful boating. Around 140 species of wetland birds can be seen at different times of year. Many waterside plant species thrive despite the nearby roads. The area has been designated a Site of Special Scientific Interest by the Nature Conservancy Council.

Barn Hill/Fryent Way Nature Trail

Fifty acres of woodland and 200 acres of conserved farmland. A nature trail takes approximately two hours. A remnant of a much larger estate once belonging to Richard Page in the late eighteenth century. Close to Wembley Park and Kingsbury tube stations.

Bromley

Chelsfield Circular Walk

A 5-mile walk taking in the village of Chelsfield, Goddington Park and surrounding woodland including Griff's Wood and Crown Wood, in Bromley's Green Belt. Buses and trains to Chelsfield can be picked up in Orpington.

Crystal Palace Park

Large area of open parkland on site of remains of Crystal Palace. Includes ponds, trees, gardens and children's zoo.

Cudham Circular Walk

A 3½-hour walk taking in churches and village pubs as well as large areas of Green Belt land. Particularly interesting are Twenty Acre Shaw, an area of high woods on chalky soil rich in flowers like orchids and cowslips; Downe Village Conservation Area, an area of less dense woodland; Cuckoo Wood, an area of managed woodland providing home for badgers, squirrels and birds and a variety of plant life; and Downe Bank, an area of beech and hazel woodland with its associated flora. Buses to Cudham leave from Orpington Bus Station.

Ravensbourne Nature Trail

Originally a private estate, now offering a fascinating nature trail with wildlife in many settings: ponds, streams, marsh and woods. Foxes, weasels, moles and bats have been seen along with woodpeckers, flycatchers, wagtails, siskins and blackcaps. Marsh flowers and butterflies abound in summer. The walk starts near Keston Ponds off Fishponds Road.

Hayes Common

A 200-acre common close to Hayes BR station. Farmed and settled for at least 1,200 years, now colonised by birch, oak and many flora.

Jubilee Country Park

Access via Thornet Wood Road, Southborough Lane or Blackbrook Lane. Previously a golf course, now a park and important conservation site.

Nash Circular Walk

A 2½-hour walk through rolling countryside taking in the old commons of Hayes and Keston, Well Wood and open farmland. Bus services from Bromley North.

Scadbury Park Nature Reserve

Three hundred acres of countryside that started life as a Saxon estate. Trees, flora and pondlife abound in beautiful woodland and open country. Access from Old Perry Street.

Camden

Camley Street Natural Park (see above)

Hampstead Heath

An ancient area of heathland whose character has changed over the years but whose range of woodland and open grassy areas still attracts thousands of people. Over forty species of birds breed on the heath including grebes, kestrels, whitethroats and tawny owls. Kenwood, which is part of the general area known as 'The Heath', is a particularly good spot for birdwatching. More than 200 species of fauna are known to grow on the heath, not including grasses, sedges, mosses and ferns. A range of trees, some very old indeed, grace the common, notably a number of ancient oaks.

Highgate Cemetery

An overgrown Victorian graveyard in Swains Lane, N6 with restricted access. Details of guided tours and of the cemetery's wildlife are available from Friends of Highgate Cemetery, c/o 5 View Road, N6.

Queen's Park

Site of the Royal Agricultural Show in 1879, now a 30-acre public park.

Adelaide Road, Chalk Farm

A nature reserve alongside the Euston railway line. Used for study by local schools.

The City of London

The City claims over 190 open spaces. In fact many of these are no more than a tree and a couple of seats but there are several attractive churchyards and gardens. Pressure for building space usually means that office blocks take precedence over green areas, even if the City of London Corporation encourages builders to incorporate open spaces into their plans. A number of gardens remain, however, such as the one adjoining Wren's church of St Anne and St Agnes in Gresham Street, Postman's Park, St Dunstan-in-the-East, Finsbury Circus and St Paul's Churchyard, injecting the odd splash of colour into the encroaching brick jungle.

Many people do not realise that the Corporation has responsibility for the management of several parks and commons outside the City, and indeed outside London. A century ago an Act of Parliament authorised the Corporation to acquire land within 25 miles of the City 'for recreation and enjoyment of the public'. These areas include Epping Forest (stretching from Wanstead Flats to Epping, a 6,000-acre wood with deer, fox and other woodland mammals and birds); Burnham Beeches (a heavily wooded area in Buckinghamshire extending over 500 acres between Slough and Beaconsfield); Hampstead Heath (see Camden); Highgate Wood (see Haringey); Queen's Park (see Camden); Coulsdon, Farthingdown, Kenley and Riddlesdown commons in Surrey; West Wickham Common and Spring Park in Kent and West Ham Park in Essex.

Croydon

Selsdon Wood

Originally oak woodland, now supplemented by larch, spruce and beech. Also boasts a wide range of grasses and herbs. Parts of the wood are enclosed as bird sanctuaries.

Bramley Bank

An area of mixed woodland with a pond overlooking a residential area at Riesco Drive, Addington.

Addington Hills

An area of heather and grassland offering remarkable views over the whole of London.

Ealing

Horsenden Wood

In Greenford, a large area of oak and hornbeam, now being restored to its original condition with meadowland, hedgerows and woodland plants.

Perivale Wood

Also in Greenford, one of the seven woods in North London named as being of metropolitan importance by the GLC London Habitat Survey. Fine examples of field maple, crab apple, oak and hazel, a beautiful display of bluebells and buttercups and a host of birds. Access is limited but visits can be arranged with the Selborne Society, 12 Hall Drive, Hanwell, N7.

Fox Wood

Adjoining Hanger Hill Park, 2 hectares of woodland surrounding a former reservoir. Hawthorn and bramble offer suitable habitat to nuthatches, blackcaps and tawny owls among others.

Enfield

Capel Manor Environmental Centre

Woodlands, meadows, lakes, ponds, educational farm and information centre.

Trent Country Park

A remnant of the Royal Forest of Enfield Chase covering 470 acres of woodland and meadows with a large amount of interesting wildlife. Also offers five suggested nature trails and a Pets Corner.

Forty Hall, Whitewebbs and Hilly Fields Parks

Three adjoining parks covering a total of 44 acres of wood and parkland with riding, wildlife, picnicking and golf.

Greenwich

Greenwich Park

Adjoining Blackheath (see Lewisham).

Oxleas Wood and Shepherdleas Wood

(See above.) Also adjoining Jack Wood, Avery Hill Park, Eltham Park and Pippenhall meadows. The Green Chain Walk takes in all of this highly attractive area.

Tump 53

The remains of a nineteenth century ammunition stores, now used as an educational nature reserve for the adjoining school. A small island in a lake with surrounding reed beds and a bird haven. Situated on Bentham Road.

Hackney

Stoke Newington Reservoirs

Attracting many waterfowl, swallows and swifts, these are the closest reservoirs to the centre of London.

Abbey Park Cemetery

Run as a nature reserve after a local campaign. Probably the most important site for birds in the borough.

Hammersmith and Fulham

Wormwood Scrubs

Formerly Old Oak Common but now mostly barren scrubland. Lizards and birds frequent the grassy areas with their wild strawberry patches.

Haringey

Haringey Park Walk

A wildlife park and footpath following the old railway line which links Finsbury Park with Alexandra Palace. Steep, grassy embankments and wooded cuttings full of fascinating wildlife including 230 species of flowering plants. Currently under threat from proposed road schemes.

Alexandra Park

A large open space surrounding Alexandra Palace with corridors of wood, scrub and grass. Many birds visit the park, forty-six of which are known to have bred. A pond has been added to the nature reserve on the east side alongside the King's Cross BR line.

Highgate Wood

Seventy acres of beautiful, peaceful woodland managed by the Corporation of London since 1886. Originally part of the Old Forest of Middlesex, now home to a great variety of woodland wildlife.

Railway Fields

A conservation park for adults and children built on a former BR goods depot. Off Green Lanes, near Umerville Road.

Harrow

Bentley Priory Walk

A 7km-walk through woods and parks, streams, ponds and historic settlements. Covers Grim's Ditch, a saxon earthwork; Grim's Dyke House, once home of W. S. Gilbert (of Gilbert and Sullivan fame); Stanmore Hall, built in the nineteenth century and containing William Morris interiors; Little Common and Caesar's Ponds, reputedly a Roman camp; Copse Farm; Bentley Priory, a house on the site of a thirteenth-century Augustine priory. The walk also takes you through a deer park, Bentley Priory Nature Reserve, Harrow Weald Common and Stanmore Common.

Havering

Duck Wood

A traditionally managed coppiced woodland extending over 20 acres. Close to Sheffield Drive in Harold Wood. Wild fungi, herbs and grasses grow amongst the trees and many species of birds feed around the trees and the wood's ten ponds where frogs and toads breed freely. Foxes, deer and hedgehogs have all been spotted.

Rainham Marshes

A highly important site for bird life. Over 10,000 birds spend winter on the meadows. Sheep and cattle still graze on the grassland. Short-eared owls and hen harriers are regularly sited. Unfortunately, part of the area has already disappeared under The Watermeads industrial estate.

Bedfords Park

Not far from Gallows Corner, the 215-acre park overlooks the Thames Valley and the Kentish Hills. Contains woodland, open grassland, deer, a lake and a stream. Set in the grounds of Bedfords House.

Hillingdon

The Grove

Once the grounds of a 450-year-old house of the same name, now demolished to make way for a modern housing development. Five acres remain and are managed by the London Wildlife Trust. There are remnants of the original garden as well as areas of woodland and scrub supporting both native or non-native trees. Kestrels, green woodpeckers and tawny owls make their homes in The Grove as do foxes, squirrels and deer.

Bayhurst Wood Country Park (90 acres), Copse Wood (150 acres), Mad Bess Wood (186 acres), and Old Park Wood (238 acres) were all part of the ancient Middlesex Forest. They now form the largest remaining remnant and are a fascinating habitat for wildlife.

There is particular concern, however, that certain sites in Hillingdon are in danger of destruction. The proposed London–Heathrow rail link will pass through Little Harlington Playing Fields, a 19-acre recreation area. Furthermore, developments on the A40 at Swakeleys Road and Long Lane are having an impact on wildlife, including the great crested newt at Park Road Ponds. The London Wildlife Trust is working with the council to find alternative habitats.

Hounslow

Chiswick House Grounds

(Off Great West Road, at Hogarth roundabout.) The grounds of this interesting building, designed and built by the 3rd Earl of Burlington in the 1720s, boast a nature trail, on whose route you are likely to see parakeets, holly trees, coppiced woodland, woodpeckers and many fascinating plants, shrubs and insects.

Boston Manor Nature Trail

A trail starting at the lake in Boston Manor Park and proceeding through a wood, crossing the River Brent on to Clitheroe's Island then along the Grand Union Canal towpath. A range of animal and plant life can be seen, including common shrews, kingfishers, woodpeckers, giant hogweed and many riverside herbs and flowers.

Hounslow Heath

A large area of woodland and open common where it is not unusual to see squirrels, rabbits, weasels and voles as well as less common birds such as the stonechat.

Gunnersbury Triangle

Saved by local residents from a BR campaign to develop factories and warehouses. Now managed by the London Wildlife Trust. Formerly agricultural land, used as allotments in the 1930s, now developed into woodland containing birch and sallow, ferns and sedges.

Islington

Islington Park Walk

A plan to link Highbury Fields to Gillespie Park (created as an inner city habitat) and Finsbury Park, thus connecting the existing park walk to Highgate Wood and Alexandra Park. The New River canal built in 1613 also passes through Islington and the council has created a nature reserve on it at Canonbury.

Kensington and Chelsea

Holland Park

Close to the western end of Kensington High Street. A private estate until as late as 1952. Still contains Holland House built in the early seventeenth century. Fifty-five acres of land including a Dutch garden, an iris garden, pools, lawns and 28 acres of woodland containing oaks, birches, limes, chestnuts and cedars.

Chelsea Embankment Gardens

A pleasant garden with spring and summer bedding, shrubs and grass areas.

Kensal Green Cemetery

Still used but like Highgate, much of the original land is now covered by thistle and bracken with a selection of flowers and birds to enhance the peaceful atmosphere.

Chelsea Physic Garden

Botanical gardens with collections from around the world. Open Wed and Sun 2pm to 5pm. Shop selling herbs and honey.

Kingston-upon-Thames

Beverley Brook

One of London's most polluted rivers, passing through Wimbledon Common, Barnes Common and Richmond Park. Waste from Worcester Park Sewage Works flows directly into it making it a major concern for conservationists.

Hogsmill River

Also highly polluted, being the channel for any overspill from Ewell storage tanks.

Kingston has a lack of public open space but small local educational sites can be visited. Contact the council Recreation Department for details.

Lambeth

Lambeth has a large amount of open space, mostly in the form of open common land: Clapham Common, Kennington Park, Streatham Common and Brockwell Park cover around 200 hectares between them. Tooting Bec Common between Streatham and Tooting offers an interesting range of wood, brush and common habitats. Two areas of wasteland, Eardley Road and Shakespeare Road are fascinating areas of wildlife interest. Unfortunately, the former is due to disappear under a housing development and the latter was sold to developers in 1984 and cleared. The council is trying to buy it now to restore it to its original state, having refused to do so in 1984 when it could have rescued the site whole with its rare plants like the bee orchid and muck thistle.

Lewisham

Blackheath

Wild open common, site of historical battles, used as camp for Danish invading armies.

Beckenham Place Park

Believed to be England's largest municipally owned golf course, also a haven for wildlife. Includes 40 acres of ancient woodland and a Nature Conservation Centre open on weekend afternoons.

Hither Green Nature Reserve, Baring Walk SE12

Part of the Green Chain Walk and containing nineteen butterfly species and 300 moths, as well as lizards and grass snakes.

Devonshire Road Nature Reserve

Saved from clearance by a public campaign in 1979. Now an educational reserve. A similar site is being prepared at Dacres Road.

Merton

Cannizaro Park, Commonside West, Wimbledon

A favourite with horticulturalists and the public covering 35 acres with plants and gardens.

Ravensbury Park, Morden

A riverside park with quiet walks and playground areas.

Wimbledon Common

Saved from development in the 1860s. A Site of Special Scientific Interest with rough grassland, gorse and birch scrub. Newts and lizards abound and about half of Britain's varieties of insect have been seen. Bird life is active all year round.

Mitcham Common

Situated in the south-east of Merton, much of the original grassland has been destroyed by infilling although Arthur's Pond was saved from a similar fate in 1984. Moths, butterflies, amphibians and birds all inhabit this third largest common in London.

Newham

Newham is not exactly overflowing with sites of natural importance but the London Wildlife Trust is managing Bully Fen, a stretch of marshland alongside the River Lee and Thames Wharf, is an area of wasteland used for feeding and nesting by a number of waders.

St Michael's Churchyard (High Street)

A mixture of grass and woodland surrounding a peaceful graveyard supporting a number of birds and butterflies.

Redbridge

Hainault Forest Country Park

Also crosses into the London Borough of Havering and into Essex. A large area of forest and grassland including an area of ancient pollarded hornbeams, designated a Site of Special Scientific Interest.

Wanstead Park

A large lake and wooded area with a heronry and Rook Island. Now also a golf course.

Richmond-upon-Thames

Richmond Park with its herds of deer and miles of open common is one of Richmond's greatest claims to fame, along with the ever fascinating Kew Gardens and Hampton Court Park (entrance fees payable). These three account for 2,000 hectares of open space. Copious information on all three areas is available in most London guide books.

Crane Park Island

Formerly part of Hounslow gunpowder mills, the remains of whose buildings can still be seen. Stands on the River Crane but was largely neglected until 1981 when the local Friends of the Earth began to manage the island as a nature reserve. Transferred to the London Wildlife Trust in 1986. The river boasts a wide range of habitats attracting water animals of all kinds. Trees include oak and sycamore, birds include herons, kestrels and blackcaps and the wild flowers attract many butterflies in the summer months.

Ham Lands, Riverside Drive

An area of grassland and hawthorn scrub supporting many plants including three species of orchid. More than forty species of birds breed here including all three British woodpeckers.

Lonsdale Road Reservoir

A great success story of resistance to the developers. Saved in 1968, 1972 and 1975 from various developmental threats. Now a nature reserve with several species of duck and a developing woodland.

Barnes Common

Hawthorn scrubland with much active birdlife. Currently under threat from the East London River Crossing like Oxleas Wood (see above).

Barn Elms Reservoir, Barnes

A favourite site for birdwatchers for its remarkable range of birdlife. The oldest of London's reservoirs.

Southwark

Sydenham Hill Wood

A remnant of the ancient woodland once covering London. Disturbed by the railway cut through it to serve Crystal Palace at the end of the last century but still an area of considerable interest despite regular threats.

Dulwich Wood

Adjacent to Sydenham Hill. Only a few hedgerows remain between the present golf course and recreation ground.

Benhill Road Nature Garden

A reserve in Bantry Road attracting birds and butterflies, with a pond drawing frogs and dragonflies.

Nunhead Cemetery

A fine overgrown Victorian cemetery part of which is now a nature reserve.

Sutton

Beddington Park

A park containing a nature reserve and a stretch of the River Wandle.

St Philomena's Lake, Carshalton

A pond supporting a variety of amphibians and invertebrates. Limited access.

Tower Hamlets

Victoria Park

Opened in 1845 as a result of public demand for a park in the East End. Boating lakes, rose garden, deer park, several buildings and monuments of interest.

St Jude's Nature Park

A nature garden built in 1980. Offers a mixture of trees, shrubs and wild flowers, hedgehogs, kestrels and frogs.

Waltham Forest

Epping Forest

Stretching out into Essex, Epping Forest is a historic area of woodland containing the famous Queen Elizabeth Hunting Lodge. A vast area of nearly 2,500 hectares with the full range of woodland wildlife. Also adjoins Walthamstow Forest with its coppiced hornbeam.

Walthamstow Reservoirs

A large heronry and nesting site for a variety of birds. Snipes, sandpipers and many species of duck have been seen here on a regular basis.

Walthamstow Marshes

Saved from development into a water sports centre in the early 1980s. Remains an interesting area for wetland wildlife.

Ainslie Wood

Once part of Epping Forest. Now boasts a range of wildlife including tawny owls, treecreepers and flycatchers. Unfortunately, the site has suffered from public overuse and rubbish dumping.

Wandsworth

Wandsworth Common

Heath and scrubland surround the Central Pond. A nature trail is available from the Nature Study Centre at Neal's Farm in the north-west of the Common.

Putney Heath

An extension of Wimbledon Common.

Battersea Park

A formally designed park with lake, river walk, deer enclosure and nature reserve.

Westminster

The Royal Parks (Hyde Park, Green Park, St James's Park, Kensington Gardens and Regent's Park/Primrose Hill) all lie within the City of Westminster and information on them is freely available in any tourist guide. All offer wide areas of grassland, some with areas of water and gardens. However, they are almost always very busy, especially in spring and summer.

There are many private squares and gardens in Westminster, details of which are available from the Recreation Department. Many well-known squares (Belgrave, Berkeley, Grosvenor, Hanover, Soho) are in the area, again a list is available; and a number of gardens such as Paddington Street, Millbank, Riverside Walk and Victoria Embankment.

Just Beyond the Borders

Box Hill and the North Downs Way

Near Dorking or Leatherhead, Surrey. Woodland, ancient fort, River Mole, panoramic views.

Bushy Park

Near Hampton Court Palace. Deer park, gardens, ponds, walks, Longford River, play area.

CITY FARMS

City farms have been created all over Britain as places where children in particular can experience farm life on a small scale, and can help with feeding the animals, harvesting crops and learning farm and village crafts. London has a number of such farms which are fascinating for adults and children alike. It is wise to phone first as opening times vary although most if not all can cater for individuals and small groups of children. Most are run as working farms and sell their produce to visitors.

Beckton Meadows
Community Smallholding
519 2439

Corams Fields
93 Guildford Street
London WC1
837 6138

Dean City Farm
1 Batsworth Road
Mitcham
Surrey
648 1461

Elm Farm
Gladstone Terrace
Battersea
London SW8
627 1130

Freightliners Farm
Paradise Park
Sheringham Road
London N7
609 0467

Goat Farm
The Lodge
Honeywood Walk
Carshalton
Surrey

Hackney City Farm
1a Goldsmiths Row
London E2
729 6381

Kentish Town City Farm
1 Cressfield Close
London SW5
482 2861

Mudchute Farm
Pier Street
Millwall
London E14
515 5901

People's Farm
Shacklewell Lane
London E8
806 5743

**Spelthorne Farm Project for the
    Handicapped**
6 Burrows Hill Close
Heathrow
Hounslow
Middlesex
0753 49330

Spitalfields Farm Association Ltd
Weaver Street
London E1
247 8762

Stepping Stones Farm
Junction Stepney Way/Stepney
    High Street
London E1
790 8204

Surrey Docks Farm
Commercial Dock Passage
Gulliver Street
Surrey Docks
London SE16
231 1010

Thameside Park Association
40 Thames Road
Barking
Essex
594 8449

Vauxhall City Farm
24 St Oswald's Place
Vauxhall
London SE11
582 4204

Walworth City Farm
230 Amelia Street
London SE17
582 2652

Wellgate Community Farm
Collier Row Road
Romford
Essex
599 0415

ENVIRONMENTAL EDUCATION, CONCERN AND ACTION

Major London Bodies

The London Ecology Centre
45 Shelton Street
London WC2
379 4324

Set up in 1985 by the GLC to act as a focus for ecological and environmental activities and to promote public education and awareness of London's natural environment.

One of its major functions is to refer members of the public to a specific organisation able to deal more thoroughly with an inquiry or to a campaign dealing with the person's particular concerns.

The LEC acts as a shop window for many environmental organisations based in London and elsewhere. As a first port of call it is unique in the broad service it offers which includes a growing database. There are also regular talks, films, videos and slide shows.

Other facilities in the centre include a gallery where artists can display their work, usually on environmental or related subjects for a relatively low hire fee. There is also a National Trust shop and a shop called 'Yours Naturally' stocking a range of books, cards, posters, and cruelty-free toiletries and household products. The centre also boasts a cafe serving organic vegetarian and wholefood snacks and light refreshments, including a selection of organic wines and beers. Open 10.30am–11.00pm Monday to Saturday.

Unfortunately, property developers have bought much of Covent Garden and the lease on the current buildings runs out in 1992–3 so the future of the centre is uncertain.

London Ecology Unit
Berkshire House
168 High Holborn
London WC1
379 4352

Set up by the GLC, the LEU now works with borough councils, writing reports on sites of ecological interest and how best to preserve them, especially if they are under threat from developers or pollution. Their advice is thorough and practical but, unfortunately, is not always heeded by those to whom it is given, whose priorities are often other than environmental.

London Waste Regulation Authority
Room 174 (N)
County Hall
London SE1 7PB
633 2786/7346
(Flytipping Action Line – 24 Hours 928 9988)

Established under the Local Government Act 1985 to undertake the regulation of London's waste after the abolition of the GLC. Its function is to protect public health and the environment and to ensure the proper procedures of waste disposal are carried out.

LWRA is responsible for the controlling of disposal of all hazardous waste and has special schemes to monitor the disposal of clinical waste and asbestos collection or removal. They will answer queries on any of these subjects. The LWRA will collect or accept waste for disposal provided it does not exceed 50kg or 50 litres (1cwt or 10 gallons) and which is packed in containers of 'manageable size and weight'. Special arrangements are made for explosives, nerve gases and drugs. Radioactive waste is not accepted.

Books for a Change
52 Charing Cross Road
London WC2H 0BB
836 2315

Named as 'the best green bookshop in the UK' by Jonathan Porritt of Friends of the Earth, Books for a Change stocks an extensive range of books, posters, cards and recycled stationery. Specialising in ecology, aid and development, the Third World, and peace and disarmament. Also stocks selections of children's books, books on food and nutrition and a range of Third World literature.

Friends of the Earth London Unit
26–28 Underwood Street
London N1
490 1555

FoE London Unit was set up in 1987 to provide a service for Londoners dealing with recycling, pollution and road safety, as well as providing general information and advice on many other topics of national and international importance such as the ozone layer, forests, etc. Most London boroughs have a FoE group. Details from the above address.

British Trust for Conservation Volunteers
London Regional Office
London Ecology Centre
80 York Way
London N1 9AG
278 4293

A charity aiming to involve people of all ages in conservation work. Activities include working holidays, local groups working in their spare time and special projects for schoolchildren and unemployed people. The BTCV works in all seasons and weathers in London and the surrounding countryside, carrying out everything from hedge-laying to creating nature areas. Transport, tools and training are provided.

The London Wildlife Trust
80 York Way
London N1 9AG
278 6612

Established in 1981 the LWT is Britain's leading urban wildlife group. LWT manages forty-five sites across Greater London and appears at public inquiries when green areas are under threat. Work includes everything from planting trees to advising on development plans. LWT is supported in its work by a large number of volunteers. Projects under way in Dartford (Crayford Marshes), Neasden (Neasden Grange Roundabout), Camden (Camley Street), Lewisham (New Cross Cutting). Also running a Kestrel Count after its successful 'Foxwatch' and 'Owl Prowl' schemes. Organises walks, talks and guided events of all kinds.

London Boroughs Joint Ecology Committee
Camden Town Hall
Euston Road
London NW1 2RU
278 4444

Thames Water
New River Head
Rosebery Avenue
London EC1R 4TP
Leaflets on Thames wildlife and birdwatching at London reservoirs.

Miscellaneous

Amateur Entomologists Society
355 Hounslow Road
Hanworth
Feltham
Middx TW13 5JH
755 0325

Animal Aid
7 Castle Street
Tonbridge
Kent TN9 1BH
0732 364546
*Education, exhibitions and
parliamentary lobbying to campaign
against animal abuse.*

Ark
498–500 Harrow Road
London W9
968 6780
*Originally set up with the support of
celebrities such as Chrissie Hynde,
David Bowie, Sting, and Peter
Gabriel, concentrating on producing
environmentally friendly products.*

Beauty without Cruelty
11 Lime Hill
Tunbridge Wells
Kent TN1 1LJ
0892 25587
*A campaigning organisation
opposing the commercial use of,
and killing of, animals to provide
clothing, fashion accessories or
beauty products.*

Blue Cross Animals Hospital
1 Hugh Street
London SW1
834 5556
*Cares for animals whose owners
cannot afford a private vet.*

Body Shop plc
Brighton
Sussex BN16 3LR
*Britain's major retail outlet for
cruelty free cosmetics. Branches all
over London, including Piccadilly,
Oxford Street, Covent Garden, etc.*

**British Butterfly Conservation
  Society**
Tudor House
Quorn
Loughborough
Leicestershire, LE12 8AD
0509 412870

British Ecological Society
Burlington House
Piccadilly
London W1V 0LQ
434 2641
*Researches into ecological issues.
Supports ecological education.
Publications, meetings, grants.*

British Naturalists Association
69 Marlowes
Hemel Hempstead
Herts
0933 314672

The British Trust for Ornithology
Beech Grove
Tring
Herts HP23 5NR
*National ornithological research
body.*

**British Union for the Abolition of
  Vivisection**
16a Crane Grove
London N7 8LB
700 4888
*Campaigns locally and nationally
for the abolition of vivisection.
Publishes* Liberator *magazine
monthly.*

Care for the Wild
26 North Street
Horsham
West Sussex RH12 1BN
Information service for groups.

Christian Ecology Group
58 Quest Hills Road
Malvern
Worcs WR14 1RW
06845 2630

Civic Trust
17 Carlton House Terrace
London SW1Y 5AW
930 0914
Aims to uphold standards of environmental quality and management in Britain. Works in places where people live and work. Projects include 'face-lifts' for shopping streets and 'greening' projects for housing estates.

Common Ground
45 Shelton Street
Covent Garden
London WC2H 9HJ
Aims to forge links between the practice and enjoyment of the arts and the conservation of landscapes and nature through projects involving the arts.

Compassion in World Farming
20 Lavant Street
Petersfield
Hants GU32 3EW
0730 64208

Conservation Foundation
Fairholt House
2 Pont Street
London SW1X 9EL
235 1743
Umbrella organisation for a variety of conservation groups. Organises schemes, grants and awards in Britain and Europe.

Council for National Parks
45 Shelton Street
London WC2
235 9481

Council for the Protection of Rural England
4 Hobart Place
London SW1
235 9481

Countryside Commission
John Dower House
Crescent Place
Cheltenham, Glos GL50 3RA
0242 521381

Department of the Environment
Romney House
42 Marsham Street
London SW1
212 5464

Environmental Data Services Ltd
Finsbury Business Centre
40 Bowling Green Lane
London EC1R 0NE
278 4745

Fauna and Flora Preservation Society
c/o Zoological Society of London
Regent's Park
London NW1
387 9656

Forest of London Project
247 Pentonville Road
London N1 9NJ
833 2130
Launched in 1987 to plant trees, increase awareness, appreciation and sense of responsibility for trees through community, educational and media campaigns.

Gaia Foundation
18 Well Walk
London NW3 1LD
435 5000

*Foundation based on the Gaia
principle which sees the Earth as a
living organism. Developing
alternative approaches to ecology,
health and the mind.*

Green Alliance
60 Chandos Place
London WC2
836 0341
*Organisation based on information
gathering and exchange between
the green movement and decision-
makers through lobbying, debates
and seminars.*

Green Party
10 Station Parade
London SW12 9AZ
673 0045
*Formerly the Ecology Party, now
with a number of local councillors.
Campaigning on the whole range of
environmental issues, local,
national and global, as well as
parliamentary reform, health,
education and housing.*

Greenpeace
30–31 Islington Green
London N1
251 3022
*Campaigning locally, nationally, and
internationally on a broad range of
issues from the preservation of
whales to nuclear dumping. A range
of local groups and activities exist,
details of which can be obtained
from the above address.*

Hunt Saboteurs Association
PO Box 87
Exeter, EX4 3TX
*Direct action and campaigning
against hunting and all bloodsports
such as cockfighting, badger
baiting, dog fighting, etc. Wide
network of local groups.*

Keep Britain Tidy Group
Bostel House
37 West Street
Brighton, East Sussex, BN1 2RE
0273 23585

League Against Cruel Sports
83–87 Union Street
London SE1 1SG
407 0979/403 6155
*Campaigning for a change in
legislation to make hunting with
dogs illegal, and to educate people
on cruel sports in general such as
badger baiting, hare coursing, etc.*

Living Earth
10 Upper Grosvenor Street
London WC1
499 0858
*Set up in 1987 with 'the aim of
helping to protect the environment
by working towards the sustainable
and socially beneficial use of the
world's resources', based on a long-
term and strategic approach.*

London Food Commission
88 Old Street
London EC1V 9AR
253 9513
*Educational and research
campaigns on food, nutrition, diet,
health, food production, retail,
distribution, cooking, catering, etc.*

London Natural History Society
c/o P. C. Holland, Membership
  Secretary,
Flat 9, Pinewood Court
23 Clarence Avenue
London SW4 8LB
or
36 Milton Road
Hampton, Middx, TW12 2LT

Lynx
Long Acre
London WC2
*The major campaigning
organisation opposing the fur trade.
Has a shop selling T-shirts, etc. in
Long Acre, WC2.*

Media Natura
c/o London Ecology Centre
*Aims to bring conservation issues
and the organisations involved to
the public via the media.*

National Anti-vivisection Society
51 Harley Street
London W1N 1DD
580 4034/631 0612
*Education and lobbying to convince
Parliament and the public that
animal experiments are dangerous
and unnecessary.*

**National Society against Factory
  Farming**
41 Mercator Road
Lewisham
London SE13 5EH
852 1832
*Campaigning for a return to free-
range farming and better conditions
for all factory farmed animals.*

National Trust
36 Queen Anne's Gate
London SW1H 9AS
222 9251

**Natural History Museum and
  Geological Museum**
Exhibition Road
London SW7 2DE
938 9123

Nature Conservancy Council
Northminster House
Northminster Road
Peterborough, PE1 1AV
0733 40345
*Soon to be split up by the
government and merged with the
Countryside Commissions in Wales
and Scotland, but not in England . . .*

Open Spaces Society
25a Bell Street
Henley-on-Thames
Oxon RG9 2BA
0491 573535

**People's Dispensary for Sick
  Animals (PDSA)**
PDSA House
South Street
Dorking
Surrey RH4 2LB
0306 888291

Rainforest Foundation
5 Fitzroy Lodge
The Grove
Highgate
London N6 5JU
*Education and campaigning on
saving the rainforests.*

Ramblers Association
1–5 Wandsworth Road
London SW8 2XX
582 6878
*Campaigns to protect the
countryside and its public footpaths
and rights of way, and to make it
more accessible to and popular
with the walking public.*

**Royal Society for Nature
  Conservation**
164 Vauxhall Bridge Road
London SW1V 2RB
828 1657
*The major voluntary organisation in
Britain concerned with all aspects
of nature conservation. Runs a
youth section (the WATCH club)
Coordinates the British Wildlife
Appeal.*

**Royal Society for the Prevention of
  Cruelty to Animals (RSPCA)**
(London Area)
Major Lamond
13 Knowles Avenue
Crowthorne
Berkshire, RG11 6DU
0344 771929

Royal Society for the Protection of Birds (RSPB)
The Lodge
Sandy
Beds SG19 2DL

SERA (Socialist Environment and Resources Association)
26–28 Underwood Street
London N1
490 0240
Known as 'The green wing of the labour movement and the socialist wing of the green movement', SERA aims to integrate environmental perspectives into all aspects of policy and decision-making.

The Tidy Britain Group
Head of London Operations
Premier House
12–13 Hatton Gardens
London EC1 2NH
831 1462
Campaigning for a litter-free Britain.

Tree Council
35 Belgrave Square
London SW1X 8QN
235 8854
Runs an annual National Tree week, produces useful leaflets and organises tree planting.

UK2000
Unit 101
Butler's Wharf Business Centre
45 Curlew Street
London SE1 2ND
370 1047
Promotes and supports community-based environmental projects, arranging training, supporting volunteering and managing a grants fund.

Vegan Society
33–35 George Street
Oxford OX1 2A7
0865 722166

Vegetarian Society
Parkdale
Dunham Road
Altrincham
Cheshire WA14 4QG
061 928 0793

Wildfowl Trust
Slimbridge
Gloucester, GL2 7BT
045 389 333
Working to conserve wildfowl and woodlands. Educating and researching into ecology and preservation issues.

Wildlife Link
45 Shelton Street
London WC2H 9HJ
240 9284/9289
A liaison body between major voluntary organisations in the field of wildlife preservation.

Woodland Trust
Autumn Park
Grantham
Lincs NG31 6LL
Protects native British trees by acquiring woodland and looking after it. Woods are owned in all the home counties, some on the very borders of London.

World Society for the Protection of Animals
106 Jermyn Street
London SW1Y 6EE
839 3026
Promoting cooperation between animal protection societies on an international scale.

**Worldwide Fund for Nature (World
  Wildlife Fund)**
Panda House
11–13 Ockford Road
Godalming
Surrey
GU7 1OU
04868 20551

**Young People's Trust for
  Endangered Species**
19 Quarry Street
Guildford
Surrey, GU1 3EH
0483 396000
*Aims to educate young people
about world conservation.
Information service, lectures,
courses and summer schools.*

7

HEALTH

As a symbol of the changes in London over the last decade you can't beat the state of the capital's health service. Visit the casualty department of one of London's famous teaching hospitals; Guy's, the London, Hammersmith, etc, on a busy Friday evening. The rundown waiting rooms, the peeling paint, the coffee machines that never seem to work and most noticeable, the nurses and other hospital staff dashing around with grim expressions and an often visible air of exhaustion. Compare this with the entrance lobby in one of the rapidly expanding private hospitals around the capital; the Humanae in Kensington or the BUPA hospital in Harrow; here all is peaceful, thick pile carpets on the floor, unharassed receptionists, piped music and potted palms all around. A two-tier health service is already with us.

Nevertheless, both the above mentioned private hospitals, along with all other private hospitals and the private beds in NHS facilities, depend entirely upon the NHS for their existence. The NHS trains all the staff who work in these hospitals and provides all the medical back-up required so they can concentrate on the acute 'hi-tech' medicine that is profit-making and attractive to the wealthy and more and more of the not so wealthy who are forced into private operations because of the ever expanding waiting lists for London's hospitals.

London has suffered more than any other area of the country from the policy of cuts and closures carried out by successive Tory governments in the last decade. The policy of channelling money out of the capital's acute services into the 'priority' services of care for the elderly and people with mental health problems, and into provision of better services for people in the home counties, started off as sounding like a reasonable course of action. After all, Londoners had more hospital beds per head of population than any other part of the country. However, the money from London did not go to provide new and better facilities elsewhere, but into shoring up overburdened and underfunded services outside the capital. Meanwhile, the waiting lists in London lengthened and the private sector expanded.

I would never seek to defend absolutely the present organisation of the NHS in London. It is clear that what we have is primarily a 'sickness' rather than a 'health' service. It is undemocratic, medically dominated and underfunded. What is needed is a service that genuinely attempts to meet the individual needs of people rather than fitting those people into a system. That service should also be democratically accountable in the same way that social service provision is, and planned on some all-London basis (bring back the GLC!) rather than on the present four Thames regions which stretch from Brighton to Bedford. Most of all, the developments in alternative medicine and self-help (many of whose organisations are listed in this chapter) should be recognised more by the health service and provided free at the point of use to NHS patients.

One thing is certain, however, the introduction of market forces into the NHS, as proposed by the government in their White Paper, will do nothing to improve the service and will in the main cause immeasurable harm to the most vulnerable people in our society who simply cannot afford to go elsewhere for their treatment. Markets are very good places to do your weekly shopping, I would prefer to have my health looked after on a basis of need rather than on the basis of what happens to be on special offer this week.

Pete Marshall
London Regional Officer, COHSE

GENERAL INFORMATION

Registering with a GP (General Practitioner)/ Changing Your GP

To register with a doctor, contact your local Family Practitioners Committee or look in the telephone directory, then go to the surgery and make an appointment. If you wish to change your doctor for some reason, you may do so, but it is wise to contact the local Community Health Council (CHC) or Family Practitioners Committee (FPC) for help and advice. When changing your doctor, you must ask your current doctor to sign your medical card releasing you from his or her practice. The FPC should be able to help you find a new doctor, especially if the reason you are leaving is because you are moving house.

Hospitals and Emergencies

For emergency treatment every individual has the right to go to any NHS medical practice or hospital and be seen by a doctor. Your local FPC or CHC can tell you the whereabouts of your local NHS hospital and specialist clinics and hospitals, e.g. maternity, children, drugs, sexually transmitted diseases, etc. Usually you will be referred for any necessary hospital treatment by your GP.

The following hospitals in central London are open twenty-four hours for 999 cases and other emergencies:

Charing Cross, Fulham Palace Road, W6, 748 2040
Guy's, St Thomas Street, SE1, 407 7600
Lewisham, Lewisham High Street, SE13, 690 4311
Royal Free, Pond Street, NW3, 794 0500
St Bartholomew's, West Smithfield, EC1, 601 8888
St George's, Blackshaw Road, SW17, 672 1255
St Mary's, Praed Street, W2, 725 6666
St Thomas's, Lambeth Palace Road, SE1, 928 9292
University College, Gower Street, WC1, 387 9300

Children's Casualty Hospitals:

Queen Elizabeth the Queen Mother's Wing, St Mary's, Praed Street, W2, 725 6305
Queen Elizabeth's, Hackney Road, E2, 739 8442
Sydenham Hospital, 321 Sydenham Road, SE26 778 7031

Dentists

Your local FPC or CHC can help you find a local dentist.

Dental Care Emergency Service
677 8383
24 hours, 365 days.

Emergency Dental Service
584 1008
24 hours, 365 days.

Opticians

Your local CHC or FPC can help you find a local optician.

Chemists

Police stations should have a list of emergency chemists and doctors in the locality.

Boots at Piccadilly is open until 8pm Mon–Sat, Bliss Chemists at 5 Marble Arch, W1 (723 6116) are open 9am to midnight, and Bliss Chemists at 54 Willesden Lane, NW6 (624 8000) 9am–2am, seven days a week.

Alternatives

Some NHS doctors will recommend or even use alternative therapies, but they are still a small minority. Some homoeopathic treatments are available on the NHS. In order to find practitioners of alternative treatments in your area, contact the Institute for Complementary Medicine, the British Holistic Medical Association or the Concessions Register for a Natural Health Service (see below).

District Health Authorities

The DHAs are responsible for coordinating, planning and running local services. They are also responsible for collaboration with the local authority. They should not be confused with Regional Health Authorities which cover a much wider area.

Family Practitioner Committees

Every borough has one or more FPCs (see telephone directory) concerned with questions of general practice. FPCs are responsible for making sure that medical, dental, optical and pharmaceutical services are provided in their area. FPCs are legally obliged to find you a GP if you request it. They will also find you a dentist or optician if you do not know where your local practice is situated. They publish lists of dentists, chemists, ophthalmic medical practitioners, opticians and GPs which are available from Post Offices, libraries, CHCs and the FPC itself. If the White Paper proposals became legislation, FPCs would be merged with Regional Health Authorities (RHAs).

Local Authorities

Local authorities are responsible for some services, mainly those connected with care and support.

Joint Consultative Committees

JCCs are responsible for integrating local health and local authority services.

Community Health Councils

CHCs represent the interests of the public in the NHS. Each DHA has a CHC, theoretically independent of NHS management but having to review NHS operations and be consulted about planning. They can help with complaints and are involved in many local health initiatives. See below under 'Community Medicine' for address of Association of CHCs.

Complaints

Any complaint about the treatment you receive from a GP, dentist, optician or pharmacist working for the NHS can be made through the FPC. Your local Community Health Council can also help and advise you on who should take up a complaint. There is also an NHS Ombudsman who can deal with certain complaints such as failure to provide a service, e.g. a necessary operation or a disability aid; faulty services, such as bad handling of medical records; or bad administration.

Health Service Ombudsman
Great Smith Street
London SW1P 3BW
276 2035

Patients' Rights

Health Rights Limited
(Health Advisory Association trading as Health Advisory Group)
344 South Lambeth Road
London SW8
720 9811
Seeks to represent NHS users. Advice, information, research, campaigning on maternal and child welfare, medicines and safety, democracy in the NHS.

National Association for Patient Participation
13 Manor Drive
Surbiton
Surrey, KT5 8NE
399 4122
Conferences and workshops for local groups concerned with fostering higher standards of primary medical care through patient participation.

Patients' Association
Room 33
18 Charing Cross Road
London WC2H 0HR
240 0671
Represents patients. Advice and information for individuals. Promotes understanding between patients and all those in the health service.

Prescription Charges and Other NHS Costs

1. Prescriptions

Prescription charges have risen dramatically under the Conservatives. It is now far more expensive to be ill than it was in the 1970s. Those not entitled to free prescriptions have to pay £3.05 for each item on a prescription. If you are likely to require regular prescriptions over a long period, you might save money by getting a 'season ticket' for four months or a year. Forms are available from Post Offices, chemists, social security offices and Family Practitioner Committees.

In some cases, treatments can be bought more cheaply over the chemist's counter than if they are given on prescription. It is always wise to check this.

The following groups of people are automatically entitled to free NHS prescriptions and should claim using DSS form P11:

Men over 65, women over 60, anyone under 16, people between the ages of 16 and 19 in full-time education, people on Income Support or Family Credit or their partners, pregnant women,

women who have had a baby in the last twelve months, people receiving a War or MoD Disablement Pension, people suffering from any of the following: permanent fistula requiring continuous surgical dressing or an appliance, Addison's Disease or other forms of hypoadrenalism, diabetes insipidus and other forms of hypopituitarism, diabetes mellitus, hypoparathyroidism, myasthenia gravis, myxoedema (hypothyroidism), epilepsy requiring continuous anti-convulsive therapy, a continuing physical disability which prevents you from leaving home without the help of another person.

People on low income may be entitled to free prescriptions. It is wise to contact a Citizens Advice Bureau, Law Centre or Independent Advice Centre first (see Appendix).

2. NHS Dental Charges

Three categories of people are entitled to free dental treatment. If you believe you are entitled, tell your dentist on your first or next visit.

a. Automatic Entitlement

People under 18, people between 16 and 19 in full-time education, people on Income Support or Family Credit and their partners, women expecting a baby, women who have had a baby in the last twelve months before treatment began. DSS form D11 tells you how to claim.

b. Low-Income Entitlement

See above under prescription charges.

c. Certain War Pensioners

If the treatment you need is due to the disability for which you receive a war pension, you may receive help.

If you are not entitled to free dental treatment, you will pay 75 per cent of the cost of a course of treatment up to a maximum of £150.

3. Sight Tests

The Conservatives have abolished free sight tests for all but a very few people. Figures already show that this has discouraged many people, especially older people, from getting their eyes tested and treated.

Free tests are now only available for people under 16, full-time students aged 16–19, people on Income Support or Family Credit or their partners, people with certificate AG2 from the Department of Social Security, people needing complex lenses as defined in the NHS voucher scheme, people who are registered blind or partially sighted, people who are diagnosed as a diabetic or glaucoma patient, and people aged 40 or over who are the brother/sister/parent/child of a diagnosed glaucoma patient.

You can get help with costs if you are on a low income. Contact a CAB, Law Centre or other independent advice centre for help.

If you need glasses, or new glasses, you may be entitled to vouchers to help pay for them. It does not cover the full cost. If not you must pay the full cost yourself.

The following are entitled to NHS vouchers:

a. Automatic Entitlement

People under 16, people between 16 and 19 and in full-time education, people on Income Support or Family Credit or their partners. DSS form G11 tells you how to claim.

b. Low-income Entitlement

The value of your voucher will depend on your exact income. Contact a CAB, Law Centre or other independent advice agency or the DSS for help.

c. People who need complex lenses.

d. Certain war pensioners.

If the glasses are needed as a result of the disability for which you are receiving a pension.

4. Other Costs

Some people are entitled to help with hospital travel costs, NHS wigs and fabric supports, and milk and vitamins. A Citizens Advice Bureau, Law Centre or other independent advice agency (see Appendix) can give information, as can DSS form AB11.

Health Authorities are entitled to charge £15 when an ambulance is called out to an accident. This has often been overlooked in the past but recently the authorities have become more strict. The charge can be claimed against insurance.

NHS REFORMS

The government's White Paper on the future of the National Health Service, *Working for Patients*, was published on 31 January 1989. If implemented, the changes it proposes for the NHS will remain fundamental to health service provision for years to come. Even if there is a change of government, the outstanding priorities for the NHS pinpointed in the reactions to the White Paper will remain the same.

Most if not all the major bodies working within the NHS, as well as many individual doctors, nurses, ancillary staff, and the general public, expressed grave concern about the government's plans.

Government spending on the NHS since 1979, whatever claims are made about expansion and financial input, has resulted in the closure of wards and hospitals, the decline of facilities and buildings, and the suffering of patients as a result of insufficient money and staff to deal with existing problems.

The government uses its statistics selectively. It is true that spending has increased on the health service, but it has not increased at anything like the same rate as NHS pay and prices. In any case, the government failed fully to fund many of its pay awards over the last ten years, leaving the NHS to meet the shortfall.

The government makes great show of its expansion of hospital building programmes but fails to mention that this only accounts for 6 per cent of the NHS budget, and that in any case more and more building developments (currently about 20 per cent) are funded by land and property sales. Furthermore, when compared to other Western European countries, Britain spends less on its health service as a proportion of GDP than anyone except

Portugal and Greece. The health service is desperate for an injection of funds, not a major step towards privatisation, with competition and market forces taking priority over patients' needs.

The British Medical Association (BMA), the major organisation representing doctors, writes in its report on the White Paper: '[The BMA Council] is convinced that many of the proposals would cause serious damage to NHS patient care, lead to a fragmented service and destroy the comprehensive nature of the existing service . . . The Government's main proposals would appear to be to contain and reduce the level of public expenditure devoted to health care.'

The report goes on:

> The underfunding of the National Health Service by successive governments has placed great strains on the service and on its staff. However, more serious problems have arisen in recent years, and there is a large and increasing gap between the resources required for services and the funds which have been made available to them . . . The Government's proposals do not make reference to increased funding for the health service.

The nursing unions share many of the BMA's fears. The Royal College of Nursing (RCN), in its response to the White Paper, says that the government's proposals 'threaten the principles and effectiveness of the National Health Service'.

The White Paper's proposals and the responses to them can be divided into eight major areas. (NB The sections of the White Paper dealing with Practice Budgets for GPs and Indicative Prescribing Budgets for GPs, might well have been considerably altered by the time this book is published.)

1. Self-Governing Hospitals

The White Paper states that hospitals will be encouraged to become 'self-governing', 'separate legal entities' within the NHS. They will be governed by a board of directors with powers not available to existing NHS hospitals.

They will earn money according to the services they can offer, or according to their ability to borrow money and dispose of assets such as land or buildings. They will be able to set up their own management structures independent of health authority or central control. They will also be able to determine their own levels of pay and conditions for their staff within certain contractual limits. The government claims that this represents a move towards healthy competition and more consumer choice.

A common response to these claims has been to point out that in effect, self-governing hospitals will reintroduce divided health care. That is to say, in order to remain financially viable, hospitals will have to put greater emphasis on cheaper services or fast turnover acute care, in order to appear competitive to the GPs and Health Authorities who make contracts with them for services (see below). This could well lead to sacrificing many essential but expensive services or long-term care for older people or people with a disability.

This in turn will threaten the continuity of care and reduce access to comprehensive local health services, as well as separating the acute sector from the primary health care services. Long-term planning would be made more difficult and administrative costs would inevitably rise. Groups of hospitals may form into business cartels in order to fix the level of prices and suppress competition.

Another fear is that the hospitals that 'opt out' and choose to become self-governing may be taking a step towards the full privatisation first of that hospital and later of the entire health service. Highly specialised self-governing hospitals, as they will undoubtedly become, will be perfect candidates for total independence and privatisation at some time in the future.

Self-governing hospitals will be expected to provide a number of 'core services' that are considered vital to every local community such as accident and emergency, immediate admissions for most general medical cases, geriatric and psychiatric services, out-patient services, services for elderly, mentally ill or mentally handicapped, such as district nursing and health visiting.

However, there is little detail about these services and some rather obvious services have been excluded. For example, how can immediate access to maternity care not be seen as vital to a local community?

2. Funding and Contracts for Hospital Services

The White Paper states that General Practitioners (GPs) and District Health Authorities (DHAs) will have to place contracts for care with either NHS directly managed hospitals, self-governing hospitals or private hospitals. Regional Health Authorities (RHAs) will pay each other for services. Most GPs will send patients to the hospital used by the DHA but some will be allowed to make their own contracts (see below).

DHAs will buy the service offering the best 'value for money', even if it is many miles away. There is therefore no guarantee that there will continue to be a comprehensive local health service. It is not beyond the bounds of reason that in the future patients may be forced to have two separate but related operations in different parts of the country, with no guarantee of suitable after-care when they return home.

The requirements in terms of administration costs for such arrangements will be immense, not to mention the fact that hospital or DHA staff are not necessarily trained in the right skills to deal with tendering, contracts and business deals.

3. Practice Budgets for GPs

Doctors in general practice with more than 11,000 patients will be encouraged to hold their own budgets. They will then buy NHS or private care on a contractual basis.

Doctors would become responsible for their own drugs bill, a full range of primary health care facilities and arranging in-patient treatment at hospitals. If budgets are cash-limited, it is worrying in the extreme that a patient will now go to visit the doctor unsure as to whether the drug prescribed to him/her will be based on the diagnosis made by the doctor or on financial concerns stemming from budget restrictions.

Doctors may even be forced to send patients elsewhere if they consider the treatment necessary for their condition too expensive. Doctors may well hesitate to take on elderly or disabled patients requiring long-term treatment. Doctors will also be forced to employ administrative staff or spend more time themselves on administrative and business duties.

GPs outside the budget scheme will have to use whatever services have been negotiated by the DHA (see above), reducing both the patient's and the doctor's choice.

4. Indicative Prescribing Budgets for GPs

RHAs will be given an annual block grant to fund prescribing needs of their Family Practitioner Committees, the local bodies with whom GPs are registered. FPCs will then allocate GPs a budget depending on the number of patients covered by that GP and in some cases depending on the part of the country. This has been welcomed by many in the NHS but with certain provisos. For instance, it should be made clear that budgets must be adaptable to local population and incidence of diseases, and that AIDS patients will not be denied AZT treatment because of its cost and because it is not ultimately a cure for the illness.

5. Capital Charges

A new system of charging for capital within the NHS will be introduced, but this will not affect the amount of money available for health care.

6. Medical Audit

A new comprehensive system of medical audit will be introduced covering primary health care, hospitals and community services. It is generally welcomed as long as it is not introduced over-hastily and does not apply only to doctors, as appears to be the case at the moment.

7. NHS Consultants

A hundred new consultant posts will be created to help reduce waiting lists. In order for such a move to be effective, there would have to be a corresponding increase in the number of registrars, nurses and administrative staff to support the new consultants.

8. Family Practitioner Committees/DHAs and RHAs

For the third time in recent history, a new management structure is being introduced in the NHS. Regional, district and family practitioner management bodies will be reduced in size and modified along business lines. RHAs will take over responsibility for FPCs. This will reduce the local autonomy of FPCs. Many would prefer to see FPCs merged with DHAs to provide a better coordinated local service.

Furthermore, the government is removing local authority representatives from DHA boards. This follows the government line of reducing the influence of the local authorities on local services. It is a move towards centralisation as seen already in education, housing, transport, etc.

General Conclusions

So much for what is in the White Paper. What about what is left out? There is virtually no mention of community care. Emphasis is given to the acute sector (GPs and hospitals). The enforced slimming down of health authorities and the severing of links with the local authority (which is responsible for many community services) by removing local authority representatives from management boards, will make joint planning and continuity even more difficult than it already is.

The elderly are hardly mentioned, people with disabilities are largely ignored, and people with learning difficulties or mental health problems are given only minimal attention. It is far from clear whether there will be safeguards to long-term treatment for those who most need it.

Maternity care, too, is given poor coverage. As Jenny Langford, Senior Professional Officer at the Royal College of Midwives (RCM) said, the RCM is concerned about 'the fragmentation of maternity care into a hospital based service which may be situated distant to the mother's home and community care'.

There is no serious mention of preventive medicine, yet there is a general feeling that health service priorities should be shifted towards preventing ill health rather than simply curing it.

As for complementary or 'alternative' medicine, there is no mention whatever of expanding local health resources to include complementary treatments, many of which are now recognised and used by GPs and patients.

Furthermore, there is a failure to recognise the importance of linking health care to wider social issues. Poor quality housing and homelessness, education, pollution, food production, welfare benefits; all these contribute to the health of the capital and the country. And yet all have suffered over the last decade and there is no sign of a comprehensive strategy which recognises the links between all these factors, other than a desire on the part of the government to centralise decision-making in all these areas and turn over as much as possible to the dictates of the market, rather than planning to meet people's needs.

At the core of opposition to the White Paper, however, are two key principles. First, the government has ignored the real agenda, namely, how to cope with the problems posed to the health service by an ageing population, shortages of skilled workers and the results of years of underfunding. There is no mention of more money for the health service, indeed, many of the proposals in the White Paper will inevitably result in massive costs to account for necessary increase in administration and organisation of the proposals.

There is a blind reliance on the principles of the market. Most people involved in the health service recognise the need for a major overhaul, but the introduction of market forces is *not* the kind of reform that is required.

Second, the White Paper represents a threat to the whole principle of a health service free for every individual at the point of delivery under which the NHS was founded in 1948 after years of campaigning. It replaces long-term planning with the principle of competition and short-term gain. Hospitals will survive by out-competing other hospitals which will then go to the wall. In the meantime, successful hospitals, often miles from their users' homes, will move ever closer to privatisation. The end result will be a reduction in choice for patients, GPs and hospital staff. Health authorities will be cut off from the local representatives of communities (councils) and all vestiges of democratic accountability within the health service will disappear.

PRIVATE HEALTH CARE

Despite the fact that private health care implies the provision of faster and better quality health care only for those can afford it, and a drain on highly trained staff who can earn higher wages than in the NHS, many people understandably feel themselves pushed into using private health facilities simply because it means that they or their loved ones can be treated more quickly. In many cases, this can mean the difference between life and death, or at the very least, the difference between long suffering and fast relief.

Long NHS waiting lists and declining facilities should not be the justification for a private health service but rather a spur to more investment in a top quality health service that is free to all at the point of use. However, the government continues to use the red herring of 'greater choice for the consumer' to justify the private sector, and what is more, under the new plans for the NHS outlined above, is moving towards privatisation of the entire health service.

Some health authorities offer single-cost treatments, which in effect gives NHS patients the chance to jump the queue for certain kinds of treatment. At any time after a GP or consultant makes a diagnosis suggesting that an operation or other treatment is necessary, a patient may pay the set fee for that treatment and receive it immediately. The treatment is then given in an NHS hospital. (It is not necessary to be a member of BUPA or any other private health insurance scheme in order to 'go private'.) If there is a subsequent problem relating to the treatment, the patient reverts to NHS care.

It should be noted, however, that when a patient 'goes private' within the NHS system, the staff who treat them do not receive any more money and are the same nurses providing care in the non-paying parts of the hospital. Even in private hospitals the vast bulk of nurses and all doctors and paramedics are NHS trained. Similarly, the ambulance and casualty staff who deal with accident victims with private health insurance are NHS trained and NHS paid. Private health care is thus a drain on the already limited resources of the NHS.

Indeed, private health insurance can only exist in its present form because of the existence of the NHS; a 'universal' system of health insurance such as in certain other countries would be very expensive indeed to introduce.

ALTERNATIVE OR COMPLEMENTARY HEALTH CARE

Complementary or alternative medicine is the general name given to a range of therapeutic techniques. Such therapies tend to be holistic; they regard health and disease in terms of the whole person. They complement conventional medicine and in some cases may be considered as an alternative to it. In most cases, alternative therapies are not covered by the NHS although homoeopathic treatments are available at the NHS Royal Homoeopathic Hospital and some treatments are available in those well-women, mental health and other clinics where there is a sympathetic consultant.

The cost of complementary treatment varies and some practitioners charge lower rates to people on low incomes.

It is important to check before accepting treatment from a

practitioner of alternative medicine that s/he is in fact genuine. There are very few 'fakes' but most therapies have some kind of organisation with whom one can check. Some institutes and bodies have registers of recognised practitioners. It is perhaps wise to find practitioners through institutes or therapy centres, but many practitioners can be found in the Yellow Pages.

There are many books available on alternative therapies. A good general introduction to many of the therapies available can be found in the *London Guide to Mind, Body and Spirit* by Kate Brady and Mike Considine (Brainwave). There follows a brief list of some of the therapies available in London and a selection of centres and institutes. The list is not exhaustive.

A major source of information on complementary therapies is:

The Institute for Complementary Medicine
21 Portland Place
London W1N 3AF
636 9543

The ICM was established as a national charity in 1982 to increase public awareness of natural therapies through education and research. It is a meeting place for the official therapy bodies. Among the services it offers are public information points staffed by volunteers providing information, public classes and lectures, self-help schemes and at-home discussions. Particularly useful is the institute's *Directory of Registered Practitioners* working with some of the major disciplines. The institute also has clinic facilities for osteopathy, chiropractic, kinesiology, Alexander Technique, medical herbalism, homoeopathy, radionic analysis and counselling.

Public Information points in the London area are as follows:

Miss C. McNab Hampstead 485 7656
Mrs J. Pleshette Finchley 839 6495
Mrs S. Warlow Blackheath 858 0157

Also useful in finding alternative therapists and general information are:

Concessions Register of the Natural Health Service
55A Longridge Road
London SW5 9SF
244 7578
Since comparatively little in the way of complementary health care is available on the NHS, the Concessions Register aims to link low and unwaged people with qualified practitioners of complementary therapies who offer treatment at special rates.

British Holistic Medical Association
179 Gloucester Place
London NW1 6DX
262 5299
Run by a group of doctors interested in holistic approaches to health. Runs campaigns, courses and seminars.

Women's Natural Health Centre
1 Hillside
Highgate Road
London NW5 1QT
482 3293
Offers a variety of alternative therapies for women and children living on low income.

Acupuncture

Acupuncture is part of a system of medicine which originated in China several thousand years ago. The principal method is the insertion of fine needles into points lying beneath the skin. It also uses burning herbs. It aims to regulate bodily functions and thereby promote the restoration of health. Acupuncture is suitable for many conditions from lumbago to psoriasis and from asthma to depressions. It has been successfully applied to drug addiction (including smoking and alcohol).

The British Acupuncture Association and Register
London Office
34 Alderney Street
London SW1V 4EU
834 1012
Not all acupuncturists are registered as such and the law does not yet require this to be the case. The BAAR therefore aims to register practitioners if they have sufficient qualifications. If an acupuncturist in your area does not appear on the BAAR register (available from their London office) contact the BAAR and they will make inquiries for you.

Alexander Technique

Alexander Technique, named after its founder, aims to teach correct body posture and movement and the 'unlearning' of misuse of the body. It is often used by actors or musicians.

Society of Teachers of Alexander Technique
10 London House
266 Fulham Road
London SW10 9EL
351 0828

The governing body of Alexander Technique. Does not refer patients to practitioners.

Allergy Therapy

Individuals can suffer allergic reactions to many stimuli. Hay fever is one of the most common. Allergic reactions themselves can be extremely varied, as is the range of possible treatments, including homoeopathy and osteopathy.

Allergy Clinic
44 Harley Street
London W1
323 0657

Action Against Allergy
43 The Downs
London SW20 8HG
947 5082

Anthroposophical Medicine

An extension of orthodox medical practice (anthroposophical doctors have always trained first in conventional medicine) based on the teachings of Rudolf Steiner. Anthroposophical medicine starts from the premise that as well as the physical body, our thinking, feeling, will, and our 'I', all contribute to our health and well-being. Illness is seen as a result of an imbalance between these aspects. Among the treatments used in anthroposophical medicine are massage, hydrotherapy, artistic therapy, and eurythmy (a specialised movement therapy). (See also Steiner Education in Chapter 4: Education.)

Anthroposophical Society
Rudolf Steiner House
35 Park Road
London NW1 6XT
723 4400
Will give details of anthroposophical doctors working in London, both within and outside the NHS. Information on all aspects of Anthroposophy can also be obtained.

Aromatherapy

Aromatherapy uses concentrated oils from plants, flowers, trees and spices, usually applied externally. They are used to treat a wide range of ailments, especially skin complaints, from skin cancer to cuts and bruises.

London School of Aromatherapy
PO Box 780
London NW6 5EQ

Institute of Clinical Aromatherapy
22 Bromley Road
London SE6 2TP
690 2149

Bach Flower Remedies

These are herbal remedies used to treat the negative emotional states seen as the cause of illness. There are few practitioners, but the remedies are freely available and can be self-administered using the *Handbook of Bach Flower Remedies*.

Edward Bach Centre
Mount Vernon
Sotwell
Wallingford
Oxfordshire OX10 0PZ
0491 39489
Mail order books and remedies.

Biodynamic Massage

Developed by the Norwegian Gerda Boysen, biodynamics works on the premise that mind and body function together in emotional processes. Fluids built up between muscles and nerves are seen as blocked up energy which, when dispersed, allow the release of tension and the ability to absorb trauma and shock.

Gerda Boysen Centre for Biodynamic Psychology and Psychotherapy
Acacia House
Centre Avenue
Acton Park
London W3 7JX
743 2437

Chiropractic

Chiropractic concentrates on the manipulation of joints, especially the spine. Similar in some ways to osteopathy, but more likely to use mainstream methods such as blood tests and X-rays as part of the diagnosis. Can be used for back pain, headaches, digestion and many other complaints.

Chiropractic Advancement Association
38A Upper Richmond Road
London SW14 8DD
878 3989
Holds a register of members of the British Chiropractic Association.

Colour Therapy

Colour therapy uses colour or coloured light as an aid to healing. Based on research that has shown how colours can affect mood, blood pressure and the nervous system. Colours may be administered through food, direct coloured light, clothes or many other methods. Usually used as a supplement to other treatments.

Living Colour
33 Lancaster Grove
London NW3
794 1371

Your True Colours
12 St Mark's Crescent
London NW1 7TS
482 2038

Both run courses on colour analysis.

Feldenkrais Method

A movement therapy used to improve posture and flexibility. Slow exercises are used involving no strain or pain. Can be used to help people with disabilities or serious injuries, including disabilities suffered as the result of, for example, a stroke. Also used to help dancers, singers and athletes.

Feldenkrais Method
18 Kemplay Road
London NW3 1SY
435 8145

Feldenkrais PTP Information Centre
188 Old Street
London EC1V 9BP
549 9583

Healing

Healing by the laying on of hands has a long history. Different healers have different beliefs as to where the power of healing comes from; some believe it comes from a holy or guiding spirit, others say it is a natural human power. Often used to treat ailments like backache or terminal illnesses that have not been offered a cure by traditional methods.

Confederation of Healing Organisations
Pleasant Lodge
The Common
Berkhamsted, Herts HP4 2QF

Herbalism

Herbs have been used to cure disease since time immemorial. There are probably as many different kinds of herbal remedies as there are countries, climates or environments in the world, but European and Asian forms are the most popular in this country.

School of Complementary Medicine
9 Sharpshall Street
London NW1 8YN
586 1263
Information on herbalism and many other treatments.

Homoeopathy

Homoeopathic remedies are substances diluted up to thousands of times that in their pure state would produce the same symptoms as the illness for which they are prescribed. Homoeopathy treats like with like, instead of the conventional method of suppressing symptoms. Diagnosis is very thorough. Family medical histories and personal characteristics are important. Homoeopathy can be used to treat most reversible illnesses. Opinions vary as to their effectiveness for terminal illness or cases that would normally be treated with surgery.

British Homoeopathic Association
27A Devonshire Street
London W1N 1RJ
935 2163
A national charity that can provide any amount of information on homoeopathy, including a list of homoeopathic doctors in London and chemists stocking homoeopathic remedies.

Hahnemann College of Homoeopathy/Homoeopathic Health Centre
342 Barking Row
London E13 8HL
476 7263

Royal London Homoeopathic Hospital
Great Ormond Street
London WC1
837 3091 ext. 72

Iridology

Iridology uses the eye to diagnose physical and psychological problems. Practitioners believe that the body is reflected in the eye, the point where the nervous system comes to the surface. Parts of the eye are thought to correspond to parts of the body. It is usually used in conjunction with other therapies.

National Council and Register of Iridologists
80 Portland Road
Bournemouth BH9 1NQ

Massage

There are many forms of massage, using techniques developed all over the world. Massage is used to relieve tension in the body and for the relief of stress as well as physical pain. Many health centres, both conventional and alternative, offer forms of massage.

Naturopathy

Based on the idea that Nature itself can cure illness if the right conditions prevail. It suggests that animals, unlike humans, have not lost touch with natural mechanisms of healing or removing toxins, such as fasting or eating medicinal plants. Naturopaths therefore encourage fasting followed by maintenance of a healthy diet, or perhaps hydrotherapy, osteopathy, etc.

British Naturopathic and Osteopathic Association
Frazer House
Netherall Gardens
London NW3 5RR
435 8728
Has a register of practitioners as well as general information.

Osteopathy

Osteopathy employs joint and spine manipulation to restore bones, muscles, ligaments and nerves to their correct alignments, thus curing the patient. Can be used for a number of complaints, not just back and joint pain. Osteopathy is now one of the most widely recognised forms of alternative therapy and is used by many people in conjunction with or as an alternative to other methods.

British College of Naturopathy and Osteopathy (see above)

British Osteopathic Association
8–10 Boston Place
London NW1 6QH
262 5250

Polarity Therapy

Polarity therapists believe that the body is made up of a universal energy of which both the material and spiritual worlds are composed. It uses a number of techniques including manipulation, stretching and diet to remove blocks to the correct flow and balance of this energy.

Polarity Therapy Association
33 Dudley Court
Upper Berkley Street
London W1H 7PH
Has a list of qualified practitioners.

Reflexology

A technique whereby points on the soles and sides of the feet are seen to correspond to organs of the body and are massaged to treat complaints. Crystalline deposits are thought to be left at the points on the feet corresponding to the affected organ.

Reflexology Centre
8 Russel Court
London Lane
Bromley
Kent BR1 4XH
464 9401

Rolfing

Taking its name from Ida Rolf, rolfing attempts to realign the body into its correct symmetry by manipulating connective tissue. Rolfing has been likened to a deep massage. It has been used to relieve pain from a number of ailments.

Institute of Structural Bodywork
Hyatt Carlton Tower
c/o Roger Golten
The Peak Club
Cadogan Place
London SW1X 9PY
235 5411

Shiatsu and Acupressure

Shiatsu is a type of massage concentrating on the pressure points used in acupuncture and therefore working on a similar principle.

Used to treat a variety of ailments including tension, PMT, stress related pains and insomnia.

British School of Shiatsu
188 Old Street
London EC1V 9BP
251 0831

Shiatsu School of Natural Therapy
7 Health Villas
Vale of Health
Hampstead
London NW3
435 8787

T'ai Chi Chu'an

Often described as a 'moving meditation' using slow flowing movements to harmonise mind, body and spirit. It can be used as a form of healing.

British T'ai Chi Association
7 Upper Wimpole Street
London W1M 7TD
935 8444

School of T'ai Chi Chu'an
5 Tavistock Place
London WC1
459 0764

Yoga

A means of self-help towards spiritual and physical health. There are a number of forms of yoga, some placing more emphasis on the spiritual. All forms use basic poses designed to strengthen muscles and ligaments and stimulate internal organs.

British Wheel of Yoga
Grafton Grange
Grafton
York YO5 9QQ
09012 3386
Training, information and support for local groups on all aspects of yoga.

Iyenga Yoga Institute
223A Randolph Avenue

London W9 1NL
624 3080
Classes, training, workshops, lectures, library, information.

Yoga Centre
13 Hampstead Hill Gardens
London NW6
794 4119
Hatha and Raja yoga.

Alternative Health Centres

The London Guide to Mind, Body and Spirit (Brainwave, 1988) has a useful list of alternative health centres around London where the above and other various treatments are practised. There are too many to list here, but two of the best known are:

Community Health Foundation
188 Old Street
London EC1V 9BP
251 4076

City Health Centre
36–37 Featherstone Street
London EC1Y 8QX
251 4429

MENTAL HEALTH

What people call 'mental illness' is not a virus. It is a painful experience shared by one in six people! Obviously it affects families and friends as well as the sufferer. Often all these people will require some kind of help and support. Complaints such as depression, schizophrenia, anxiety and phobias are so common as to make them almost invisible but to those suffering from them and those close to them, they are only too clear.

Arbours Association
6 Church Lane
London N8
340 7646
Crisis centre, consultation, residential treatment, training.

Association for Humanistic Psychology
62 Southwark Bridge Road
London SE1 0AU
928 7102
Workshops, lectures, conferences and a referral service for alternative (non-Freudian) psychotherapists.

British Association of Psychotherapists
121 Hendon Lane
London N3 3PR
346 1747
Training for adult and child therapy, meetings, conferences, clinical service.

CMH – Campaign for Valued Futures with People Who Have Learning Difficulties
12A Maddox Street
London W1
491 0727

Federation of Phobic Care Organisations
Greater London House
547/551 High Road
London E11 4PR
558 3463
Coordinates activities of local organisations, should be able to tell you about local activities.

Good Practices in Mental Health
380–384 Harrow Road
London W9 2HU
289 2034
Information service for planners and professionals.

London Alliance for Mental Health Action
5 Anglers Lane
Kentish Town
London NW5 3DG
485 3021
An umbrella organisation of progressive user-led groups. Can put people in touch with local groups.

Mental After-care Association
Bainbridge House
Bainbridge Street
London WC1A 1HP
436 6194
Care and rehabilitation after mental illness.

Mental Health Foundation
8 Hallam Street
London W1N 6DH
580 0145/6
*Fundraising and promotion of
treatment for mental disorders.*

**MIND (National Association for
  Mental Health)**
22 Harley Street
London W1N 2ED
637 0741
*The UK's largest mental health
charity supporting those affected by
mental illness. Helps to find homes
for those with mental health
problems, tries to promote local
services, offers help, advice and
information. Two hundred local
groups.*

National Schizophrenia Fellowship
79 Victoria Road
Surbiton, Surrey KT6 4NS
390 3651
*Advisory service, local groups,
publications.*

Phobic Action
Greater London House
547–551 High Road
London E11 4PR
558 3463
*Telephone help lines, local
branches, classes and home
visiting.*

**Psychiatric Rehabilitation
  Association**
21a Kingsland High Street
London E8 2JS
254 9753
*Evening and day centres, education,
teaching aids, staffed and other
accommodation.*

**Richmond Fellowship for
  Community Mental Health**
8 Addison Road
London W14 8DL
603 6373/4/5
*Provides residential
accommodation, therapeutic
communities and workshops for the
rehabilitation of those recovering
from mental illness or an addiction.*

Psychotherapy

Psychotherapy is a general term describing many different approaches to the care and treatment of emotional problems. All methods attempt to help clients better understand themselves and their problems.

The London Guide to Mind, Body and Spirit, mentioned previously in this chapter, gives much useful information on the differences between psychotherapy, psychology and counselling. It also describes many different forms of therapy and lists organisations offering different forms of psychotherapy, such as art therapy, assertion training, Freudian psychoanalysis, gestalt therapy, hypnotherapy, Jungian analysis, Kleinian analysis, rebirthing, sex therapy, and stress management.

Paddington Centre for Psychotherapy
63 Lancaster Road
London W10
221 4656
An NHS-run psychotherapy centre.

Counselling

Counselling is not necessarily a form of psychotherapy. The term can describe services which offer specific help and information on, for instance, careers or education, or it can describe sessions to help with drug and alcohol abuse, sexual, emotional and personal problems.

British Association for Counselling
37a Sheep Street
Rugby
Warwickshire CV21 3BX
0788 78328/9
Can answer questions on counselling and find you a practitioner in your area.

Help Advisory Centre
3 Adam and Eve Mews
London W8
937 7687/937 6445
You can phone to talk confidentially on problems involving relationships, sexual problems, pregnancy, drugs, VD, etc. Also offers pregnancy testing, counselling and groups and workshops.

Samaritans (Central London)
46 Marshall Street
London WC1V 1LR
439 1406
Twenty-four-hour telephone service for the suicidal and despairing. Absolutely confidential.

Samaritans London Numbers

Central	439 2224	Brent	459 8585
Croydon	681 6666	Ealing	560 2345
Enfield–Haringey	889 6888	Harrow	427 7777
Havering–Romford	751111	Hillingdon–Uxbridge	53355
Kingston	399 6676	Lewisham	692 5228
Orpington	33000	Putney	789 9121
Redbridge	478 7273	Waltham Forest	520 1181

FAMILY PLANNING AND CONTRACEPTION

Men and women are entitled to free contraception. The local Family Planning Clinic (see telephone directory) or your GP will tell you how to go about obtaining the kind of contraception you require and offer information and advice on the kinds available.

Margaret Pyke Centre
15 Bateman's Buildings
Soho Square
London W1
734 9351
The largest and most central family planning clinic.

Family Planning Association
27–35 Mortimer Street
London W1N 7RG
636 7866
General information and details of local clinics.

AIDS INFORMATION AND COUNSELLING

AIDS has been constantly in the news over the last few years. Questions relating to the government's belated realisation that AIDS is a serious problem and its still inadequate funding of research and publicity campaigns are well documented and will not be repeated here. Suffice to say that as long as the government continues to give insufficient priority to AIDS/HIV and does not allow frank and accurate advertising on safer sex and the use of condoms in the papers and on the television (and not just late at night), then progress will probably continue to be slow in the quest for a cure.

The following organisations can offer advice and information on AIDS/HIV transmission, safer sex, the law, support for people with AIDS/HIV and their family and friends. See also Chapter 9: Lesbians and Gay Men and Chapter 15: Women.

Body Positive
51B Philbeach Gardens
London SW5 9EB
835 1045 (office)
373 9124 (helpline)
From 7pm to 10pm daily. Help for people who are HIV positive and their friends and families.

Frontliners
831 0330 ext. 433–4 office hours
AIDS Healthline 980 4848
  2pm–10pm
National organisation run by and for people with AIDS.

Lantern Trust
72 Honey Lane
Waltham Abbey
Essex, EN9 3BS
0992 714990
Publishes teaching packs for the school, college and workplace.

London Lesbian and Gay Centre
67–69 Cowcross Road
London EC1M 6BP
608 1471
Have produced the National AIDS Manual, an indispensable 500-page information source.

London Lighthouse
111–117 Lancaster Road
London W11 1QT
792 1200
AIDS centre linking with community care groups and educational courses for carers.

Mainliners
738 7333 (Mon–Fri 4pm–8pm)
Assistance and information for intravenous drug users with HIV/AIDS.

National AIDS Helpline
0800 567123
Twenty-four-hour helpline.

Positively Healthy
c/o Cass Mann
63 Priory Road
Kew
Surrey, TW9 3DH
940 5355
Self-health group with a holistic approach to HIV infection. Seminars, distributes information and holistic products.

Positively Women
333 Gray's Inn Rd
London WC1
837 9705
Support group for women around
the issues of HIV and AIDS.

Terrence Higgins Trust
52–54 Gray's Inn Road
London WC1
242 1010 (helpline)
831 0330 (office)

VD/SEXUALLY TRANSMITTED DISEASES CLINICS

James Pringle House
Middlesex Hospital
73–75 Charlotte Street
London W1
323 4819

Marlborough Dept
Royal Free Hospital
75 Hampstead High Street
London NW3
435 5747

Praed Street Clinic
St Mary's Hospital
London W2
927 1696
(No appointment necessary.)

John Hunter Clinic
St Stephen's Hospital
Fulham Road

London SW10
352 8161 ex221/223
(No appointment necessary.)

Lloyd Clinic
Guy's Hospital
St Thomas Street
London SE1
407 7600 ex2292

Lydia Clinic
St Thomas Street
Westminster Bridge
London SE1
(No appointment necessary.)

Alexandra Clinic
St Giles Hospital
St Giles Road
London SE5
703 0898 ex6024

DRUGS

London has a serious drugs problem. Heroin, cocaine and crack are widely available. Thousands of people are suffering and dying as a result of drug misuse. The connection between drug injection and the transmission of the AIDS/HIV virus is now generally recognised. Failure to tackle the real culprits, namely the drug traders, and too much police time spent arresting young people for possession of minute quantities of cannabis, means that there has been little sign of slowing down drug traffic into London.

However, the reasons why people take drugs are many and varied and this is not the place to discuss the social, moral or political arguments relating to drug addiction and its treatment. The purpose here is merely to provide a list of contacts for people who need help with their addiction or advice and information on drugs generally and how to recognise their effects in others. The list below is not exhaustive. These organisations might also be able to refer you to a local clinic or support group, which might be NHS run, voluntary or private.

Accept
200 Seagrave Road
London SW6
Drugs helpline: 286 3339
Alcohol helpline: 381 3155
Advice on drugs, alcohol and tranquillisers, treatment services and family support. Local branches.

Accept Ethnic Network for Greater London
170A Heston Road
Hounslow, Middlesex
577 6059
Counselling in five languages.

Action on Smoking and Health (ASH)
5–11 Mortimer Street
London W1N 7RH
637 9843
Attempts to keep smoking and the related problems in the public eye through the dissemination of information, links with other organisations and lobbying the appropriate bodies.

Angel Project (Inner City Action on Drugs)
38–44 Liverpool Road
London N1
226 3113

Association for the Prevention of Addiction
5–7 Tavistock Place
London WC1H 9SS
383 5071
Training courses, counselling for drug misusers, public education.

Beresford Project
8 Beresford Square
London SE18
854 9518
Advice, information and counselling.

Blenheim Project
7 Thorpe Close
London W10
960 5599
Support and counselling for people with drug-related problems.

Campaign Against Drug Abuse
359 Old Kent Road
London SE17
854 9518
Telephone advice for users and families.

City Roads Crisis Intervention Centre
356–358 City Road
London EC1
278 8671/2
Residential centre for drug users and twenty-four-hour advice line.

Community Drug Project
30 Manor Place
London SE17
703 0559
Support, advice, counselling, referral service for detoxification and rehabilitation.

Drug Advice Workshop
145a Putney High Street
London SW15
788 1199
Support group for relatives and friends of drug users.

Drugline
9a Brockley Close
London SE4 2AB
692 4975
Telephone advice and counselling, individual counselling, meetings for parents and for tranquilliser users, prison and hospital visits.

Families Anonymous
88 Caledonian Road
London N7
278 8805
A chain of self-help groups set up

by parents. Will tell you if there is a group near you.

Narcotics Anonymous
PO Box 417
London SW10 0RS
351 6794
For people with a major drug problem.

National Campaign Against Solvent Abuse
The Enterprise Centre
444 Brixton Road
London SW9 8EJ
733 7330
Educates young people and adults about dangers of abuse through schools, clubs and other organisations.

Non-users Group
Clare House
St George's Hospital
London SW17
Group of ex-addicts offering mutual support. Meets 6pm, Weds.

Release
169 Commercial Street
London E1 6BW
377 5906 (daytime)
603 8654 (24-hour emergency helpline)
An independent national agency concerned with all aspects of the welfare of people using drugs, including legal problems.

Standing Conference on Drug Abuse
1–4 Hatton Place
London EC1N 8ND
430 2341
Have a full list of drug abuse services throughout London and the whole country.

TRANX UK
National Tranquilliser Advice Centre
25a Masons Avenue
Wealdstone
Middlesex HA3 5AH
One-to-one counselling and walk-in service, advice and information for people suffering withdrawal symptoms or other problems as a result of the long-term use of tranquillisers.

Turning Point (Hungerford Drug Project)
26 Craven Street
London WC2 5NT
930 4688
Advice, information and counselling for people with drug-related problems and for their families and friends.

Women's Tranquillisers Group
Women's Centre
2–6 Peckham High Street
London SE15
701 2564

ALCOHOL

Counsellors recommend that people should try to visit these organisations in a sober condition.

Accept (see above under 'Drugs')

Action on Alcohol Abuse (Triple A)
Livingstone House
11 Carteret Street
London SW1H 9DL
222 3454/6
A pressure group concerned with the dissemination of information on alcohol abuse. No direct work with clients.

Alanon
403 0888
Help for families and friends of alcoholics.

Alcohol Concern
305 Gray's Inn Road
London WC1X 8QF
833 3471
Works with government, statutory and voluntary organisations, supports existing services and helps set up new ones. Information, education and onward referral.

Alcohol Counselling Service
34 Electric Lane
London SW9
737 3570
Counselling and other services by and for lesbians and gay men.

Alcohol Education and Research Fund
Abell House
Room G6
John Islip Street
London SW1P 4LH
211 8513
Administered by a council appointed by the Home Secretary. Concerned with both preventive measures and treatment.

Alcohol Problem Advisory Service
National Temperance Hospital
Hampstead Road
London NW1
387 8354
Counselling, groupwork, onward referral.

Alcohol Recovery Project
68 Newington Causeway
London SE1 6DF
403 3369
Advice, information, counselling, group meetings, residential services, training.

Alcoholics Anonymous
352 3001
10am–10pm advice line.
Fellowship of men and women who share their experiences to help each other combat drink problems.

B-Sharp
302 Devons Road
London E2 2PN
987 1765
Residential, training and other services.

Greater London Alcohol Advisory Service
91–93 Charterhouse Street
London EC1M 6BT
253 6221
Coordinates agencies in Greater London and offers training.

Haringey Alcohol Project
530–532 West Green Road
London N15 3DX
888 7737
Thirteen-week residential assessment, onward referral. Fast decision on admission.

Turning Point
9–12 Long Lane
London EC1A 9HA
606 3947
Will also give details of Turning Point Southall Alcohol Advice Service – advice and counselling in Punjabi, Hindi, Urdu and Bengali. Also a number of local projects.

Women's Alcohol Centre
66 Drayton Park
London N5
226 4581
Individual counselling, information and advice about alcohol and its effects. Also maintains a residential service.

ADDRESSES

General

Action for Victims of Medical Accidents
24 Southwark Street
London SE11 1TY
403 4744
Advice and information for people who have suffered as a result of medical treatment or non-provision of treatment.

Association for Improvements in the Maternity Services
163 Liverpool Road
London N1 0RF
278 5628
Acts mostly as a pressure group, disseminates information and provides support and advice.

British Library of Tape Recordings for Hospital Patients
12 Lant Street
London SE1 1QH
407 9417
Operates a postal library of books on cassette and supplies playback equipment to hospitals at cost price.

College of Health
14 Buckingham Street
London WC2N 6DS
839 2413
Health education for members, information on making the most of health services, publishes a consumers' guide to health.

Department of Health
Whitehall
London SW1
210 3000

Health Information Trust
18 Victoria Park Square
London E2 9PF
980 6263
Operates a telephone information service on a number of topics and a
twenty-four-hour service giving advice about AIDS. Disseminates information on health.

Healthline
A confidential health information service by phone.
980 4848 (evenings)

Hospice Information Service
St Christopher's Hospice
51–59 Lawrie Park Road
Sydenham
London SE26 6DZ
778 9252 ext. 262/263
Information about hospice services, both for members of the public and those planning to set up a hospice.

Institute of Religion and Medicine
St Marylebone Parish Church
Marylebone Road
London NW1 5LT
935 6374 ext. 133
Publications, conferences, meetings and discussion groups on the relationship between religion and medicine.

London Food Commission
88 Old Street
London EC1V 9AR
253 9513
Educational and research campaigns on food, nutrition, diet, health, food production, retail, distribution, cooking, catering, etc.

London Health Emergency
446 Uxbridge Road
London W12 0NF
749 2525
Information providing and campaigning organisation in defence of the Health Service in London. Also runs the 'Hands-Off' Campaign, against the NHS White Paper and will put people in touch with local groups.

Medic-Alert Foundation
11–13 Clifton Terrace
London N4 3JP
263 8596/7
*Carrying the medic-alert emblem
warns police, ambulance and
medical services of a hidden allergy
or medical condition.*

**Medical Association for the
    Prevention of War**
16b Prince Arthur Road
London NW3 6AX
794 1430
*Conferences, etc. on the ethical
responsibilities of doctors in
relation to war.*

**Medical Campaign Against Nuclear
    Weapons (MCANW)**
3 Stamford Street
London SE1 9NT
261 1266
*Information, speakers, etc. on the
health implications of nuclear
weapons.*

**Medical Foundation for the Care of
    Victims of Torture**
2nd Floor

National Temperance Hospital
110–114 Hampstead Road
London NW1 2LT
388 8204
*Care for those who suffer injury as
the result of torture.*

Radical Statistics
c/o BSSRS
25 Horsell Road
London N5 1XL
607 9615
*Prepares publications revealing the
misleading use of statistics in many
areas including health, education,
race, nuclear disarmament, etc.
Meetings, research, etc.*

Socialist Health Association
195 Walworth Road
London SE17 1RP
703 6838
*Affiliated to the Labour Party,
campaigns for the development of a
fully comprehensive health service,
both preventive and curative,
funded from taxation and free at the
time of use. Publish a quarterly
journal, 'Socialism and Health'.*

Women's Health

NB   A more extensive list of addresses relating to pregnancy,
childbirth, abortion, and other aspects of women's health appears
in Chapter 15: Women.

Well Women Clinics

There are many well women clinics across the capital, some of
which are attached to family planning clinics. Your local
Community Health Council can give you the address of your
local clinic.

Breast Cancer Research Trust
7 Soho Street
London W1V 5FA
437 9727
Promotes research.

**Breast Care and Mastectomy
    Association of Great Britain**
26 Harrison Street
London WC1H 8JG
837 0908/278 3529

Non-medical information and support service for women coping with breast surgery. Voluntary helpers provided to complement professional care. Helpers have had some form of breast surgery.

Hysterectomy Support Group
11 Henryson Road
London SE4 1HL
690 5987
Information and support for women and their partners.

Medical Women's Federation
Tavistock House North
Tavistock Square
London WC1H 8HX
387 7765
Promoting the education, study and practice of medicine among women. Career advice and general information.

National Abortion Campaign
Wesley House
4 Wild Court
London WC2B 5AU
405 4801
Campaigns to secure the right of women to make their own decision about abortion on the NHS.

National Association for Premenstrual Syndrome
25 Market Street
Guildford
Surrey GU1 4LB
0483 572715
Campaigning group working for greater recognition of PMS.

National Childbirth Trust
Alexandra House
Oldham Terrace
London W3 6NH
992 8637

Women Against Cervical Cancer
50A Pall Mall
London SW1Y 5JQ
823 4467
Aims to heighten public awareness of cervical cancer.

Women's Health Concern
Ground Floor
17 Earls Terrace
London W8 6LP
602 6669
An inquiry service, counselling service and educational service to promote research on women's health problems.

Women's League of Health and Beauty
Rooms 29–31
18 Charing Cross Road
London WC2H 0HR
240 8456
Physical education and promotion of health.

Women's Health Information Centre
52–54 Featherstone Street
London EC1
251 6580

Women's National Cancer Control Campaign
1 South Audley Street
London W14 5DQ
499 7532
Screening, campaigning, information on cancers of the breast and cervix.

Women's Reproductive Rights Information Centre
52–54 Featherstone Street
London EC1
251 6332

Professional, Advisory and Trade Union Organisations

British Medical Association
Tavistock Square
London WC1H 9JP
387 4499
Representative body for doctors.

Confederation of Health Service Employees (COHSE)
112 Greyhound Lane
London SW16
677 3622

Health Education Authority
Hamilton House
Mabledon Place
London WC1H 9TX

Health Visitors Association (HVA)
50 Southwark Street
London SE1 1WN
378 7255

Institution of Environmental Health Officers
Chadwick House
48 Rushworth Street
London SE1 0QT
928 6006

Medical Research Council
20 Park Crescent
London W1N 4AL
636 5422

Medical Women's Federation
Tavistock House North
Tavistock Square
London WC1H 9HX
387 7765

National Association of Women Pharmacists
c/o Pharmaceutical Society of Great Britain
1 Lambeth High Street
London SE1 7JN
735 9141

National Union of Public Employees (NUPE)
20 Grand Depot Road
London SE18 6SF
854 2244

Royal College of Midwives (RCM)
15 Mansfield Street
London W1M 0BE
580 6523/4/5

Royal College of Nursing (RCN)
20 Cavendish Square
London W1M 0AB
409 3333

Royal Institute of Public Health and Hygiene
28 Portland Place
London W1N 4DE
580 2731

Royal Society of Health
13 Grosvenor Place
London SW1X 7EN
235 9961

Royal Society of Medicine
1 Wimpole Street
London W1M 8AE
580 2070

Community Medicine

Association of Community Health Councils
30 Drayton Park
London N5 1PB
609 8405
An independent body representing the interests of the public in the NHS. Responds to health policy matters, promotes good practice. Can give you the address of your local CHC.

British Red Cross Society
9 Grosvenor Court
London SW1X 7EJ
235 5454

**Institution of Environmental Health
 Officers**
Chadwick House
48 Rushworth Street
London SE1 0QT
928 6006
*Your local EHO will be listed in the
phone book.*

Queen's Nursing Institute
57 Lower Belgrave Street
London SW1W 0LP
730 0355
Works with District Health

*Authorities to provide information
and advice on community nursing
care.*

St John Ambulance
1 Grosvenor Crescent
London SW1X 7EF
235 5231

Society of Community Medicine
c/o Royal Institute of Public Health
 and Hygiene
28 Portland Place
London W1N 4DE
580 2731

Carers

Carers National Association
29 Chilworth Mews
London W2 3RG
262 1451
*Support, counselling and advice on
benefits and help availability.*

**Association of Crossroads Care
 Attendant Schemes**
Greater London Office
Victoria Chambers
16–18 Strutton Ground
London SW1P 2HP
222 6858
*Helps carers with opportunities for
breaks from their caring role.*

Specific Maladies

Action Against Allergy
43 The Downs
London SW20 8HG
947 5082
*Information for sufferers,
campaigning for better diagnosis
and treatment, raising funds for
research.*

**Action for Research into Multiple
 Sclerosis**
4a Chapel Hill
Stansted
Essex CM24 8AG
0279 815553
*Promotes awareness and research.
Twenty-four-hour counselling
service.*

Alzheimer's Disease Society
158–160 Balham High Road
London SW12 9BN
675 6557/8/9/0
*Support for families, promoting
awareness, fundraising for support
services.*

Amnesia Association
25 Prebend Gardens
London W4 1TN
747 0039

**Anorexia and Bulimia Nervosa
 Association**
Tottenham Women's Health Centre
Annexe C
Tottenham Town Hall
London N5 4RX
885 3936

Runs a confidential helpline, organises workshops, etc. nationwide, maintains a national network of self-help groups.

Arthritis Care
6 Grosvenor Crescent
London SW1X 7ER
235 0902
Runs many local branches; offers services such as adapted holiday accommodation.

Arthritis and Rheumatism Council
41 Eagle Street
London WC1R 4AR
405 8572
Finances research and encourages better treatment facilities.

Association for All Speech-impaired Children
347 Central Market
Smithfield
London EC1A 9NH
236 3632

Association for Spina Bifida and Hydrocephalus
22 Woburn Place
London WC1H 0EP
388 1382
Concerned with both welfare and research. Departments dealing with accommodation, social work, disabled living, education, training and employment.

Association for Spinal Injury Research, Rehabilitation and Reintegration (ASPIRE)
16 East Heath Road
London NW3 1AL
209 1072 or 209 0868
Runs 'half-way homes', buys aids for patients and the London Spinal Unit.

Association for Stammerers
c/o The Finsbury Centre
Pine Street
London EC1R 0JH

Association for the Study of Obesity
c/o 50 Ruby Road
London E17 4RF
521 0653
Promotes medical research and facilitates contact between individuals and organisations.

Asthma Society and Friends of the Asthma Research Council
300 Upper Street
London N1 2XX
226 2260
Help and advice, promotion of research, local groups.

Blood Transfusion Service
628 9540

British Association of Cancer United Patients (BACUP)
121–123 Charterhouse Street
London EC1M 6AA
608 1785
Free, confidential cancer information service, by telephone or letter, counselling service for patients and their families.

British Diabetic Association
10 Queen Anne Street
London W1M 0BD
323 1531
Advice, fundraising, educational and holiday activities for diabetics through local groups.

British Digestive Foundation
3 St Andrew's Place
London NW1 4LB
Information on and fundraising for treatment of gastro-intestinal disease.

British Heart Foundation
102 Gloucester Place
London W1H 4DH
935 0185
Research, information, local groups.

British Lung Foundation
12A Onslow Gardens
London SW7 3AP
581 0226

*Awards grants to research workers
and disseminates information to
sufferers.*

British Migraine Association
178A High Road
Weybridge
Surrey KT14 7ED
09323 52468
*Encourages sufferers to participate
in research and offers help and
reassurance.*

British Polio Fellowship
Bell Close
West End Road
Ruislip
Middlesex HA4 6LP
0895 675515
*Social welfare work for those
suffering the after effects of polio.*

British Tinnitus Association
105 Gower Street
London WC1E 6AH
387 4803
*Brings together sufferers and
lobbies MPs and relevant
organisations, fundraising and
publicity.*

Cancerlink
17 Britannia Street
London WC1X 9JN
833 2451
*Information and support on all
aspects of cancer and practical help
available to sufferers, their family
and friends.*

Cancer Relief Macmillan Fund
Anchor House
15–19 Britten Street
London SW3 3TY
351 7811
*Skilled care and support for cancer
patients at home, in-patient and
day-care facilities. Training for
doctors and nurses.*

Cancer Research Campaign
2 Carlton House Terrace
London SW1Y 5AR
930 8972

*Raises funds for research and
treatment.*

Chest, Heart and Stroke Association
Tavistock House North
Tavistock Square
London WC1H 9JE
387 3012
*Research, education, counselling
and welfare services.*

Children's Cancer Help Centre
PO Box 4
Orpington
Kent, BR6 8Q7
0689 71587
*Individual support for children and
their families. Sessions of relaxation
and meditation designed to
complement traditional treatment.*

Colostomy Welfare Group
38–39 Eccleston Square
London SW1V 1PB
828 5175
*Advice, information and support
based on personal experience.*

Coronary Prevention Group
60 Great Ormond Street
London WC1N 3HR
833 3687
*Information and advice on healthy
eating, food labelling, stress,
exercise, smoking, etc.*

CRUSAID
83 Clerkenwell Road
London EC1R 5AR
831 2595
*Raises money for the care and
treatment of people with AIDS.*

Down's Syndrome Association
12–13 Clapham Common Southside
London SW4 7AA
720 0008
*Parents' self-help organisation,
meetings, support, etc.*

Dyslexia Institute
133 Gresham Road
Staines
Middlesex TW18 2AJ
0784 459498

Dystonia Society
Omnibus Workspace
39–41 North Road
London N7 9DP
700 4594
*Telephone helpline, local groups,
support and advice.*

Endometriosis Society
65 Holmdene Avenue
Herne Hill
London SE24 9LD
737 4764
*Information, help and advice for
sufferers, self-help groups,
workshops, etc.*

Haemophilia Society
123 Westminster Bridge Road
London SE1 7HR
928 2020
*Advice on education, training,
employment, etc. Lobbies local and
central government. Local groups.*

Herpes Association
41 North Road
London N7 9DP
609 9061
*Runs a helpline, answers written
inquiries, acts as a pressure group
for research, coordinates local self-
help groups.*

Imperial Cancer Research Fund
PO Box 123, Lincoln's Inn Fields
London WC2A 3PX
242 0200
*Runs fundraising groups, shops, a
cancer research institute and
supports many laboratories.*

International Glaucoma Association
c/o King's College Hospital
Denmark Hill
London SE5 9RS
274 6222 ext. 2934 (Mon and Thurs
only)
*Discussion forums and information
for patients and those interested in
the condition.*

Leukaemia Research Fund
43 Great Ormond Street
London WC1N 3JJ
405 0101
*National charity. Newsletter,
information booklets.*

**LINK – The Neurofibromatosis
 Association**
D15 London House
26–40 Kensington High Street
London W8 9PF
983 2222 ext. 2226
*Mutual support group for sufferers,
provides advice counselling and
information.*

Lupus Group – Arthritis Care
6 Grosvenor Crescent
London SW1X 7ER
235 0902
*Provides communication between
sufferers and educates sufferers, the
general public and the medical
profession.*

Manic Depression Fellowship
51 Sheen Road, Richmond
Surrey TW9
332 1078
*Runs local self-help groups and
attempts to educate the public and
fund research into manic
depression.*

Marie Curie Memorial Foundation
28 Belgrave Square
London SW1X 8QG
235 3325
*Concerned with cancer prevention
and the well-being of cancer
patients. Runs nursing homes,
community care and night nursing
service, provides advice and
information.*

Menieres Society
59 Emmanuel Road
London SW12 0HP
675 5808
*Provides information to sufferers.
Local groups.*

**Michael McGough Foundation
  Against Liver Disease in Children**
PO Box 494
Western Avenue
London W3 0SH
992 3400 ext. 6131
*Advice and support for families,
grants for research, fundraising.*

Migraine Trust
45 Great Ormond Street
London WC1N 3HD
278 2676
*Information, advice, counselling,
research grants, self-help groups.*

Multiple Sclerosis Society
25 Effie Road
London SW6 1EE
*Welfare and support service for
sufferers and families. Promotes
and funds research.*

Muscular Dystrophy Group
Nattrass House
35 Macaulay Road
London SW4 0QP
720 8055
*Fundraising to promote research,
conferences to promote
information.*

**National Ankylosing Spondilitis
  Society**
6 Grosvenor Crescent
London SW1X 7ER
235 9585
*Advice and information for
sufferers, training for professionals.*

**National Association of
  Laryngectomee Clubs**
4th Floor
39 Eccleston Square
London SW1V 1PB
834 2857
Information, advice, lectures, etc.

National Autistic Society
276 Willesden Lane
London NW2 5RB
451 3844
*Advice and information for parents
and professionals. Runs schools
and adult centres.*

National Back Pain Association
31–33 Park Road
Teddington
Middlesex TW11 0AB
*Information, activities, funding
research.*

National Diabetes Foundation
177a Tennyson Road
London SE25 5NF
656 5467
*Non-medical advice on twenty-four-
hour advice line, other advice in
office hours. Help for parents of
diabetic children.*

National Eczema Society
Tavistock House North
Tavistock Square
London WC1H 9SR
388 4097
*Local groups, social functions,
meetings, promotion of information
on eczema.*

National Rubella Council
33–39 Pancras Road
London NW1 2QB
837 0623

New Approaches to Cancer
Addington Park
Maidstone
Kent ME19 5BL
0732 848336
*Encourages use of complementary
methods alongside traditional
treatments. Developing Cancer Help
Centres.*

Renal Society
41 Mutton Place
London NW1 8DF
485 9775
Information for kidney patients.

Scoliosis Association
380–384 Harrow Road
London W9 2HU
289 5652
Counselling, information, education.

Sickle Cell Society
Green Lodge
Barrett Green Road
London NW10 7AP
961 7795
Financial support for sufferers and their families, fundraising, information and advice.

Society for the Prevention of Asbestosis and Industrial Diseases
38 Drapers Road
Enfield
Middlesex EN2 8LU
0707 873025
Help for sufferers, information on causes and prevention.

Spastics Society
12 Park Crescent
London W1N 4EQ
636 5020
Information on schools, education and residential centres, family services. Local groups.

Spinal Injuries Association
Newpoint House
76 St James Lane
London N10
444 2121
Advice and information for people with spinal injuries. Membership open to all.

United Kingdom Rett Syndrome Association
Freepost
Orpington
Kent BR5 1SZ 0689 26760
Parent-to-parent support, information and advice for families and carers of children suffering from Rett Syndrome.

United Kingdom Thalassaemia Society
107 Nightingale Lane
London N8 7QY
348 0437
Fundraising, meetings, counselling and advice for sufferers and carriers.

Vitiligo Group
PO Box 919
London SE21 8AW
670 7175
Information, support and advice for members, promotion of research and awareness.

VOCAL – (Voluntary Organisations Communications and Language)
336 Brixton Road
London SW9
274 4029
Support and link services for people with speech, language and voice disabilities, advice on therapy and technical help.

8

HOUSING

London faces a housing emergency. The number of people without a home has reached scandalous proportions. In 1988 over 30,000 families became homeless. Thousands more are sleeping rough or living in squalid, insecure homes.

London councils have to cope with the crisis but have been hit by huge cuts in the money they are able to spend on building new homes. In fact fewer new homes were built in London in 1988 than at any time since the First World War. So local councils have far fewer homes to let to new tenants. Lets to new tenants have fallen by half to about 25,000 over the last ten years. There are simply not enough homes to house the homeless, let alone people who have been waiting years on the list.

Many councils are forced to use various kinds of temporary accommodation. The most depressing, cramped and often downright unhealthy and dangerous are 'bed and breakfast hotels'. Over 7,500 families spent last Christmas living in such hotels in London. Another 2,500 were found places in hostels, and nearly 9,000 were offered short-term houses in run-down old properties.

The word 'temporary' implies that these families are soon found decent long-term accommodation. But many have been living in bed and breakfast for over a year. Stays of over two years are not uncommon any more.

This is bad enough, but the final lunacy is that it would be cheaper to provide homeless people with decent council homes. The government admits that it costs more to keep a family in bed and breakfast than it would cost in interest payments and management charges to build a new council flat for the same family. But councils' hands are tied. Government rules prevent them building these badly needed new homes. Instead Londoners pick up the £100 million a year hotel bill, when about half as much would provide new homes for all those in bed and breakfast. It would also provide work for the thousands of London's jobless building workers – one in four are estimated to be out of work.

Homelessness set against the city which is the playground of the rich and powerful is a shocking indictment of the 'new Britain'. It's a waste of human lives. It's a waste of money, too. It must be prevented. Only the political will appears to be lacking to mount a successful housing programme.

Single people who usually have no legal right to housing and who are not able to find affordable accommodation in the shrinking private rented market have little choice but to squat or sleep rough. The sight of very young women and men forced by poverty to spend their lives in and around the West End is no longer a rare phenomenon. There is nothing attractive or glamorous about London after hours. Many are led reluctantly into a life of begging, prostitution or stealing.

Rising homelessness is far from the only problem. The city's housing is beset by decay and disrepair. One-fifth (over half a million homes) of the housing stock is either unfit for human habitation, lacking modern facilities or in disrepair. The worst conditions are found in homes which are rented privately. More than one out of every six London houses are over one hundred years old yet home improvement grant spending has been halved in the last few years.

Housing costs are rocketing way beyond the means of many ordinary people. House prices have more than doubled since 1979. The same is true of private rents. And the government has introduced new legislation which will force council rents up double in some cases. What about the social security help that is available? Housing benefit help with rent and rates has been cut almost every year since 1983. Racial harassment, even physical abuse and violence, and discrimination in housing disfigure many parts of London.

To meet these problems little of practical help has been attempted. The government's new Housing Act promises even higher rents and reduced security for private tenants. Council tenants have not been forgotten. The Act contains measures designed to transfer their homes into the private sector. Nothing was done to provide extra help for the homeless. And in 1990 we all face the poll tax which is bound to have damaging effects on the financial stability of many families. It could even lead to young people having to leave their parental home because the poll tax burden will be too great.

It is impossible to be optimistic about the future. Unless policies and priorities change soon the outlook for many Londoners is bleak. More will find themselves trapped in the vicious spiral of homelessness, unemployment and poverty. Time is short. Action is needed now.

Paul Walentowicz
Researcher, SHAC
(The London Housing Aid Centre)
April 1989

HOMELESSNESS IN LONDON

A 1988 report by the housing charity Shelter showed how the Conservative government's policies had contributed to homelessness in Britain as a whole and in London in particular. There has been a drive towards increasing private sector housing and reducing the level of state provision of housing to those most in need of cheaper accommodation. Up to now one of the principal means of achieving this has been the restriction of local authority building programmes.

In 1978, the number of council houses completed in Britain was 79,733. By 1987, the annual figure had fallen to 18,880, a fall accompanied by sharp rises in the cost of private housing and in property values generally. Private rented accommodation in London is moving out of the price range of more and more people. Homelessness is on the increase and the general situation has now been dramatically worsened by the introduction of the 1988 Housing Act.

In 1987, it was estimated by Shelter that between 25,000 and 40,000 young people were sleeping rough or squatting in London. Hostels and hotels are overflowing, and in 1986 513 children were taken into care for no other reason than the fact that their families were homeless. Women with children account for two out of three of those designated 'homeless' in London. SHAC estimated the number of households in London accepted as homeless in 1988 as 32,160, a third of whom were black.

A survey published by the Salvation Army in July 1989 went some way to bringing homelessness figures up to date. It estimated 75,000 homeless in London (including those in hostels or squats). In the seventeen boroughs covered by the survey 753 people were counted actually sleeping on the streets. Even this figure was thought to be a vast underestimate as around twice that number were estimated to have gone uncounted. In October 1989, a survey by Centrepoint Soho estimated that the number of young people sleeping rough on London's streets had risen by more than 50 per cent in two years. Four out of ten of the young people questioned in the survey had previously been in care, one in three had begged for money and one in three had been approached for prostitution.

The legal definition of homelessness actually ignores many groups such as single people and couples without children who, despite their situation, are not necessarily designated as homeless. Only about half of those applying to be recognised as homeless are accepted as such by local authorities. Of that 50 per cent, only about half are provided with permanent accommodation. Stories of people in real need of immediate housing, but who are not granted it, are more and more common. It might be tempting to suggest that local authorities are not fulfilling their obligations, but resources are severely limited in the wake of GLC abolition, rate capping and government spending limits, not to mention the lack of available housing, and councils' hands are often tied.

One of the most obvious and certainly most disturbing illustrations of London's homelessness crisis is the number of people sleeping on London's streets. It is no longer just the Embankment arches that are lined with cardboard box and newspaper covered bodies, but the South Bank Centre car parks, doorways in the Strand and Charing Cross Road and just about every tube entrance in the capital.

I spoke to a man begging on Hungerford Bridge, a man in his early 30s, intelligent and well spoken, who told me he was sleeping under the Festival Hall and that he had counted over 300 people on his patch of the South Bank the previous night.

A further aspect of the problem is largely a result of the so-called Care in the Community programme. In the past ten years, 23,000 psychiatric hospital beds have been cut with only 4,000 residential places being created to replace them. This would be understandable if sufficient resources were available to provide for those displaced by these cuts. In fact another 29,000 places are due to be lost and the responsibility for the patients passed to local authorities with neither the capital, the available places nor the expertise to deal with the arrival of many more people, often ex-psychiatric patients who require special care or at least proper supervision.

Between 1980 and 1987 more than 1,000,000 local authority and new town homes were sold in order to promote owner occupation. Frequent changes in housing benefit rules mean that many people, especially young people, will be forced out of accommodation they are no longer able to afford. The street is often the only place for them to go. There have been cuts in housing benefit every year since 1980 except 1986. Clearly, the policies of the Thatcher government are largely responsible for the sharp increase in homelessness, but Labour Party members and supporters should also realise that Labour councils are not blameless; they have often been involved in producing badly designed, poorly serviced accommodation.

THE HOUSING ACT 1988

The Housing Act 1988 is just one aspect of a much wider assault by the Conservative government on the Welfare State. Health and social security measures coming into force will mean that the less well-off are going to suffer on more and more fronts.

The Housing Act aims to transform the way in which rented accommodation is provided. It is part of a wider attack on the powers of local government and on state ownership, shifting political power ever more towards the centre and placing still more emphasis on private enterprise at the expense of affordable accommodation for those most in need. The 1988 Act is merely the culmination of measures gradually introduced since 1979 to reduce the role of council housing.

Withdrawal of subsidies, penalising expenditure and 'Right to Buy' schemes have all played a part. Now the government plans to speed up the erosion of council property provision and the transfer of accommodation to private landlords approved by the Housing Corporation.

The government's claim is that the Housing Act simply offers tenants a choice of landlord – Council, private landlord, housing association, or tenant coop. In reality, any private landlord can offer to buy an estate from a local council. Once accepted by the Housing Corporation as a bona fide purchaser, the landlord can challenge the council's asking price and ask for lists of all residents on the estate and many other details such as their record on prompt payment of rent.

Under the 'Tenants Choice' scheme, the tenants of an estate or group of flats will be able to vote on the landlord's offer but anyone who does not vote for any reason, even if they are ill or on holiday, will be counted as having voted in favour of the private landlord's offer. The only rule is that at least 50 per cent of the tenants must have voted one way or the other. In theory, this means that in a block of forty council flats, if five people voted for the landlord, fifteen voted against and twenty did not vote, the landlord would gain possession. Of course, this system is open to gross abuses such as sending ballot forms to empty flats or houses and counting them as 'yes' votes. Only secure tenants are allowed to vote in any case. Lodgers, subtenants or squatters will have no vote. Joint tenants will only have one vote between them.

In the case of blocks of flats and maisonettes, those tenants who vote against a transfer will remain as council tenants if the rest of the block is sold, with the new landlord leasing the property back to the council for as long as the tenants remain in residence. In the case of housing estates, those tenants who vote against the sale will remain as council tenants with the council retaining possession of the property. Council house tenants also have the right to opt out of council ownership individually if they so desire and if they can find an alternative landlord.

If the vote goes against the landlord the estate cannot be taken over but there is nothing to stop the same or a different landlord coming back with a new offer and forcing another ballot.

If an estate is taken over the landlord will be at liberty to replace rents set by the council with 'market rents'. This will undoubtedly lead to major rent increases for those who can least afford them, and who may well have to move out to seek cheaper accommodation allowing wealthier tenants to move in, thus boosting the profits of the landlord and displacing those most in need of housing.

New tenancies under the new private landlords will be less secure than under council tenancy arrangements. They will be known as 'assured tenancies'. Eviction will be easier and rights fewer. For example, rights to transfers, subletting and so on will be lost. In a few cases, the landlord will be able to impose 'assured shorthold tenancies', initially of a minimum of six months, subsequently of as little as two months, after which a tenant can be evicted.

Some councils will decide themselves to sell all or part of their housing as a 'voluntary' sale. The word 'voluntary' might not be entirely accurate as a council could well be under extreme financial pressure to sell off an estate. In such cases tenants must be consulted but there need not even be a vote! However, it is unlikely that the government would approve a voluntary sale without a ballot.

If council properties are transferred to private landlords, the new landlords will not be under the same compulsion to provide special facilities for the elderly or disabled, nor are they likely to follow the policies of certain councils in assuring equal access to council housing for ethnic minorities, people with disabilities or lesbians and gay men; discrimination is almost certain to increase. There is a 'Code of Practice' for approved landlords but it is not legally binding.

There will be no opportunity for any new private tenant to seek a fair rent assessment. (As with council tenants taken over by a private landlord, new private tenants will be known as 'assured tenants'.) This is bound to lead to rent increases and it implies an incentive for landlords to encourage existing tenants to leave, since they are 'protected tenants' whose rent can still be assessed by a Rent Officer. If a landlord offers a tenant a move to another flat, though, that tenant will not lose his/her existing security of tenure.

It is worth remembering, too, that as the general level of rents in an area rises, the 'fair rent' for the area is likely to be reassessed as well. What is more, there is no guarantee that Housing Benefit will cover any rent increases. It will also become easier to evict new tenants who fall behind with their rent.

Tenancies that are transferred to housing associations, which can also bid for council estates, will also become 'assured tenancies' with the associated loss of rights and protection. Also, since the government is planning to cut the amount of funding it gives to housing associations, they will have to increase rents in order to remain solvent, especially if they are forced to attract funds from private investors who will insist on making a profit on their investment. This would be the case with banks and building societies, for example. Existing housing association tenants will not lose their existing rights.

A major cause of opposition to the government's plans has been the proposed setting up of Housing Action Trusts (HATS), government appointed bodies given control of all or parts of council estates. The plan is for HATS to spend money on improving the state of these estates then sell them off to private landlords under the ballot scheme mentioned earlier. In theory, the estate could be bought back by the council but it is unlikely that the local councils will have sufficient funds to bid against private landlords and their backers. A last minute concession by the government, in response to the overwhelming opposition to the proposal on the estates where the first HATS were due to be set up, made it possible for tenants to vote on the setting up of a HAT.

Tenancy

The 1988 Housing Act introduced new types of tenancies from 15 January 1989.

Private Tenancies

1 Tenancies started after 15 January 1989 where the landlord lives in a different property from the tenant. These are called assured tenancies.
2 Tenancies started before 15 January 1989 where the landlord lives in a different property from the tenant. These are often called protected tenancies. In a few cases there may be certain restrictions on the protection. Assured and protected tenants can only be evicted for reasons specified by law and can exercise other rights.
3 Assured shorthold tenancies: fixed-term tenancies which must, at this stage at least, be for at least six months. Landlords must serve notice at the beginning of the tenancy.
4 Tenancies where the landlord lives in the same property as the tenant. Such tenants have few rights.

NB When a person is offered a tenancy, they must choose between a sole or joint tenancy (see elsewhere).

Security of Tenure and Eviction

The Department of the Environment Housing Booklet Number 21 has this to say about illegal eviction.

A landlord cannot usually enforce his right to get property back from a residential tenant, or in many cases a licensee without going through the courts. A landlord seeking possession from a periodic residential tenant (other than a tenant under the 1988 Housing Act) or licensee must generally serve a written notice to quit giving at least four weeks notice. A landlord seeking possession from an assured tenant under the 1988 Housing Act must tell the tenant of his intention to start court proceedings by serving a notice on him. Depending on the grounds on which the landlord is seeking possession, the period of notice will be either two weeks or two months except in a few cases where the tenancy agreement entails longer notice. The tenant is not required to leave the property until the notice expires, and even then may not be evicted without an order from the court.

In simple terms, if a tenant has security of tenure it means his/her landlord cannot evict him/her without convincing a court of law that for one of the reasons laid down by law the landlord wants the tenant to leave.

Private tenants with assured or protected tenancy (see above); council tenants (secure tenants); housing association tenants who are secure or assured tenants can only be evicted for certain legal reasons. Tenants with a landlord living in the same house or flat have very little security, but there are possible courses of action available to them.

Housing Law is extremely complex. If you are not sure of your position you should contact a Housing Advice Centre, Law Centre, Citizens Advice Bureau (see Appendix) or the Housing Advice Switchboard.

Rent and Rates

Assured tenants no longer have the right to have their rent registered with the fair rent officer and must either pay the rent asked by the landlord or not accept the tenancy. Protected tenants can still register their rent and have it assessed by the rent officer. If a rent rise is found to be too high then it goes down to the original level. If not, the increase can be phased in over two years.

For council tenants, rents are fixed by the local council which is the landlord and cannot be controlled by the tenant. Housing association tenants whose tenancies began before 15 January 1989 have always had their rents set by the Fair Rent Officer. Those whose tenancies began after this date are assured tenants and must pay the amount asked by the housing association.

Help With Rent and Housing Benefit Regulations

See Chapter 13: Social Services, Benefits and Taxation.

The Poll Tax

The Poll Tax has implications for housing since it will be

replacing the payment of domestic rates. It is discussed more fully in Chapter 13: Social Services, Benefits and Taxation.

Harassment

The one area where the 1988 Housing Act actually improves the lot of the tenant, at least in theory, is that of harassment. Already under the 1977 Protection from Eviction Act, it is an offence to commit acts likely to interfere with the peace or comfort of a tenant or anyone living with him/her; or persistently withdraw or withhold services for which the tenant has a reasonable need to live in the premises as a home. Doing any of these things intending, knowing or having reasonable cause to believe that they would cause a tenant to leave his/her home or stop using any part of it is an offence. It is also an offence to take someone's home away unlawfully.

Under the 1988 Housing Act a person who is convicted by a magistrates court for harassment may have to pay a maximum fine of £2,000 or be sent to prison for six months, or both. If the case goes to the Crown Court, the sentence can be up to two years, with or without a fine. (Details taken from Department of the Environment Housing Booklet Number 21.)

Harassment can cover many things such as violence, withdrawal of services, failure to do repairs or anti-social behaviour by an agent of the landlord. If a tenant feels s/he is being harassed, s/he should go to the <u>local council tenancy relations officer</u>, a <u>Citizens Advice Bureau,</u> Law Centre or other independent advice agency (see Appendix) or a solicitor. If violence is involved, the police should also be contacted. (See also Chapter 5: Ethnic Minorities.)

FINDING A HOME – GENERAL INFORMATION

Finding a home in London is a daunting task whatever your available funds or desired type of accommodation. From reasonably priced owner-occupied property to a space under the arches among the rough sleepers, living space is increasingly difficult to find. SHAC (The London Housing Aid Centre) suggests three golden rules when looking for accommodation in London: if you have a home, do not give it up before you are absolutely certain you have a place to go to; always seek advice from an advice agency; do not be too optimistic about the quality of home you expect to find.

It may seem obvious to mention that you should not consider coming to London if you have no money and are not prepared to end up sleeping on the streets within a few weeks.

Within the available limits, there are a number of organisations that can help you to find somewhere to live, even if the accommodation you end up with is not what you were expecting.

Citizens Advice Bureau
Numbers of local Citizens Advice Bureaux will be in the phone book, otherwise see Appendix.

Housing Advice Switchboard
47 Charing Cross Road
London WC2 0AN
434 2522
Perhaps the first number you should call if you are single or a childless couple. A twenty-four-hour telephone advice service. If you have nowhere at all to stay they will almost always be able to find you somewhere. They will also give you advice on homelessness and the law. Publishes the invaluable booklet 'Finding a Place to Live in London' (£2 from HAS). Advice Line open from 10am to 6pm every weekday; emergency line open at all times.

SHAC
(The London Housing Aid Centre)
189a Old Brompton Road
London SW5 0AR
373 7276
Provides advice to thousands of people and other organisations and produces a range of leaflets, guides and reports. Publications currently available include 'The Housing Rights Guide', and guides for both single and married women. Undertakes research into homelessness, housing benefit etc. Offers legal advice and cooperates with local housing aid centres in all areas of its work.

EMERGENCY ACCOMMODATION: WHERE TO SLEEP TONIGHT

Temporary accommodation is not secure. It may not be in good condition. Some places may not take you if you are unemployed, black, Irish or Asian. Racism in housing is common. The Housing Advice Switchboard may well be able to find you a place to stay temporarily, as may Centrepoint, the hostel in the West End.

Centrepoint Soho
33 Long Acre
London WC2E 9LA
379 3466
(Nearest tube, Tottenham Court
Road; entrance to night shelter in
Shaftesbury Avenue.)
Charity working with young
homeless, primarily in the West
End. Runs an emergency night
shelter, a long stay supportive
hostel and a series of bedsit
schemes.

Bethany Hostel
for Pregnant Women and Homeless
   Mothers
583 Commercial Road
London E1

Homeless Action
52–54 Featherstone Street
London EC1Y 8RT
251 6783

For single homeless women.

The Salvation Army
101 Queen Victoria Street
London EC4P 4EP
236 5222
Hostels, residential homes etc.
Operates a nightly soup run to
those sleeping rough. A midnight
patrol visits London's railway
stations looking out for young
people at risk at night. Also a
missing persons bureau. Individuals
can offer voluntary help.
Missing Persons Bureau: 387 2722
Soup-run Route: Starting at 11pm at
Euston Station, visiting Lincoln's Inn
Fields, Temple Underground station
(around midnight), Embankment,
Strand, Royal Festival Hall
(underneath), Waterloo 'Bullring'
(around 2am). More details, 236
5222 ext. 2186.

Hostels

Usually for single people. May be private or voluntarily run, e.g.
Salvation Army, YWCA/YMCA, Simon Community, women's
hostels, housing associations or some other voluntary associations. Most have an age limit and are single sex. Very few cater
for couples.

If you have no money there are a few short-stay hostels in
central London. Some of these ask for identification. They fill up
early. If you are working and have spent all your money, it will
be hard to find somewhere which will take you without payment.
If you have a little money, there are hostels which cater for such
groups as claimants or working people. The average cost is £7.
Contact Housing Advice Switchboard for details of London's
hostels. The Salvation Army also has a number of emergency
hostels (see above).

Longer stay hostels are often full. You will probably have to
wait for a vacancy. Cost and standard varies as do facilities.
Contact Housing Advice Switchboard for details.

National Association of Voluntary Hostels
33 Long Acre
London WC2
836 0193

Bed and Breakfast

Usually more expensive than hostels. Privately run and with varying prices. <u>Very expensive in the centre.</u> Breakfast sometimes means no more than a cup of coffee.

COUNCIL HOUSING

There is a shortage of council accommodation in London and what there is tends to be concentrated in the inner boroughs. Lack of council funds, rate capping, the cutting of central government grants and the selling off of council property to private landlords are not likely to improve matters!

Of course, the quality of council house provision varies somewhat from borough to borough, as does the attitude of each borough towards 'right-to-buy' and the 1988 Housing Act. Some councils, for example Wandsworth, have an active policy of selling off council properties thereby keeping rate levels down, but at the expense of council house availability.

There are two ways of becoming a council house tenant:

1. Applying to be placed on a waiting list

In order to register on a waiting list, certain conditions must be satisfied, most important of which is that you must register in the area in which you live. Certain councils will also allow you to register in the area in which you work, or if you have a family connection in the area, but this varies considerably and should be checked with the council in question. Different councils have different guidelines as to how long you have to live in an area before becoming eligible. You must be aged 18 or over.

You will have to apply to the council Housing Department and complete an application form. Waiting lists can be literally years long and being on such a list does not guarantee the eventual offer of accommodation. In 1987, there were 264,000 people on Greater London Council waiting lists (GLC and London Research Centre statistics). The accommodation you are offered will depend on the number of bedrooms you need. For instance, if you are a single parent with a young child, you are likely to be offered a one-bedroomed flat or bedsitter.

Each council has its own section designed to deal with waiting lists. Your place on the waiting list may be determined initially by the number of points allocated to you by your council. Your points total depends on your current circumstances.

Different councils have slightly different criteria for points allocation, but you are likely to get points for such things as living in accommodation with no kitchen or bathroom, having to share these facilities with other people, having too little space for living and sleeping if you have a family, living in conditions likely to endanger health. It is important to check with the housing department of your council to see if it operates a points system and if so, what kind.

In urgent cases it is possible for the council to find accommodation for someone who is not on the waiting list, for example if an individual's circumstances or health make it necessary to find new accommodation in a hurry.

In certain cases there may be schemes to house single people or single sharers in council accommodation.

Lack of funds and government restraints on local council spending have meant that, in many cases, councils are unable to offer accommodation to anyone other than registered homeless and those who are considered to have priority need on the waiting list, even if there are many people who have the necessary points total. In some cases, people have camped outside council offices in order to draw attention to their plight.

Each borough council has a stock of different kinds of accommodation which it can let out to people on a permanent basis. Accommodation normally available includes flats and maisonettes in small blocks or tower blocks on estates; flats in converted houses and individual houses. You can state the kind of accommodation you would prefer but if you wish to be housed at all in council housing, you will have to accept whatever is available. Individual councils may have different policies on how many properties you can be offered before refusing to offer further properties. When you apply to go on a waiting list you can state whether you would be prepared to or would like to live in another borough or to have your name put forward to a housing association, as some councils have agreements with other boroughs and housing associations. Indeed, people who are prepared to live in any part of London stand a greater chance of being found council or housing association accommodation.

2. Applying to be registered as homeless

If you are a single person without children or a couple without children you have very little chance of being housed by the council unless you have special needs (see below).

If you are homeless or about to become so go to your local Homeless Persons Unit at the council Housing Department or ring Housing Advice Switchboard.

You are considered to be homeless if you are at the present time without a home or if you are threatened with being in that situation within twenty-eight days.

If it is agreed that you satisfy the conditions listed in the Homeless Persons Act, the local council has a duty to find you accommodation. Every borough council has a Homeless Persons Unit (it may be called the Homeless Families Unit or the Housing Emergency Unit, it may also fall within the remit of the Housing Department).

If you are coming out of hospital or prison, a social worker or probation officer should help you apply to the council.

It is necessary to satisfy *all* the following conditions in order to be legally homeless.

1. You must be considered to have a 'priority need'. In order to satisfy this condition you must fit into one of the following categories.

You or someone you live with have children aged under 16.
You are a pregnant woman.
You have an elderly or disabled dependant.
You are an elderly or disabled or mentally ill person.
You have been made homeless by an emergency such as fire or flood.

Victims of domestic violence or victims of sexual exploitation, especially women, who have been forced to move out of their home, even if they are not theoretically 'homeless', are also usually treated as homeless by the council. The usual course of action is for such people to be referred to a refuge (see also section on relationship breakdown in Chapter 15: Women).

2. You must not be intentionally homeless. If you are considered to be 'intentionally homeless', that is you have left accommodation of your own accord and not for one of the reasons listed in the Act, or have been asked to leave for such things as non-

payment of rent, the council is only likely to give you temporary accommodation.

3. You must normally live in the area to which you are applying for accommodation or have some direct local connection.

If you fulfil *all* these conditions you *must* be offered accommodation by the council. If you only satisfy one or two, you might only be given advice on finding somewhere to live.

The quality of advice varies. It is wise to contact Housing Advice Switchboard, Citizens Advice Bureau, Law Centre or other advice agency (see Appendix), too. Any council decision will be put in writing if requested.

If you are a refugee, you may well qualify as homeless but you will need to contact one of the specialist advice agencies listed in this chapter.

If a council home is not available immediately, as is quite likely to be the case, you may be put into temporary accommodation such as a bed and breakfast hotel, hostel or house waiting for improvements to be made.

Moving to a Different Council Property

There are three ways of moving from your current council home to another one.

1. Transfer Scheme

If you want to move to another home in the same council area, apply to the council but do not expect it to be easy. You may be given priority if the size of your family has increased, if you require a smaller property, or in some cases if you are experiencing racial harassment. (Address as MEB, below.)

2. Tenants Exchange Scheme

It may be possible to exchange your council property for that of another council or housing association tenant in another borough or another part of the country. Permission must be granted first by the local councils concerned but the process can be self-initiated.

Council Housing Departments should be able to provide you with a list of people wishing to exchange properties through the

Tenants Exchange Scheme. You can also advertise in local shop windows or approach a private organisation, information on which can be obtained from the Housing Department, although these usually charge fees.

The London Mutual Exchange Bureau (MEB) is a computer assisted scheme jointly run by the London boroughs, designed to help find suitable exchange partners. Inquiries can be made by phone and there is also a regular list of people wishing to exchange properties. It is a free service. Any tenant of council property, housing associations or if the landlord agrees, private rented accommodation, can apply for an exchange.

Tenants Exchange Service
PO Box 170
London SW1P 3PX

MEB Central Office
164–168 Westminster Bridge Road
London SE1 7RW
928 8081 (open 9am–4.45pm)

3. National Mobility Scheme

A scheme agreed between most public housing authorities to help tenants or people high on housing waiting lists who have to move because of their job, or in order to care for a friend or relative. You must fill in a form at your council offices in order to register. Councils use their discretion in nominating people for exchanges.

There is a housing association equivalent.

HALO (Housing Advice Liaison Office)
189a Old Brompton Road
London SW5 0AR
370 6591/373 2005
The mobility scheme can also be used by private tenants.

Buying a Council House

It is now possible to buy the council home you are occupying. The Housing Department and many advice agencies can provide information. Political arguments aside, it should be remembered that anyone buying their council house will be taking full responsibility for such things as repairs. It might also be wise to consider whether it would be possible to sell the house, especially if the other houses around it are still council properties, or are in poor condition, should the owner wish to move.

Council Housing for People with Special Needs

People who might need special accommodation are: elderly people unable to live entirely alone, people with a physical disability, people with a mental handicap, people recovering from mental illness, people recovering from drug or alcohol dependence. Such people may be offered one of the following types of accommodation:

1 Local authority residential care accommodation, residential care accommodation provided by a voluntary organisation on a non-commercial basis, or by private organisations on a commercial basis. Local authorities have a responsibility to provide this kind of accommodation to those who need it, usually the elderly, but lack of available accommodation is always a problem.
2 Nursing homes run by voluntary organisations, charities or private organisations. This kind of accommodation should be provided to those who need nursing care from qualified staff.
3 Sheltered housing with a warden. May be run by local authorities, voluntary or private organisations.
4 Extra help from social services for those otherwise able to stay at home. Aids and adaptations to the house may be possible. (See also Chapter 11: People with Disabilities.)

HOUSING ASSOCIATIONS

These are usually non-profit organisations which build or convert existing properties and set a fair rent with the help of the Rent Officer. Rents are usually higher than in council houses. They often work in association with councils. Some are supported by the councils but their spending is controlled by the government.

Most money for housing associations comes from central or local government so about 50 per cent of vacancies tend to be let to those nominated by the council. It is therefore necessary to inform the council waiting-list department if you are interested. Only a few housing associations have their own waiting lists. Due to reductions in the amount of money granted to housing associations by central and local government, associations are now forced to seek funds elsewhere – from banks and building societies or other private funders. Clearly this implies having to pay interest so it is likely that rents will rise to cover this requirement.

Associations often choose people from council waiting lists although some will accept self-referral or agency referral.

The most common conditions imposed by housing associations are: homelessness, poor accommodation, no security of tenure, local connection (living, working or relatives) or low income. Most existing tenants have security from eviction which will only occur for specific reasons such as non-payment of rent. The 1988 Housing Act's provisions mean that conditions for new tenants are likely to be different. For more details contact Shelter, SHAC, Housing Advice Switchboard, Citizens Advice Bureau, National Federation of Housing Associations.

Special projects do exist for women, gays and lesbians, ethnic minorities or those with disabilities. For further information, contact National Federation of Housing Associations.

The Housing Advice Switchboard has a (quite expensive) book called *The Directory of Housing Associations and Cooperatives operating in the Greater London Area.*

However, the Housing Act has altered some of the conditions of new tenancies (see above). Housing associations will also be able to bid against private landlords for ownership of council estates. Thus the character of housing associations is likely to change considerably in the future.

PRIVATE RENTED ACCOMMODATION

Private rented accommodation covers houses, flats, mobile homes and hostels but the first two are the most common. It is often the only available option for someone seeking accommodation in London if s/he is not a priority need homeless person. Single people are unlikely to be given council housing. There is often a good deal of (legal and illegal) discrimination by landlords. Be prepared to pay at least £40 per week for a single room which may well be less luxurious than you would like.

It is not hard to find lists of accommodation but it is very difficult to find accommodation that is: (a) suitable, (b) affordable, (c) not already snapped up by someone else before you get to it. Newspapers and magazines such as the *Evening Standard*, *Loot*, *NME*, *City Limits* and *Time Out* have listings but by far the best bets are local newspapers or shop window advertisements. The University of London Union, councils (sometimes) and advice agencies also have lists of accommodation.

Accommodation agencies are numerous but prospective tenants should be careful. It is only legal for an agency to charge a fee if accommodation is found. The equivalent of one to two weeks' rent is usually the amount charged. The agency may also draw up the agreement for you. Do not sign an agreement without checking with a Citizens Advice Bureau or other advice body if at all possible. Housing Advice Switchboard has a list of accommodation agencies. If you have any problems with an agency, contact your council Housing Department, a Citizens Advice Bureau, Law Centre or other independent advice centre (see Appendix). SHAC can provide a list of accommodation agencies in the London area.

Levels of rent in an area tend to reflect the general property values in that area. As far as it is possible to generalise, the boroughs with the lowest average rent levels are Bexley, Newham, Tower Hamlets, Waltham Forest, Barking, Greenwich, Enfield, Lewisham, Redbridge and Southwark, that is the outer, eastern and some of the south-eastern boroughs. The most expensive are Westminster and Kensington and Chelsea. It should be pointed out, though, that the type of accommodation is often rather different from one borough to the next, especially in the more expensive boroughs. Similarly, the quality of available accommodation for £60 a week in a central borough will be rather different from accommodation of a similar cost in an outer borough.

Flats

A self-contained flat with kitchen, bathroom and toilet will normally cost you at least £70–£80 per week and usually more. This does vary from one borough to the next (1989 figures).

Non-self-contained accommodation with shared bathroom and toilet may be cheaper depending on the area.

Bedsits

One room with shared kitchen, bathroom and toilet (maybe small cooker in room) or studio flat (expensive self-contained bedsit) start from an absolute minimum of around £35 per week, and are usually much more (1989 figures).

Campaign for Bedsit Rights
5–15 Cromer Street
London WC1H 8LS
278 0598

Flat Sharing

Often the cheapest way of living in rented accommodation. Shared flats are advertised in the same places as other rented accommodation.

Rooms/Shared Houses

Often share all rooms except bedroom. From around £30 pw.

Lodgings

Digs are a more expensive option but may be possible in the short term. Usually advertise in newspaper small ads.

Mobile Homes (Caravans)

Sites are usually licensed with the local council. They may be either residential or holiday sites. There are very few in London. Residential sites are open all year, holiday sites for only part of the year. Lists are available from borough councils. Tenants of mobile homes have some rights including protection against eviction except for special reasons.

Camping

There are a few local camp sites if you have a tent or the money to hire one. Details can be obtained from local councils.

Signing Agreements

It is often not made clear that in most cases, a prospective private tenant has statutory rights that cannot be affected by the signing of a tenancy agreement. Indeed, if a landlord/lady is pushing for you to sign a contract, it is often because s/he wishes to limit your rights in some way. It is therefore rarely in the tenant's interest to push for a written agreement. However, details of deposits, rent, rates, bills and repairs (both inside and out) must be written down for you. Tenants should purchase a rent book if one is not provided. They are widely available in stationery shops. The landlord/lady should sign this whenever you pay rent. If for any reason you cannot get hold of a rent book, make sure you get receipts for any money paid.

The terms of any tenancy agreement may well affect such things as ability to register for fair rent, length of notice, and so on. If the landlord insists on you signing an agreement, check with an advice agency first if at all possible, otherwise read very carefully or get someone to be with you who knows about contracts. Otherwise get copies of anything written and keep a record of all phone calls/conversations. It is also important to check whether the landlord will be living in the same building as this affects tenants' legal protection.

It is sensible to work on the assumption that you will need a minimum of £400 for a deposit. Make sure you get a receipt. Landlords might not accept tenants who are on the dole. The DSS no longer pays deposits – applications for rent in advance should be made to the Social Fund but it is unlikely that you will be lucky. You should go to an advice agency first. The low-waged may get some help with rent.

HOSTELS AND HOTELS

These may be run by charities, housing associations, or commercial organisations. Hostels for those with special needs, including people with drug and alcohol problems, are quite common. Most advice agencies will have lists. Also hostels may cater for particular groups of people such as students.

Cheap hostels or B&B hotels are often of poor quality and sometimes rooms have to be shared. Such accommodation is most useful in an emergency. Some hostels provide short-term free accommodation for homeless people, e.g. Centrepoint (see above).

Bed and breakfast hotels are advertised in local newspapers, shop windows, telephone directories, housing advice and aid centres and other advice centres. At local advice centres you should be able to discover what is available and whether a particular hostel is run on a charitable basis, whether short-stay or residential rooms are available, quality of rooms and whether income support would cover the rent. There is no security from eviction by the landlord.

London Hostels Association
54 Eccleston Square
London SW1V 1PG
828 3263

London Tourist Board
26 Grosvenor Gardens
London SW1
730 3450
Provides a list of bed and breakfast hotels and hostels.

HOUSING COOPERATIVES

Coops are independent non-profit-making organisations whereby properties can be bought or rented as a group. There are different forms of ownership. Coops are always run by tenants which implies more control over the home but also responsibility for all administration, repairs, etc. Local advice agencies or housing departments can provide information, as can the Cooperative Services Unit at the Housing Corporation. The Housing Advice Switchboard has a directory of housing coops in the London area. Housing coop tenants will be affected by many of the provisions of the 1988 Housing Act but such tenants should seek advice. Like other types of accommodation, there are usually long waiting lists for a place in a coop.

Types of Coop

Fair Rent Coops

The coop owns or has leases on the properties and lets them to their tenants. No profit is made and rent is set by the fair rent officer.

Management Coops

Owned by council or housing associations and managed by tenants.

Short-life Coops

Use properties owned by council or housing association due for redevelopment or demolition. May last for several years. Coop issues licences to occupants who may have to carry out some repairs. Coop will try to find a new property if owners take back possession.

Mortgage Financed Coops

This kind of coop is very rare. Properties are bought by mortgage from building societies. Rents are paid to cover the mortgage repayments and may therefore be higher than a fair rent.

Most coops concentrate on certain groups, e.g. single parents, black people, lesbians and gay men. Prospective tenants must first join a coop then wait to be housed by them.

National Federation of Housing Cooperatives
88 Old Street
London EC1
608 2494/253 0202

'Setting up a Housing Coop'
from The Carlton Centre
Granville Road
Kilburn NW6

'Outlines'
from The Housing Corporation
149 Tottenham Court Road
London W1P 0BN
387 9466 (free)

SHORT-LIFE ACCOMMODATION

This is temporary, often poor condition accommodation, often communal or of uncertain life expectancy. It is usually cheaper and with fewer regulations but is less secure. Terms usually last for about six months and a weekly fee is charged. As a rule the property concerned is awaiting demolition or repair. There are almost always waiting lists.

Such accommodation is run as a cooperative let on licence from the owners. Licence fees tend to be quite low but rights are reduced. The accommodation is rarely self-contained. It is usually owned by non-commercial organisations, e.g. councils or housing associations.

The life of the house can vary from around six months to in excess of five years. Advice centres have lists of short-life accommodation. There may be conditions such as homelessness and low income.

People in short-life housing have a licence agreement which means they can be evicted at short notice. If this occurs, the group organising the accommodation will usually try to arrange for another house or flat, but not always.

More information can be obtained from the Housing Advice Switchboard, a Citizens Advice Bureau, Law Centre (see Appendix) or local Housing Advice Centre (see end of chapter).

SQUATTING

Squatting in itself is not illegal, although forcing an entry or causing damage is. However, you will always be evicted unless the owner permits you to stay. Basic rights do exist, and it is very rare for someone to be physically thrown out. The most useful source of information on squatting is *The Squatters Handbook*. It costs 60p and is available from the Advisory Service for Squatters (see below). It is an excellent guide to all the possibilities and pitfalls, pros and cons of squatting, and if you are already squatting or are considering it as a possibility your first and immediate move should be to get hold of a copy. It is very comprehensive and I do not intend to reproduce its contents here. However, there are a few essential pointers that you need to be aware of if you are contemplating taking this course.

Squatting is not a crime! The Public Order Act made certain changes to existing laws affecting travelling people and derelict land, but the changes did not affect squatting. If you can gain entry to a property which is not being used by anybody else, without causing any damage, you can make it your home and expect the same rights as any other home occupier, including privacy, rubbish collection, post, social security, water, gas and electricity. You might never be sure how long you are going to be able to stay but it is frequently seen as a feasible option for a person who has nowhere to go but does not qualify as a 'homeless' person according to the law.

It is essential to be fully aware of the law relating to squatting and *The Squatters Handbook* is excellent in this respect. If you know your rights, you can't be easily conned (or forced to leave).

It is important to think carefully about where you choose to squat as it may affect your eligibility for more permanent housing at a later stage. You can get advice from the ASS or a local squatting group.

As a rule it is not too difficult to find empty property, especially in London. Most people know of an unused building in their area. The points to establish are how long you are likely to be able to stay and how easily you are likely to be evicted without a court order. A court order may result in your having to face criminal charges so be certain before moving in.

There are local squatters groups who can help you find a suitable property. If not, get advice from ASS or someone else. Don't take action on your own or blindly. There are believed to be around 35,000 squatters in Greater London so it shouldn't be difficult to find someone with first hand experience.

The Empty Property Unit at Shelter may be able to help especially if you and a group of others find a block of unoccupied properties. They may even be able to negotiate a short-life group or housing association.

In the case of council properties, budgetary cuts and central government pressures have forced local councils to spend a lot longer in regenerating old properties. Councils tend to have a much more flexible attitude towards squatters and don't usually evict people under section 6 of the Criminal Law Act. If you don't cause problems either to the building or with neighbours, a council may let you stay unofficially until they actually need the property.

Other possible properties are housing association or trust property which can be regarded as similar to council properties as far as squatting is concerned. Hospitals, BR and government departments all have empty property but attitudes vary as does the period of availability.

Properties belonging to private landlords tend to be unpredictable and squatters may either be ignored for a long time or removed by heavies. It may even be possible to come to some arrangement with the landlord.

Privately owned houses are rarely considered worthwhile by potential squatters unless they have been bought or are about to be, by a Council or Housing Association. If a house is furnished and therefore occupied, however infrequently, it is dangerous to squat as the DRO provisions of section 7 apply (see below).

The Squatters Handbook provides thorough information on practical measures such as locks, gas, electricity, water and so on, together with full details of the law, advice, how to deal with the police and eviction.

Unless you are evicted under sections 6 or 7 of the Criminal Law Act or illegally by the owner or police, the usual way is for the owner to apply to the courts for a possession order. Usually it is cheaper to find another place than to fight a case which has no real defence. The first warning that eviction might be on the way is often just a letter rather than a visit. You do not have to *do* anything until you receive a summons, to which you have a right.

Licences

A licensee is half way between a squatter and a tenant. Basically, a licence is permission given by the owner or someone entitled to act for them to someone else to occupy premises. It carries more weight if it is in writing.

Advisory Service for Squatters
2 St Paul's Road
London N1 2QN
359 8814
Legal and practical advice for squatters and homeless persons. Produces essential booklet on squatting. Contacts with local groups. Open Mon–Fri 2–6pm, always phone first.

The following groups are able to help you find somewhere to squat in their area and provide advice and support. They are not alternative estate agents and only exist because groups of squatters have come together to support each other and exchange information.

Brixton Squatters Aid
121 Railton Road
London SE24
274 6655
Open most Sundays but always phone first.
Tube: Brixton.

Camden Squatters
Culross Hall
Battle Bridge Road
London NW1
Tuesdays 7–8pm. Tube: King's Cross.

Haringey Homes for All
Unwaged Centre
72 West Green Road
London N15
Tuesdays 6pm. Tube: Seven Sisters.

Limehouse Squatters
17 Turners Road
London E3
Tues and Thurs 6–9pm.
Saturdays 1–4pm. Tube: Mile End.

Squatters Network of Walworth
362 Old Kent Road
London SE1
Mon–Fri 4–7pm. Tube: Elephant and Castle.

Stoke Newington Housing Action
61 Leswin Road
London N16
Mondays 6–8pm. Buses: 67, 73, 76, 149, 243, 253, 276, 106.

OWNER OCCUPATION

Before attempting to buy a house, make sure you have enough savings for a deposit, solicitors' fees, surveyors' fees, moving fees, furnishing etc.

Mortgages

Building societies or banks, including the Post Office Girobank, will usually provide loans of two to three times basic salary/wages. Joint borrowing is possible. Estate agents will provide lists of accommodation in your price range on request. Councils can also provide money for mortgages or make special arrangements with a building society.

Mortgage brokers also exist but are more expensive than building societies. They usually give you an endowment mortgage where you pay only the interest then pay back after twenty-five to thirty years. The other possibility is capital payments, whereby one pays a regular monthly amount plus interest for twenty-five to thirty years.

Finance companies also exist but have higher interest rates, and severe penalty clauses. Councils and employers also provide mortgage schemes.

Other expenses are likely to include payment to the surveyor for checking the property's condition, solicitors' fees, insurance of building and contents, removal expenses, tax (stamp duty) on property over a certain value.

Advice can be obtained from advice agencies or from building societies or banks but potential buyers should remember why such organisations are in business . . . Local solicitors can be approached, too, but their advice does not come cheap. A local estate agent will offer help, too, but remember that they are always acting on behalf of the seller.

Shared Ownership

In certain cases a shared ownership scheme will be available. This is a kind of 'half-way house' where the property is half rented and half paid for by mortgage, usually with a fifty-fifty split between the two. Such schemes are usually run by housing associations.

ADDRESSES

General

Catholic Housing Advice Society (CHAS)
189a Old Brompton Road
London SW5 0AR

CHAR (The Housing Campaign for Single People)
5–15 Cromer Street
London WC1H 8LS
833 2071

Child Poverty Action Group (CPAG)
21 Queen Anne's Gate
London SW1H 9BU
222 5622

The Housing Corporation
149 Tottenham Court Road
London W1P 0BN
387 9466
Cooperating with government plans to sell off council housing to private landlords. Regional offices have details about housing associations and cooperatives in the area.

London Housing Unit
4th Floor
Berkshire House
168–173 High Holborn
London WC1

Shelter
157 Waterloo Road
London SE1
633 9377
*Campaigning housing charity.
Publications, advice and
information. Runs several special
housing projects and campaigns for
the homeless.*

The Simon Community
129 Malden Road
London NW5
485 6639
*Works with the long-term homeless
for whom it has a night shelter and
some residential housing.*

Simon Community Night Shelter
32 Pancras Road
London NW1

Local Housing Aid Centres

Councils usually have their own advice-givers for information on council housing, but some will direct you to independent agencies. If you have a problem with the council itself, contact another advice centre. Housing Advice Centres offer advice on all kinds of problems. Most deal with both private sector and council house problems. Your council will have lists of advice centres and independent housing aid centres as well as details of your local Law Centres.

The list below gives the addresses of Housing Aid or Housing Advice Centres for those boroughs that have them. For those boroughs without a HAC a contact address or number for further information is given.

Association of Housing Aid
c/o Brent Housing Aid Centre
Robert Owen House
192 High Road
London NW10
451 0911

**Barking and Dagenham Borough
   Housing Department**
Dagenham
Essex
592 4500

Barnet Housing Aid Centre
1 Friern Park
Finchley
London N12 9DE
446 2504

Bexley Housing Advice Section
Civic Offices
Broadway
Bexleyheath
Kent DA6 7LB
303 7777

Brent Housing Aid Centre
Hampton House
1b Dyne Road
London NW6 7XG
908 7401

Bromley Housing Advice Centre
United Reformed Church
Widmore Road
Bromley
313 3375

Camden
No single housing aid centre but a
network of local offices. In the first

instance, phone the council on 278
4444 and they will give you the
address of your local office.

City of London Housing Section
Guildhall
London EC2P 2EJ
606 3030

**Croydon Association for the Young
 Single Homeless**
98–100 Lodge Road
Croydon
683 0227
(Also has a hostel.)

Croydon Housing Aid Society
10A Station Road
West Croydon
688 7900

Ealing Housing Advice Centre
Town Hall Annexe
Ealing
London W5
579 2424

Enfield Civic Centre
Silver Street
Enfield
Middlesex, EN1 3XN
336 6565

**Greenwich Housing Aid and Advice
 Centre**
122 Powis Street
Woolwich
London SE18
854 0055

Hackney Housing Aid
287 Mare Street
London E8 1EB
986 3191

**Hammersmith and Fulham Housing
 Centre**
77 Glenthorne Road
London W6 0UJ
748 3020

Haringey Housing Advice Centre
13–27 Station Road
Wood Green
London N22
975 9700

Harrow
No Housing Aid Centres.
For advice on council housing,
apply to council Housing
Department, otherwise, contact
Citizens Advice Bureau.

Havering Housing Aid Centre
Mercury House
Mercury Gardens
Romford
Essex RM1 3DT
0708 766999

Hillingdon Housing Advice Centre
Civic Centre, Uxbridge
Middx UB8 1UW
0895 50111 ext 2116

Hounslow Housing Aid Centre
94 High Street
Hounslow
Middx
862 5746

Islington
Islington operates a system of
twenty-four neighbourhood advice
centres. For details of the nearest
office, contact:
Housing Department
292 Essex Road
London N1
226 1234

**Kensington and Chelsea Housing
 Action Centre**
Westway Information and Advice
 Centre
London W10
969 2433

**Kingston-upon-Thames Housing
 Advice Section**
Guildhall
1 St James's Road
Kingston-upon-Thames
Surrey KT1 1EU
546 2121 ext 3631 or 3644

Lambeth Housing Advice Centre
3–7 Town Hall Parade
Brixton Hill
London SW2
274 7722 ext 2665 or 2011

Lewisham Housing Dept
Leegate House
Lee Green
London SE12 8RN
695 6000

Merton Housing Advice
Crown House
London Road
Merton SM4 5DX
543 2222

Newham Housing Aid Centre
c/o Town Hall
East Ham
London E6 2RD
472 1430

Redbridge Housing Aid Centre
9–13 York Road
Ilford
Essex IG1 3AG
478 3020

Richmond Housing Advice Unit
1st Floor, Regal House
London Road
Twickenham
891 7486 or 891 7409

Southwark Group of Tenants
639 6718

Sutton Housing Information
Lower Ground Floor
Civic Offices
St Nicholas Way

Sutton
Surrey SM1 1EA
661 5049

Tower Hamlets Housing Information
Mayfield House
London E2
980 4831

Waltham Forest Aid Centre
807 High Road
London E10
558 0033

Wandsworth Housing Aid Centre
17–27 Garratt Lane
London SW18
871 6847

Westminster
Housing Action and Advice Centre
(Private Sector West)
3 Mozart Street
London W10
798 3598

Housing Action and Advice Centre
(Private Sector East)
55 Riding House Street
London W1
798 1496

For Westminster council house inquiries, phone City Hall on 828 8070.

Women

NB For information on your accommodation position if a relationship breaks down, see Chapter 15: Women.

Asian Women's Resource Centre (ASHA)
27 Santley Street
London SW4
737 5901/274 8854 (24 Hour)

Asian Women's Resource Centre
134 Minet Avenue
London NW10
961 5701

Equal Opportunities Commission
Overseas House
Quay Street
Manchester M3 3HN
061 833 9244

Lesbian and Gay Switchboard
837 7324 (24 Hour)
The switchboard can also offer help in finding flat-share accommodation for lesbians and gay men.

Lesbian Line
BM Box 1514
London WC1X 0AP
251 6911

London Rape Crisis Centre
PO Box 69
London WC1X 9NJ
837 1600/278 3956

**Wesley House London Women's
  Centre**
4 Wild Court
London WC2B 5AX
831 6946

Women's Aid
52–54 Featherstone Street
London EC1
251 6537/251 6537/8 (24 hour)
*Help and support for women alone
especially victims of domestic
violence, pregnant women or
women with young children.
Advice, information, support and
accommodation. (See
also Chapter 15: Women.)*

Older People

Age Concern Greater London
54 Knatchbull Street
London SE5 9QY
737 3456

Help the Aged
St James's Walk

London EC1R 0BE
253 0253

Pensioners' Link
17 Balfe Street
London N1 9EB
278 5501/2/3/4

(See also Chapter 10: Older People.)

People with Disabilities

Disability Alliance
25 Denmark Street
London WC2
240 0896

Disabled Living Foundation
380–384 Harrow Road
London W9 2HU
289 6111

**Greater London Association for the
  Disabled**
336 Brixton Road
London SW9 7AA
274 0107

RADAR
25 Mortimer Street
London W1N 8AB
637 5400

(See Chapter 11: People with Disabilities.)

Young People

For young people who are under 18 and homeless it will be even more difficult to find accommodation, although certain councils will accept young people as homeless on the grounds that they are vulnerable, in the same way as they might accept victims of domestic or sexual violence. Under-16s must be given at least temporary accommodation by the council Social Services Department.

Under-26s may only be able to stay in B&B for a short period, if at all, since the new Housing Benefit regulations make it unlikely that young people will be able to continue paying the required rent. It may be possible for under-18s to get accommodation if the Department of Social Security guarantees rent payments as you are not old enough to get a council tenancy in your own name. The DSS will no longer provide money for deposits required by private landlords. Nor will they provide a food allowance for Bed and Breakfast claimants as they did until the 1989 benefit changes. (For more details on housing benefit see Chapter 13: Social Services, Benefits and Taxation.)

Alone in London
188 King's Cross Road
London WC1
278 4224
*Advice, counselling and information
for young homeless people.*

New Horizon
1 Macklin Street
London WC1
242 0010/242 2238
*Youth centre also providing
information and advice.*

Basement Youth Project
227 Earls Court Road
London SW5
373 2335

Piccadilly Advice Centre
100 Shaftesbury Avenue
London W1V 7DH
434 3773

Children's Legal Centre
20 Compton Terrace
London N1
359 6251
*Legal Advice centre for under-18s.
Mon–Fri 2pm–5pm.*

Portobello Project
49–51 Porchester Road
London W2
221 4413

Soho Project
142 Charing Cross Road
London WC2
836 8121

**London Council for the Welfare of
   Women and Girls/YWCA**
Accommodation Service
57 Great Russell Street
London WC1B 3BD
430 1524

For a more detailed list of groups for young people, see Chapter 2: Children and Young People.

Ethnic Minorities

Commission for Racial Equality
Elliot House
10–12 Allington Street
London SW1 5EH
828 7022

**Federation of Black Housing
   Associations**
374 Gray's Inn Road
London WC1
837 8288
Information and advice for black

*housing groups. Coordinates
national black housing campaign.
Produces* Black Housing *newsletter.*

The Irish Centre
50 Camden Square
London NW1
485 0051
*Advice, counselling and info on
many issues.*

**Irish Homeless and Rootless Project
(CARA)**
13–15 Tollington Way
London N7
833 4022/3719
*Information on accommodation for
homeless Irish single people.*

NB   For further details of specific housing problems for ethnic
minorities see Chapter 5: Ethnic Minorities.

Refugees

British Refugee Council
Bondway House
3 Bondway
London SW8
582 6922

Immigrants

**Joint Council for the Welfare of
 Immigrants**
115 Old Street
London EC1V 9JR
251 8706

UK Immigration Advisory Service
7th Floor
Bretton House
Savoy Street
London WC2 7EH

Prisoners and their Families

NACRO
169 Clapham Road
London SW9 0PU
582 6500
*Information on Housing Benefit,
housing costs, prisoners' rights, etc.*

**Prisoners' Wives and Families
 Society**
254 Caledonian Road
London N1
278 3981

Students

**British Council Accommodation
 Service**
Unit 10, Spring Gardens
London SW1 2BN
930 8466
A service for overseas students.

NUS Housing Officer
National Union of Students

Nelson Mandela House
461 Holloway Road
London N7 6LJ
272 8900

University of London Union
Malet Street
London WC1
637 8241

Legal Advice

Law Centres Federation
Duchess House
18–19 Warren Street
London W1P 5DB
387 8570
Details of local law centres and legal aid.

Legal Action Group
242–244 Pentonville Road
London N1

Release
377 5605 (10am–6pm Mon–Fri)/603 8654 (any other time).
Legal advice and information on accommodation, trouble with the police, etc.

9

LESBIANS AND GAY MEN

When I arrived in London during what was, in 1964, the old August Bank Holiday, I clutched a rather battered A6 gay guide to Europe. It ran to about sixteen pages and I had bought it for around 10 guilders in Amsterdam (when 1 guilder was worth a British florin). Probably a page was devoted to Britain with the bulk, if not all the entries, concentrating on London. There were some dozen locations – but they were all drinking clubs which had entry requirements. One of these was the need for a person to propose you. I wrote to all these clubs on the off chance that one of them would arrange for an existing member to propose me, thus providing entry to the homosexual world which I knew existed in London but had found difficult to break into. Only one club replied! The proprietor suggested I go along and that I would probably gain membership. That open door belonged to the Festival Club which used to be a gay haven opposite one of the exits of the London Coliseum. As soon as I became a member of the Festival Club I met other homosexual men ('gay' was not in use then) who were members of other clubs – and I was *in*.

The other way to become part of the 'scene' was to turn up at the monthly Winter Talks organised by the Albany Trust in the Alliance Hall in Palmer Street, just off London's Victoria Street. At the end of these monthly meetings the Secretary of the Trust would remind those present that they could continue their discussion over a drink at the regular watering hole, the Old Star public house, opposite the northern exit of St James's Park underground station. After a couple of meetings your presence would have been noted by a female Trust volunteer. By that time she had come to the conclusion that you were 'safe' (remember it was prior to the passing of the 1967 Sexual Offences Act) and there would be an invitation to one of her monthly parties. Clutching a half-bottle of gin (costing about 10s 6d), I would turn up at her Notting Hill bedsit and find thirty other gay men chatting over their drinks. During the course of the conversations, around a hundred men would turn up. Considerable information and intelligence about the latest developments on the gay scene and the progress of the 1967 Bill would be the topics of the evening before you made a solitary exit. The latest coffee bar catering for gays or the cover of the current issue of *Films and Filming* were among some of the other talking points. Such a gathering would be the way to learn about the gay scene.

This was twenty-five years ago and before such publications appeared that listed the kind of information which follows.

Griffith Vaughan-Williams
Member of the Executive Committee of the
Campaign for Homosexual Equality since 1975

DISCRIMINATION

Whatever progress has been made, discrimination and homophobia remain powerful factors in the lives of lesbians and gay men. The AIDS backlash has contributed to a new wave of anti-gay propaganda in the media and from the government. Clause 28 of the 1988 Local Government Act which limits the presentation of positive images of gay culture, while it may be virtually unenforceable, is a dangerous development, fostering hysterical reactions to all forms of gay culture. The combined force of these events has presented the gay community with new problems to overcome in a society which already treats them as second-class citizens. Nevertheless, in the view of some gay activists, Clause 28 acted as a catalyst, leading to a realisation of the real threat posed to gay lifestyles, and stirred many lesbians and gay men from a creeping complacency.

Discrimination against lesbians and gay men is rife in many areas where most people take their rights for granted. Such things as the age of consent – 16 for heterosexuals, 21 for gay men – or the refusal of certain shops to stock publications specific to gay lifestyles are the thin end of the wedge.

All discrimination is upsetting but some instances are simply heartless. For example, if a gay person dies, the body of the deceased will be returned to the family and not to the gay partner, even if the family lost all contact years ago and the gay partner was the closest person to the deceased. A gay partner is never given rights equal to those of 'next of kin'. Society still has a million miles to go before it throws off its prejudices and recognises lesbians and gay men as equal in the eyes of the law and in the eyes of fellow citizens.

Campaign for Homosexual Equality
38 Mount Pleasant
London WC1Z 0AP
833 3912
*Campaigning and lobbying
organisation.*

**Legislation for Lesbian and Gay
 Rights**
Room 221
38 Mount Pleasant
London WC1X 0AP
833 3860

*Campaign to end legal
discrimination, supported by groups
within all major political parties.*

National Council for Civil Liberties
(Lesbian and Gay Group)
21 Tabard Street
London SE1
403 3888

Discrimination at Work

LAGER (Lesbian and Gay Employment Rights) has reported an increase in requests for advice and information relating to lesbian and gay employment rights, blaming it largely on 'misinformation around AIDS, populist politics and the gutter press.'

There are no laws which specifically prevent discrimination by employers against lesbian or gay male employees, but there are statutory employment rights which give a degree of protection to all employees. LAGER suggests the following steps if discrimination is suffered at work.

1 Call LAGER for initial advice and information.
2 Keep a written record of anything that happens to you at work which you think is unreasonable. This may be used to support evidence to a tribunal, if one takes place.
3 If you are asked to accept a significant change in terms or conditions which is unacceptable to you and not in your terms of employment, ask your employer what the consequences will be if you refuse. Try to have a witness, e.g. a friend or trade union representative and write down what is said.
4 Do not accept a change of conditions if you are not happy with it. Ask for time to consider the proposed changes then seek legal advice. Do not sign anything. If you have no option but to keep on working while pursuing the matter, write to your employer stating that your continuing to work does not mean you accept the new conditions.
5 Do not take action against your employer without first checking your employment rights. If you just walk out it is possible you will not be able to claim compensation. Seek advice from LAGER before taking any action.

If you are sacked, call LAGER immediately, contact your trade union representative if you are in a union and if your employer has asked you to resign, seek legal advice before making a decision. Resignation might result in loss of social security benefits or right to claim unfair dismissal.

LAGER (Lesbian and Gay Employment Rights)
Room 205
Southbank House
Black Prince Road
London SE1 7SJ
587 1636 (Lesbians)
587 1643 (Gay men)

Fighting discrimination in the work place and in unemployment. Lesbian Employment Rights is a self organised group within LAGER. Produces a newsletter and a range of leaflets.

AIDS

Government advertising campaigns on AIDS have come in for a great deal of criticism, especially from AIDS charities like the Terrence Higgins Trust. Not enough money has been spent on AIDS education, let alone research, and what has been done has occurred only after years of campaigning. The gay community has been stigmatised by attitudes about AIDS. Tabloid headlines about 'The Gay Plague' have still not been fully combated. (More information about AIDS in Chapter 7: Health.)

ADDRESSES

Much of the information in this section was compiled with the help of *Gay Times* (incorporating *Gay News*) and Kennedy's *Gay Guide to London*. These publications have much more comprehensive listings sections than space allows here, including lists of local groups and special interest groups. Both publications are available from good newsagents, gay outlets and the bookshops listed below.

Other regular publications are *The Pink Paper*, a free national weekly newspaper for gays, *Capital Gay*, a free newspaper published by gay men, *Scene Out*, a national magazine published in Manchester, *Lesbian and Gay Socialist*, *European Gay Review*, and *Square Peg*.

Many local and specialist organisations not listed here can also be contacted through Gay's the Word Bookshop, London Lesbian and Gay Centre (LLGC), Lesbian and Gay Switchboard, Libraries, especially Swiss Cottage Library, the Association of London Authorities and all London Boroughs with a Lesbian and Gay Unit.

Bookshops

Gay's the Word Bookshop
66 Marchmont Street
London WC1N 1AB
278 7654
London's Lesbian and Gay community bookshop, stocking lesbian, gay and feminist books, both new and secondhand; pamphlets, magazines, badges, cards, records, etc. Refreshments available. Open every day including Sunday afternoons.

Collets International Bookshop
129–131 Charing Cross Road
London WC2
734 0782
*Progressive bookshop with gay and
lesbian section.*

Compendium
234 Camden High Street
London NW1
485 8944
*Gay and lesbian section in
basement.*

Housman's
5 Caledonian Road
London N1
837 4473
*Progressive books, magazines,
posters, etc.*

Reading Matters
187 High Road
Wood Green
London N22
881 3187
*Progressive literature including
range of gay/lesbian books.*

Silver Moon Women's Bookshop
68 Charing Cross Road
London WC2
836 7906

Sisterwrite Women's Bookshop
190 Upper Street
London N1
226 9782

Zipper
283 Camden High Street
London NW1
284 0537
*Books, magazines, clothing,
postcards, etc.*

Help, Advice and General Information

Albany Trust
24 Chester Street
London SW1
730 5871
*Counselling service for individuals
and couples, educational
programmes for individuals and
organisations.*

**Alcoholics Anonymous Lesbian and
  Gay Group**
352 3001
*Meets Thursdays 6.30pm–8.00pm in
Paterson Wing, St Mary's Hospital,
Praed Street, London W2.*

Al Anon
*Counselling for friends and relations
of people with alcohol problems at
London Lesbian and Gay Centre
every Saturday 7pm.*

Alcohol Counselling Service
34 Electric Lane
London SW9
737 3570
Tuesdays. Free advice.

Amici
*For shy or isolated gay people.
Second Friday of the month at
London Lesbian and Gay Centre,
2nd floor, 8pm or ring Maria (790
6409).*

At Ease
c/o St John's Church
Waterloo Road
London SE1
*Help for gay men and women in the
armed forces.*

Beaumont Society
BM Box 3084
London WC1N 3XX
730 7453
*Trustline for transvestites and trans-
sexuals. Helpline for wives of
TVs/TSs.*

Bisexual Group
Fallen Angel Public House
65 Graham Street
London N1

Meets Mondays. (Or write to BM BI, London WC1N 3XX.)

Bisexual Women's Group
BM Box LBWG
London WC1N 3XX

Black Lesbian and Gay Centre
BM Box 4390
London WC1N 3XX
885 3543

Blenheim Project
960 5599
Advice and counselling for drug addiction, Mon–Fri 10am–5pm.

Brothers and Sisters
BM B&S
London WC1N 3XX
For lesbians and gay men with hearing and speech difficulties. Meet first Friday of the month at Craven Club, 32 Craven Street, WC2, 8.30pm.

Evergreens
837 3337
Social group for gay men over 40.

FRIEND
BM National Friend
London WC1N 3XX
Counselling and befriending gay people.

Fusion Multiracial Gay Men's Group
Meet Fridays at Fallen Angel, 65 Graham Street N1, 7.30pm and Saturdays at London Friend, 86 Caledonian Road, N1, 7.30pm.

Gay and Lesbian Unemployed Support Group
854 4989 (Mon–Fri 11am–5pm)

Gay Bereavement Project
c/o Unitarian Rooms
Hoop Lane
London NW11
Phone Lesbian and Gay Switchboard for number of duty volunteer. Counselling and advice for lesbians and gay men on bereavement, writing wills, funeral services (religious and secular).

Gay Men's Disabled Group
c/o Gay's The Word
66 Marchmont Street
London WC1N 3XX
Social, support and campaigning group.

Gay Prisoners Support Group
c/o 86 Caledonian Road
London N1

GEMMA
BM Box 5700
London WC1N 3XX
Social, support and campaigning for women with disabilities.

Hall Carpenter Archives
BM Archives
London WC1N 3XX
608 1737
Gay history archives.

International Lesbian and Gay Association Support Group
c/o Nigel Warner
141 Cloudesley Road
London N1

Irish Gay Men's Network
c/o Haringey Lesbian and Gay Unit
802 8981

Irish Lesbian Network
c/o Irish Women's Centre
59 Stoke Newington Church Street
London N16

KENRIC (MO2)
BM KENRIC
London WC1N 3XX
Social activities, information etc for lesbians.

Lesbian Archive
BM 7005
London WC1N 3XX
406 6475

Lesbian and Gay Immigration Group
BM Welcome
London WC1N 3XX

Lesbian and Gay Switchboard
BM Switchboard
London WC1N 3XX
837 7324
Twenty-four-hour information and advice service for lesbians and gay men covering everything from pubs and clubs to problems faced when coming out. Also answers queries on medical problems including AIDS and HIV. People also call offering or looking for accommodation. Also running a safer sex campaign and has produced the National AIDS Manual.

Lesbian Line
BM Box 1514
London WC1N 3XX
Information advice and counselling.

London Friend
86 Caledonian Road
London N1
837 3337
(Women's line Thurs 7.30pm–10pm
837 2782)
Counselling organisation with subgroups for alcoholics, prisoner support, T/Vs. Also social groups.

London Lesbian and Gay Centre
67–69 Cowcross Road
London EC1M 6BP
608 1471
Claims to be the largest lesbian and gay centre in Europe. Has a disco, café, two bars, women's lounge, meeting rooms, theatre and resources. Also houses PACE (see below).

Married Gays/Bisexuals
BM Box 1280
London WC1N 3XX
Social groups.

PACE (Project for Advice Counselling and Education)
c/o London Lesbian and Gay Centre
67–69 Cowcross Street
London EC1M 6BP
251 2689
Counselling, advice and training service. Always interested in recruiting trainers and volunteers. Art therapy, advice and information by letter or phone; workshops and consultancy.

Parents Enquiry
c/o Rose Robertson
16 Hanley Road
Catford
London SE6 2HZ
698 1815
Counselling for parents of young gay people.

Parents and Friends of Lesbians and Gays
Phone Evelyn 523 2190 10am–10pm weekdays.
Promotes better relations between gay people and their parents.

September Group
794 5660 (Simon) or 221 4846 (Michael)
For older lesbians and gay men.

SIGMA
BM SIGMA
London WC1N 3XX
Support group for partners of married gays.

Survivors
c/o 38 Mount Pleasant
London WC1
833 3737
For victims of male rape and sexual abuse.

Turning Point
359 7371
For men who think they might be gay and want to meet others in small groups.

Youth Groups

Gay Young London Group
469 2693 (6.30pm–11pm except
Mondays)
*Meets Mondays 7.45pm–10pm at
King's Cross Neighbourhood
Centre, corner of Argyle and
Birkenhead Streets, WC1.*

Lesbian and Gay Youth Federation
c/o East London Lesbian and Gay
   Group
BM Helpline
London WC1N 3XX
520 8827

Lesbian and Gay Youth Movement
BM GYM
London WC1N 3XX
317 9690

**London Lesbian and Gay Teenagers
   Group**
6–9 Manor Gardens
London N7 6LA
*Meets Wed 7pm–10pm and Sun
3pm–7pm (Mixed). Phone 272 5741
at these times.*

Young Black Lesbian Group
387 7450
Meets Tues 6pm–9pm.

Political Groups

Campaign for Homosexual Equality
38 Mount Pleasant
London WC1Z 0AP
833 3912
*Campaigning and lobbying
organisation.*

**Association of London Authorities
   Lesbian and Gay Group**
36 Old Queen Street
London SW1H 9JH
222 7799

**Conservative Group for
   Homosexual Equality**
BM CGHE
London WC1N 3XX

DELGA
(Social and Liberal Democrats for
   Lesbian and Gay Action)
c/o SLD HQ
4 Cowley Street
London SW1
(or call Reading (0734) 588785)

Hyde Park Gays and Sapphics
422 6498 (Sharley)
*Meet 2pm at Speakers Corner, Hyde
Park, every Sunday.*

**Labour Campaign for Lesbian and
   Gay Rights**
119 Riversdale Road
London N5 2SU

Lesbian and Gay Communists
16 St John's Street
London EC1
251 4406 (Pete Shields, Thurs only,
4pm–7pm)

Lesbian and Gay Green Group
c/o London Lesbian and Gay Centre
or ring Lee (809 2468) or Hilary (278
1282)

Liberal Lesbian and Gay Action
771 0251

**National Union of Students
Lesbian and Gay Liberation
   Campaign**
Nelson Mandela House
461 Holloway Road
London N7 6LJ

**Organisation for Lesbian and Gay
   Action (OLGA)**
Room 3
38 Mount Pleasant
London WC1 0AP
833 3860

**SDP Lesbian and Gay Rights
  Section**
c/o Geoff Brown
50 Tyson Place
Brighton
BN2 2JQ

Socialist Workers Party Gay Group
PO Box 82
London E3

Stonewall
354 3187

Religious Groups

**Gay and Lesbian Humanist
  Association (GALHA)**
c/o 34 Spring Lane
Kenilworth
CU8 8HB

Gay Spiritualists
c/o J. Walters
63 Knatchbull Road
London SE5 9QR

Jewish Gay Group
BM JGG
London WC1N 3XX
958 2955

Jewish Lesbian and Gay Helpline
706 3123
Mon and Thurs 7pm–10pm.

**Lesbian and Gay Christian
  Movement**
Oxford House

Derbyshire Street
Bethnal Green
London E2 6HG
739 1249
Counselling Referral Service: 587
1235
*Ecumenical movement, open to all,
regardless of sexual orientation.
Support and counselling,
conferences, retreats and holidays,
denominational caucuses, women's
groups, youth group.*

Metropolitan Community Church
435 7507 (North London)
677 7020 (South London)

QUEST
BM Box 2585
London WC1N 3XX
For Gay Catholics.

Health

**ACT–UP (AIDS Coalition to Unleash
  Power)**
c/o LLGC
AIDS Healthline
980 4848
2pm–10pm nightly.

Body Positive
PO Box 493
London W14 0TF
*For those diagnosed as HIV
positive. Support, counselling and
social activities. New people meet
on the top floor of the centre every
other Sunday midday.*

Customers Helping AIDS Relief
c/o LLGC
69 Cowcross Street
London EC1
381 1731
*Fundraising group with money
going directly to people with AIDS.*

Frontliners
376 5752
*10am–5pm weekdays. For/by
people with AIDS/ARC offering
advice, support and organisation.*

Group B
373 6105 or 603 6516
*For those with or immune to
Hepatitis B.*

Herpes Association
39–41 North Road
London N1
340 5729

London Lighthouse
111–117 Lancaster Road
London W11
727 2018
*Centre for therapy and counselling
for people with AIDS.*

Mainliners
738 7333 (Mon–Fri 4pm–8pm)
*Assistance and information for
intravenous drug users with
HIV/AIDS.*

Mark Ashton Trust
Box 001
67–69 Cowcross Street
London EC1
Fundraising group for care of

people with AIDS and ARC.

Positively Healthy
63 Priory Road
Kew, Surrey, TW9 3DH
940 5355
*Self-help group with a holistic
approach to HIV infection.
Seminars, distributes information
and holistic products.*

Positively Women
333 Gray's Inn Road
London WC1
837 9705
*Support group for women around
the issues of HIV and AIDS.*

Terrence Higgins Trust
52–54 Gray's Inn Road
London WC1X 8JU
Helpline 242 1010
Admin 831 0330

VD/STD Clinics

See Chapter 7: Health.

Legal

Gay Legal Advice (GLAD)
BM GLAD
London WC1N 3XX
253 2043
Mon–Fri 7pm–10pm.
Advice from qualified lawyers.

**Gay London Police Monitoring
  Project (GALOP)**
38 Mount Pleasant
London WC1X 0AP
278 6215
*Monitors police activities, advises
on legal rights and offers support to
those awaiting trial.*

Immunity Legal Service
968 8909
Legal advice on AIDS/HIV.

Legal Line (Terrence Higgins Trust)
405 2381 (Wed 7pm–10pm)
*Advice on legal problems around
AIDS/HIV, employment, medical
complaints, welfare rights.*

Lesbian Policing Project (LESPOP)
c/o Wesley House London Women's
  Centre
4 Wild Court
London WC2
833 4996/404 4318

There are a number of solicitors who specialise in cases involving lesbians and gay men. Winstanley Burgess, for example (378 City Road, London EC1V 2QA, 278 7911), have done a lot of gay work specialising in crime and immigration cases. The Campaign for Homosexual Equality or Lesbian and Gay Switchboard can give more details of other 'friendly solicitors'.

The Campaign for Homosexual Equality produce a Death Advice form, available free from their office (see above). It covers such areas as making a will, dying intestate, leaving instructions to your partner or relatives, etc.

Theatre

Drill Hall
16 Chenies Street
London WC1
631 1353

Gay Sweatshop
15 Wilkin Street
London NW5
485 5799

Institute of Contemporary Arts (ICA)
Nash House
The Mall
London SW1
930 3647

10

OLDER PEOPLE

On occasional forays into bookshops, I quite often find myself spending the odd half an hour browsing through the books on display. One section I particularly enjoy is the 'Travel' section, reading about foreign countries and dreaming about holidays that never seem to happen.

There amongst the guidebooks and travelogues you can usually find chapters or pocketbooks devoted to cities both familiar and exotic. In every 'Travel' section it is guaranteed that you will find such books and booklets introducing the visitor to our own city, London. This is the picture of our city that is presented to the foreigner. Yet when I read these chapters it is I, a resident of this city for most of my adult life, who is the foreigner. Surely this varied, vibrant, exciting city bursting at the seams with culture, history and interest is not the same workaday city that I inhabit in my daily round?

But yes it is! The truth is that those of us whose lives are occupied by the routines of work, home and family do not have the time, opportunities or even energy to sample the delights of our home city and therefore tend to forget, become blasé or even blind to the fact that we inhabit one of the world's greatest cities.

This is where men and women who have reached retirement age are so lucky. As a result of improvements in health and social conditions, most people entering their 60s can expect to live and stay active for much longer than their parents' or grandparents' generation. In fact people at this stage of life can only truthfully be described as middle aged. This, taken together with the precious London pensioners' bus pass, means that retired people have the opportunity to explore and sample the full breadth of what our city has to offer.

The key to this is information. Use not only what is listed here but seek out other sources. You will find that many museums, cinemas, theatres and others offer concessionary schemes for retired people. How many people who actually live in London have seen the Crown Jewels in the Tower? Don't stop there. Seek out the unusually interesting and little-known aspects of our city. Did you know that the Post Office has its own underground railway connecting Paddington, Mount Pleasant sorting office in Farringdon and Liverpool Street and that you can visit it by appointment? Check out your family tree at St Katherine's House on the corner of Kingsway and the Aldwych. Go for a guided walking tour of the City or take a packed lunch with you on a ride on the Docklands Light Railway and see what's really happening to the Isle of Dogs.

Above all, enjoy yourself.

Michael King
Information Manager,
Help the Aged

GENERAL INFORMATION

Pensioners account for approximately 18 per cent of the population of Greater London, that is about 1,200,000 people. A total of 423,000 of these are over 75. One in five men over 65, two in five women over 60 and more than 50 per cent of women over 75 live on their own in London. One-fifth of London's elderly people claim income support and 75 per cent have a total income equal to or less than 140 per cent of income support levels. (i.e. 'poverty level'). Older people from ethnic minorities are increasing and by the year 2000 there will be 250,000 in the Greater London area.

Behind the statistics are real people with real problems. It is a great source of shame for Londoners that the capital's pensioners are much more likely to be poorer than their peers in many other parts of the country. It is one of the gross injustices of our society that once a person retires from work or takes his/her pension, s/he suddenly becomes less important to all but his/her close family. Discrimination, lack of proper care facilities and pitifully low pensions all contribute to the frightening numbers of older people living below the poverty line, in poor housing, or dying from preventable causes. The principle of community care is fine in theory but in practice there is confusion over its definition and organisation and a lack of finance for its provision.

Housing, health, transport, benefits, loneliness – all play major roles in the life of older people. Fortunately, there are organisations and individuals who take on their cause but all too often their plight is ignored or trivialised.

Government restrictions on public spending have resulted in a reduction of grants to those bodies working for or with elderly people and their carers. In the future, such groups will be forced to tailor their work more to the priorities of those who provide their funds and less to the needs of elderly people. This is not a situation to be proud of.

HOUSING

The 1988 Housing Act and its implications for all tenants is covered in Chapter 8: Housing, and this information applies equally to older tenants. Older tenants may be eligible for certain extra grants for such things as home improvements and repairs, heating or insulation. Help the Aged's free advice line can provide the relevant information on 0800 289 404. Information on Housing Aid Centres can be obtained from the same number.

Staying in Your Own Home

It is often difficult to move out of a residential or nursing home once you have moved in so all other options should be considered before such a step is taken. Staying in your own home may be possible and desirable if your needs are provided for, either by yourself or by friends, help organisations or the local Social Services Department, who can provide such things as wheelchairs, meals-on-wheels, walking aids, commodes, etc. Voluntary agencies often arrange home visits and social activities as well as help with gardening, shopping and errands. Local Age Concern groups can let you know what is available in your area.

Grants and loans are sometimes available for repairs or vital improvements to the homes of elderly people, although government limits on local authority spending have meant a reduction in money available for such grants.

Keeping Warm

Help the Aged produce a useful leaflet on keeping warm in winter, explaining about maintaining body heat, insulation, draught proofing, heating bills and help with paying them. Help the Aged Winter Warmth Line: 0800 289 404 (freephone).

Moving to Council Housing

Elderly people have to qualify for council housing in the same way as anybody else (see Chapter 8: Housing).

Housing Associations

Some housing associations specialise in rented flats for elderly people. The council should have a list of such accommodation and details of eligibility.

Private Rented Accommodation

Nowadays much private rented accommodation is often not available to, let alone suitable for, elderly people, or within their price range unless they have a private income.

Sheltered Housing

Usually a development of rooms, flats, bungalows or houses specially adapted for elderly or disabled people, all linked to a warden via an alarm system but with the residents maintaining quite a high degree of independence and privacy.

Fostering

Social Services Departments pay fostering allowances to people who take an elderly person into their home and look after them.

Almshouses and Charities

Such organisations were set up a long time ago to cater for people in a particular area, or who did a particular job. Age Concern can provide details.

Residential/Nursing Homes

A move to a residential home might be considered if more help is needed than can be provided at home, or if more companionship is desired. It is important to consider all options very carefully and to find out as much as you can about a home before moving into one. Not all homes are the same and any particular home may not suit your particular requirements.

Unfortunately, horror stories about poor standards of care, poor hygiene, and so on are common with regard to both registered and unregistered homes. It is up to councils to register homes but also to rehouse any people made homeless by deregistering a home. Therefore, whether because of lack of council finances and available housing or for some other reason, a number of homes that would not technically pass the required standards slip through the net. However, thorough investigation of a home before moving in can usually identify the level of standards.

It is important to get help from an advice or support agency such as those mentioned in this chapter, as well as talking to family and friends before taking any decisions.

Residential homes may be run by local authorities, non-profit-making voluntary bodies or commercially run private individuals and companies. Clearly, the cost of homes varies considerably.

All residential homes with four or more residents must be

registered with the council Social Services Department and inspected at least once a year by the Homes Registration Officer. Nursing homes with two or more residents must register with the District Health Authority and are inspected at least twice a year.

Nursing homes are run by voluntary organisations or by private individuals or companies. A few are run on the NHS or by health authorities.

(a) Residential Homes

Residents receive full board and personal care, although the level and quality of care varies from home to home. Care includes nursing when a person is ill but not constant nursing at other times, so some homes may not accept residents with conditions such as incontinence, Alzheimer's disease, epilepsy, diabetes or multiple sclerosis.

(b) Nursing Homes

Twenty-four-hour care by qualified nurses and auxiliaries.

(c) Dual Registered Homes

Homes where a wide range of different types of care is provided.

(d) Registered Mental Nursing Homes

Homes providing care for people suffering from a mental disorder.

(e) Hospices

Homes providing a high quality of care for the terminally ill, and offering support and counselling to patients, their families and friends.

Finding Residential or Nursing Homes

The local authority Homes Registration Officer will provide information about local authority homes and lists of all registered homes in the borough. The District Health Authority will provide information on registered nursing homes. Help the Aged, Age

Concern and Pensioners Link may be able to help but the following are more specialist organisations.

Abbeyfield Society
186–192 Darkes Lane
Potters Bar
Herts EN6 1AB
0707 44845
Acquires or builds houses to provide bedsitting rooms and accommodation for a housekeeper for residents who then furnish their own rooms and maintain their privacy within a small community atmosphere. Many local groups.

Asian Sheltered Residential Accommodation
5–5a Westminster Bridge Road
London SE1 7XW
928 9379
Information about residential accommodation for elderly Asians.

Counsel and Care for the Elderly
Twyman House
16 Bonny Street
London NW1 9LR
485 1566
Free advisory service on any matters of concern to elderly people. Helps elderly people to find nursing homes and residential care homes.

Elderly Accommodation Council
1 Durward House
31 Kensington Court
London W8 7BH
937 8709
Has a nationwide list of homes on computer. Charges £5 to match your needs to their list. Provides advice and information about all kinds of accommodation.

Friends of the Elderly and Gentlefolk's Help
42 Ebury Street
London SW1
730 8263
Manages homes for the elderly and gives grants to aid the elderly in their own homes.

Gracelink
Upper Chambers, 7 Derby Street, Leek
Staffs, ST13 6HN
0345 023300
Has a nationwide list on computer. Charges £23 to match needs to list. A Gracelink representative will visit homes once a year.

Nationwide Bed Line
0602 51896
Free twenty-four-hour information service.

SHAC (The London Housing Aid Centre)
189a Old Brompton Road
London SW5 0AR
373 7276
Independent housing advice for people of all ages.

Shelter
88 Old Street
London EC1
253 0202
Campaigning charity on homelessness.

Paying for a Residential or Nursing Home

Local authority charges depend on an individual's ability to pay. Private and voluntary homes' charges vary a great deal. A report by the National Council for Voluntary Organisations found that London charges for residential homes ranged from £140 to £355 per week.

Help may also be obtained from the Department of Social Security for those on income support. Details are quite complex and you should contact your local DSS, Citizens Advice Bureau, Law Centre or other advice agency (see Appendix).

Short Stay

In some cases, homes will accept residents on a short-term basis, for instance when someone is recovering from illness or bereavement. Individual homes have their own policies on this.

BENEFITS AND SERVICES

For general information on benefits see Chapter 13: Social Services, Benefits and Taxation. Note that the Department of Social Security has a free phone-in service for specific inquiries. The service is available from 9am to 4.30pm Monday to Friday on 0800 666555.

It can be difficult to get through to this number but if you call out of office hours and leave your name and number on the answer machine and a time when you will be at home, someone will call you back.

Unfortunately, there is a particularly low take-up rate of benefits available to older people, especially among ethnic minorities. In 1985 (the most recent figures available), there were 1.9 million elderly people on Supplementary Benefit in Britain but 1 million others eligible and not claiming. Since benefits are pitifully low in any case, it is a tragedy that what is available is not always claimed because people are not aware of their entitlements or are too shy to go to an office because of language difficulties. Citizens Advice Bureaux, the DSS or organisations working with the elderly can provide details of your entitlements.

Support Services

There is a variety of services available for older people, provided by a range of bodies including local authority Social Services Departments (SSD), voluntary organisations, charities, churches or self-help groups. The SSD will be able to provide information on services available in the area.

The following are often available: home helps, meals on

wheels, social work support, community alarm scheme, adaptations to the home, walking aids, household gadgets, laundry services for incontinent people, crime prevention advice and assistance, visiting schemes, help with shopping, gardening, decorating, repairs, free checks on gas appliances (by British Gas). Telephones are sometimes available but councils are not obliged to provide them.

Health

As well as normal NHS care, services such as chiropody, district nurses, bathing, health visitors and easy-to-open medicine bottles may be available. A person's own doctor will usually be able to provide information on these services. Women over 60 and men over 65 automatically receive free prescriptions. Pensioners may also receive free dental treatment on the grounds of low income. After recent changes by the government free eye tests are no longer available. There are a few exceptions to this (see also Chapter 7: Health).

Elderly people may be entitled to vouchers to help pay for glasses or contact lenses. A Citizens Advice Bureau or other advice centre (see Appendix) will be able to give you more details. See also Chapter 7: Health.

Clubs and Day Centres

Many hospitals run clubs for older people as do churches, local authorities and voluntary organisations such as Age Concern, Pensioners Link, etc.

EDUCATION

Age Concern and Help the Aged will be able to provide information and materials about education for older people, but there are a number of other organisations offering opportunities for older people wishing to teach or learn.

Local Adult Education Institutes will often be able to arrange for tutors to visit residential accommodation to give classes. These arrangements might change as a result of Kenneth Baker's 1988 Education Act.

Forum for the Rights of Elderly People to Education (FREE)
Bernard Sunley House
60 Pitcairn Road
Mitcham, Surrey, CR4 3LL
640 5431
Brings together groups working for educational opportunities for older people.

Greater London Association for Pre-retirement (GLAP)
560 High Road
London N17 9TA
365 1554
Organises pre-retirement courses, conferences and seminars. Helps to advise people approaching retirement and to promote pre-retirement education at work.

ILEA Education Resource Unit for Older People
West Hill School
5 Merton Road
Wandsworth
London SW18
871 0239

Open University London Region
Parsifal College
527 Finchley Road
London NW3
794 0575
Has a large number of students aged 60 and above.

Pre-retirement Association of Great Britain and Northern Ireland
19 Undine Street
London SE17 8PP
767 3225
Arranges courses in work places for pre-retirement workers.

University of the Third Age
c/o The Executive Secretary
6 Parkside Gardens
London SW19 5EY
Helps older people to become involved in teaching and learning activities, brings education resources to local communities.

Workers Educational Association
London District Office
32 Tavistock Square
London WC1H 9EZ
387 8966
Branches all over London; has several courses aimed at older people.

ARTS AND LEISURE

Age Concern Greater London (see above) has a list of entertainers available in the Greater London area. Their booklet produced in association with Thames Television, 'Help Yourself to London' also has many details about entertainment for the elderly in London. This booklet explains the vast range of concessions in theatres, cinemas, galleries, and so on that are available for pensioners. Listing magazines such as *City Limits* or *Time Out* also have information on concessions for older people.

Age Exchange
15 Camden Row
Blackheath
London SE3
318 9105/852 9293

Touring photo exhibitions, books based on reminiscence work with older people, and theatre company.

Artsline
5 Crowndale Road
London NW1 1TU
388 2227
*A free telephone advice service for
elderly or disabled people who want
to know about the arts in London.
Details about access, transport, etc.*

Senior Citizens' Matinee Scheme
c/o Society of West End Theatres
Bedford Chambers
The Piazza
Covent Garden

London WC2E 8HQ
836 0971
*Organises reductions to matinee
performances in many theatres.
Write for application forms.*

Shape
1 Thorpe Close
London W10
960 9249
*Helps older people and people with
disabilities to enjoy and participate
in the arts. Touring productions and
exhibitions available.*

Sport

The Sports Council
16 Upper Woburn Place
London WC1
388 1277

Sportsline
222 8000
Personal sport information line.

*Both these organisations can provide advice and information on sport for
older people.*

EXTEND (Exercise and Training for the Elderly and Disabled)
3 The Boulevard
Sheringham
Norfolk NR26 8LJ
0263 822479
Information on local and national facilities.

Gardening

Information on gardening in general and on gardening as therapy
can be obtained from any of the major organisations mentioned
above or from:

Horticultural Therapy
Gould's Ground
Vallis Way
Frome
Somerset BA11 3DW

TRANSPORT

Contact
15 Henrietta Street
Covent Garden
London WC2
240 0630

*Groups of volunteers organised on
a local basis who meet socially with
small groups of elderly people for
tea and conversation, trips and
tours.*

Dial-A-Ride Users Association
St Margaret's
25 Leighton Road
London NW5 2QD
482 2325
*Dial-A-Ride operates in most
boroughs providing door-to-door
transport for people who have
difficulty in using public transport.*

Elderly Persons Travel Passes
c/o Travel Concessions Officer
Hammersmith Town Hall
King Street
London W6
748 3020 ext 2029
*Free travel on buses and tube trains
after 9am and half price travel on
some BR routes in Greater London
after 9.30am.*
*Application forms available from
Post Offices.*

**London Community Transport
  Association**
Unit M2

Finsbury Business Centre
40 Bowling Green Lane
London EC1R 0NE
837 0081
*Provides transport for hire to
community groups on a non-profit-
making basis.*

Taxicard
c/o London Regional Transport Unit
  for Disabled Passengers
227 3588
*Subsidised door-to-door transport
for those unable to use buses or
trains but who can use taxis. The
first £7 of any journey will only cost
£1. Eligibility must be confirmed by
a doctor. Application forms are
available from Post Offices.*

Tripscope
63 Esmond Road
London W4 1JG
994 9294
*Advice on mobility for people with a
disability.*

ACCESS

See Chapter 11: People With Disabilities.

SAFETY

Thousands of people every year suffer a burglary or break-in, many of which could have been avoided by simple preventive methods. In fact crime against old people is statistically less common than against any other age group. However, older people can be particularly vulnerable to certain types of crime and there are a few simple steps that can make homes more secure, such as having proper locks fitted on doors and windows and taking out insurance policies. Help the Aged produce a useful leaflet entitled 'Be Safe'.

National Association of Victim Support Schemes
Brixton Road
London SW9
735 9166
Support and advice to victims of robbery or burglary.

Age Concern and Help the Aged have leaflets giving advice on safety and security for elderly people. Help the Aged produce two excellent leaflets. 'Be Sure Who's at the Door' outlines a few ideas on combating door-to-door sellers who may be trying to con you or are simply pretending to be selling something in order to gain entry to your house. Spy-holes, door-chains and so on are covered as well as asking for identification, contracts, having work done on your house, and dealing with pressure from people on your doorstep or on the telephone. This leaflet serves as a useful introduction as well as directing you to other sources of advice such as Citizens Advice Bureaux. The second leaflet, 'Who's There?', discusses burglars' artifice, that is people gaining access to your house by pretending to be a salesperson or something similar, and then robbing you when your back is turned.

VOLUNTEERING TO WORK WITH OLDER PEOPLE

Volunteers are needed by many groups working with elderly people, such as Age Concern, Help the Aged and Pensioners Link. If you wish to offer your services, the following organisations will be able to help. You can also apply directly to organisations that interest you.

Retired and Senior Volunteer Programme
c/o Community Service Volunteers
Pentonville Road
London N1 9NJ
278 6601
Encourages older people to take up volunteer work and encourages organisations to use people as volunteers.

The Volunteer Centre
29 Lower King's Road
Berkhamsted
Herts
HP4 2AB
04427 73311
Advice on different types of volunteer work and details on local volunteer bureaux.

ADDRESSES

Campaigning Groups

Age Concern Greater London
54 Knatchbull Road
London SE5 9QY
737 3456

Provides advice and information on all areas of rights, welfare and services for older people. Branches all over London.

Someone at the above address will put you in touch with your nearest source of help on, for instance, bereavement counselling, carers, charity shops, day centres, lunch clubs, pop-ins, excursions and holidays, employment, health, home help, leisure activities, aids and equipment, heaters, ethnic minorities, disablement and women's issues. ACGL produced an excellent guide entitled *Help Yourself to London* in association with Thames Television, describing in detail leisure activities in and around London with special reference to those that are free or give concessions to pensioners.

Help The Aged
16–18 St James's Walk
London EC1R 0BE
253 0253

A campaigning and fundraising organisation. Grants sometimes provided to local community groups. Produces many publications including leaflets on subjects as diverse as housing, health, bereavement, gardening and social security benefits. Has a Community Alarms Department which is the best source of information on telephone alarm systems. Advice can be given on equipment and systems and possible sources of funding. If an individual is not eligible for a grant from another source, Help the Aged may be able to help.

There is a comprehensive information and advice service which can be contacted by letter or phone (250 3399). There is also a 'Gifted Housing Scheme' whereby individuals can donate their property to Help the Aged who take over rates, maintenance and other charges for the rest of the person's life and then take possession of the property.

All-Party Parliamentary Group for Pensioners
House of Commons
London SW1A 0AA
219 4082
MPs involved include Andrew Faulds, Andrew Bowden, Nicholas Winterton.

British Pensioners and Trade Union Action Association
Norman Dodd's House
315 Bexley Road
Erith
Kent

0747 61802
A very active and vocal campaigning organisation.

Greater London Pensioners Association
28a Highgate Road
London NW5
267 6151
Campaigns for higher pensions, better services, adequate housing. Groups throughout London. Has information on many local action groups and self-help groups.

London Joint Council for Senior Citizens
c/o TGWU Retired Members Association
Room 703, Transport House
Smith Square
London SW1P 3JP
828 3806

National Benevolent Fund for the Aged
65 London Wall
London EC2M 5TU
638 2026
Provides holidays, outings, TVs and equipment for the housebound; advice and information.

National Federation of Old Age Pension Associations
Melling House

91 Preston New Road
Blackburn
Lancs BBN 6BD
0245 52606
Campaigns for higher pensions and an equal retirement age for men and women. Branches all over London.

Pensioners Link
17 Balfe Street
London N1 9EB
278 5501
Help and advisory service working in partnership with older people. Offers legal help, advice, support and social events.
Runs special campaigns on heating, older women, ethnic minorities and media resources. Has local branches.

Ethnic Minorities

Standing Conference of Ethnic Minority Senior Citizens
5–5a Westminster Bridge Road
London SE1 7XW
928 0095
An umbrella group bringing together people from many ethnic groups in London. Advice for people from ethnic minorities on

health, housing, benefits and other services.

West Indian Women's Association
71 Pound Lane
London NW10
451 4827
Cultural events, arts and crafts.

Carers

Association of Crossroads Care Attendant Schemes
Greater London Office
Victoria Chambers
16/18 Strutton Ground
London SW1P 2HP
222 6858
Helps carers with opportunities for breaks from their caring role.

Carers National Association
29 Chilworth Mews
London W2 3RG
262 1451
Support, counselling and advice on benefits and help availability.

Some London boroughs, e.g. Camden, Brent, Haringey, Southwark, and Hackney have locally based projects. Usually details can be found at the borough council Social Services Department or from one of the major organisations listed above.

General

Age Link
Suite 5, The Manor House
The Green
Southall
Middx UB2 4BR
734 9083
*A community resource for the
elderly, isolated housebound.
Establishes groups of volunteers to
visit, take out and entertain older
people who cannot go out alone.
Brings together young and old
people in recreational context.*

Alzheimer's Disease Society
3rd Floor, Bank Buildings
Fulham Broadway
London SW6 1EP
381 3177

Centre for Policy on Ageing
25–31 Ironmonger Row
London EC1
253 1787
*Encourages better services by
initiating informed debate and
stimulating greater awareness of
older people's needs.*

Cruse
126 Sheen Road
Richmond
Surrey TW9 1VR
940 4818/9047
*Counselling and social groups for
the widowed and their children.*

Holiday Care Service
2 Old Bank Chambers
Station Road
Horley, Surrey, RH6 9HW
0293 774535
*Free information and advice about
holidays for people with special
needs.*

**Women's Royal Voluntary Service
(WRVS)**
17 Old Park Lane
London W1Y 4AJ
499 6040
*Local branches often run services
for elderly people such as meals on
wheels.*

11

PEOPLE WITH DISABILITIES

Over 682,000 disabled people live in London. Whatever their disability, be it mobility disability, visual handicap, hearing impairment or learning difficulty, London offers both barriers and opportunities.

Like most capital cities, London is old. Much of it stems from a time when disabled people were not seen and not heard. There are many areas that have been built with no notion of accessibility or the needs of the disabled.

Disabled people are now making themselves seen and heard, and are coming together to demand that London becomes a city where they have physical, cultural and political access. Perhaps the most important opportunity for disabled Londoners is to become involved with the many organisations furthering the aims of disabled people in the capital.

Much has already been achieved, although there is still a very long way to go.

Nearly half a million people, one out of every fifteen, have difficulties using the capital's public transport system. As a result of the work of disabled people and their organisations, there is a network of community transport services, a scheme for cheaper travel by taxi and even a few scheduled routes with accessible buses.

As disabled people have become more able to move around in the city, so they are becoming increasingly involved in all aspects of life in the city. They are now particularly active in the arts in London. Access has gone far beyond just gaining entry to theatres and art galleries. Disabled people are now developing their own arts movement which shows positive images of disability previously unseen.

The growing political voice of disabled people in the capital is steadily increasing the pressure for change in society. While there is evidence that some progress has been achieved there is need for more.

A total of 69 per cent of disabled people are unemployed, and those who do work are generally in jobs with below average wages and few prospects for career development. As a result most disabled people are excluded from the affluence that has grown in London in the last ten years.

There are still new facilities being built with a concept of access that involves using the back door and giving a month's notice of your visit.

For people with mobility disabilities, the prospect of a fully accessible public transport system remains a very long way into the future.

The challenge for disabled people in London is to create the opportunities of the future. By breaking down the barriers, the misconceptions and the prejudices, disabled people are not only making London a better place to live in, they are creating an example for the rest of the country, and the rest of the world, to follow.

Michael Turner
Publications Officer
Greater London Association for Disabled People

TRANSPORT

Transport is of paramount importance to all disabled people. A study by the Greater London Association for Disabled People (GLAD) in 1986 entitled *All Change* showed that 465,000 people in the Greater London area, including a particularly large number of young people, identified themselves as being transport handicapped, underlining the need for a thorough review. GLAD recently published a report entitled *The Impact of Transport on the Quality of Life and Lifestyle of Young People With Physical Disabilities*. Although concentrating on the needs of young people, many of its conclusions apply to all physically disabled people, not least the fact that an improvement of the situation for young people now would prevent regeneration of current problems for the next generation of transport-disabled people.

GLAD's recommendations are clear enough, but it is for the authorities concerned to put them into practice, or for people to pressurise the authorities into doing so. Lack of transport limits disabled people's participation in leisure activities because such activity tends to be weighted towards car owners. Those disabled people who do not have access to a car or driver tend to take part in the fewest activities. The same people are less likely to be employed or to take part in full-time education, unless it is residential.

GLAD's report also found that many physically disabled people were not aware of their entitlement to local authority-provided transport facilities.

People with physical disabilities require transport that is, to quote GLAD, 'immediate, flexible and accessible', allowing unlimited trips and not restricted in their purpose. In short, disabled people should be entitled to the same degree of mobility as their able-bodied friends and families.

GLAD's recommendations include the need for both statutory and voluntary organisations to campaign for greater awareness of the needs of disabled people as drivers and passengers. It should be the responsibility of local authorities in association with the NHS and voluntary organisations to meet these needs. Of course, such work is hindered on the one hand by lack of public awareness or interest, and on the other by government restraints on local authority spending.

Tripscope
63 Esmond Road
London W4 1JE
994 9294

Transport information service seeking to expand and simplify the mobility options of people with special needs. Contact by phone or, if by post, by tape, Braille or written letter.

Bus Passes

Three kinds of bus passes are available to disabled Londoners.

(a) Blind Person's Bus Pass

Free travel at any time on buses and tubes for anyone registered blind, under retirement age and living in London. Contact your local Social Services Department (SSD) at the borough council. It will be listed in the phone book under the name of your borough, e.g. Wandsworth, London Borough of.

(b) Disabled Person's Bus Pass

Free travel after 9am on buses and tubes. Eligibility varies according to borough. Contact the Social Services Department.

(c) Elderly Person's Bus Pass

Free travel after 9am on buses and tubes for anyone over retirement age living in London. Apply at a Post Office with two passport-sized photographs.

A leaflet explaining eligibility can be obtained from LRT or your local Social Services Department.

Access to the Underground System

LRT produces a booklet entitled 'Access to the Underground' with detailed information about all 273 of London's tube stations. Also available is a leaflet entitled 'Access Around London for Disabled People'. Both are available over the counter at Travel Information Centres or from

Unit for Disabled Passengers
LRT
55 The Broadway
London SE1

Mobility Bus

LRT runs several mobility buses fully adapted for wheelchair users. Routes are now available in Waltham Forest, Newham, Hackney, Islington, Haringey, Enfield, Lewisham and South-wark. This service has been extended to include most of the north-east, north-west and south-east suburban boroughs. There are plans to extend it to the remaining areas in the near future. There is also a wheelchair accessible service between Victoria and Heathrow and between mainline BR stations.

British Rail Disabled Person's Railcard

British Rail offer disabled people a railcard costing £12 and entitling the holder and one person travelling with him/her to a half or one-third off the cost of some tickets. People receiving Mobility Allowance, Attendance Allowance or Severe Disablement Allowance or who are registered blind or deaf can get the railcard. Wheelchair users who travel in their own chairs and one person travelling with them can get the same reductions without a railcard. A leaflet is available from stations and Post Offices.

BR also has two useful publications: a leaflet entitled 'British Rail and Disabled Travellers', and a book *Travelling by British Rail – A Guide For Disabled People*, £2.00 from bookshops and £2.70 from RADAR (see p. 278).

Taxicard

To qualify for a taxicard you must be receiving either Mobility Allowance or War Pensioners Mobility Allowance, or be registered blind or have a letter from your doctor explaining why you need to use the service. Forms are available at some Post Offices or local information centres. Two passport photos and proof of eligibility will be required.

The scheme is funded by the boroughs but administered by LRT. Some councils are reluctant to pay the increasing cost of the scheme. Barnet has set up its own scheme and other councils have imposed restrictions on the number of trips that can be taken within a certain period. Check the local situation with your local disability organisation, Citizens Advice Bureau, or other independent advice centre (see Appendix).

People who have a taxicard can use black radio taxis at

reduced cost: £1 for the first £7 on the clock. You must book by phone using one of the companies listed on your card.

Metrocab

New wheelchair accessible taxis. You can use your taxicard on this service, too, but you will have to book four days in advance! Contact Computer Cab: 852 9964.

Dial-A-Ride

A door-to-door scheme for those who cannot use public transport. Each borough has its own scheme. Fares are based on bus fares. All trips must be booked. Some restrictions on distance. Can't be used to go to hospitals or day centres. Contact London Dial-A-Ride Users Association 482 2325. See also ASRA (below).

Disabled Drivers

Several organisations exist to help you learn to drive and to provide the necessary advice and assessment.

Mobility Information Service
Unit 2a, Atcham Estate
Upton Magna
Shrewsbury, SY4 4UG
0743 77489

Banstead Place Mobility Centre
Park Road
Banstead
Surrey, SM7 3EE
0737 351674

**Mobility Advice and Vehicle
   Information Service**
TRRL
Crowthorne
Berkshire RG11 6AU
0344 770456

**Disabled Drivers Association
   London Office**
Drake House
Creekside
Deptford
London SE18 3DZ
692 7141

Disabled Drivers Motor Club
Cottingham Way
Thrapston
Northants, NN14 4PL
08012 4724

Motability
2nd Floor, Gate House
West Gate
Harlow, Essex, CM20 1HR
0279 635666
Advice on financial help in buying a car.

Parking

The Orange Badge Scheme provides a national arrangement of parking concessions for disabled people either as drivers or passengers and for registered blind people. The Department of Transport is currently planning to tighten rules on eligibility for the scheme. Contact the Social Services Department for details. The scheme does not operate in the City of London, Westminster, parts of Euston Road in Camden, or Kensington and Chelsea.

'Door to Door Transport – A Guide for Disabled People' in tape or print. For details and price, contact

Dept of Transport
Disability Unit
Room 510/21
2 Marsham Street
London SW1P 3EB
276 5257

'Disability and Transport in London' is an information leaflet in tape or print of London organisations, books and publications. Free if you send SAE to GLAD.

HELP FROM SOCIAL SERVICES

Social Services Departments are bound by two Acts of Parliament to provide certain services to disabled people in their areas. It is up to the local Social Services Department to assess needs so your own assessment may not coincide with theirs. If it doesn't, contact one of the information or campaigning organisations to see whether they can help you to find what you need or whether you can help them to get the regulations changed!

The Social Services Department is allowed to charge for some services but must make the following available (each authority has its own regulations and policy): practical help at home such as home-helps; assistance with radio, TV, library and other recreational facilities both inside and outside your home; assistance in taking advantage of educational facilities; help with transport to these facilities; adaptations to your home to make it safer, more comfortable or convenient; holidays; meals such as meals on wheels; telephones and equipment required to use them.

The law demands that Social Services Departments keep a register of people with 'substantial and permanent' disabilities. Certain departments provide a range of concessions, e.g. bus passes, only to those registered (not being on the list does not affect your entitlement to other facilities). Contact your local SSD for details of services available in your area. Some authorities also offer a foreign language interpreting service if you ask for it. Local disability organisations (see end of chapter) can help you to find out about and get the services you are entitled to. If you have real problems, contact:

Network
16 Princeton Street
London WC1R 4BB
831 8031/837 7740

EQUIPMENT

Contact your local Social Services Department in the first instance if you have a specific requirement. You may well be able to get the aid you require free of charge, either permanently or on loan. Aids for washing, dressing and feeding are available, for example. Some SSDs may make a charge for certain aids. Certain types of wheelchairs, artificial limbs and appliances are provided free by local health authorities.

It is also possible to acquire aids from the Disablement Advisory Service if you need them to carry out your employment. Contact the Disablement Resettlement Officer via a Job Centre. If you are intending to buy an aid get advice first. The following may be useful contacts.

Disabled Living Foundation
380–384 Harrow Road
London W9 2HU
289 6111

Rehabilitation Engineering Movement Advisory Panels (REMAP)
(Technical Equipment for Disabled People)
c/o RADAR (see p. 278)
Develops aids often on a one-off basis that fill gaps left by standard commercial aids for disabled people.

If you need adaptations to your home (e.g. door widening or ramps) you may be able to get financial help from the SSD or the local Housing Department. Two kinds of grant are also available:

intermediate or home improvement. The former has to be paid for certain types of work, the latter is discretionary. The amount you are entitled to will depend on the policies of your particular local authority; whether you are a council tenant, a private tenant or an owner-occupier and whether the particular adaptation you have requested qualifies for a grant. Again the local SSD, Citizens Advice Bureau, independent advice agency (see Appendix) or a local disability advice service (see end of chapter) should be your first point of contact.

HELP AT HOME

Home help may be provided by the local SSD or health authority and in some cases a local voluntary organisation. The National Association of Volunteer Bureaux will send you details of your nearest voluntary organisation, many of whom provide services such as shopping or driving.

National Association of Volunteer Bureaux
St Peter's College
College Road
Saltley
Birmingham B8 3TE
021 327 0265

Services available from the SSD are home-helps for cleaning and household chores, meals on wheels and laundry services. What you are entitled to depends on an SSD assessment. Services available from the local health authority include district nurses, community physiotherapists and special beds.

Other sources of help:

Association of Carers
243 Lower Mortlake Road
Richmond
Surrey, TW9 2LS
948 3946
Helps to set up local carer groups and provides information on services available.

Association of Crossroads Care Attendant Schemes
Victoria Chambers
16–18 Strutton Ground
London SW1P 2HP
222 6858

Runs schemes in nineteen London boroughs for providing care attendants who give practical help to disabled people and their carers at home.

Community Service Volunteers
237 Pentonville Road
London N1 9NJ
278 6601
Runs a programme of placing volunteers with disabled people and their families. Usually work full time.

RIGHTS AND DISCRIMINATION

Discrimination against people with disabilities is common in all walks of life and there is no statutory protection against this. If you feel you have been unfairly discriminated against, for instance at work, at school or college or elsewhere, contact one of the local or London-wide bodies listed in this section.

The Disabled Persons Act 1986 is supposed to make it easier for people with a disability to voice their needs and opinions about the services they receive. People with a disability will have the right to a representative to put their views to the local authority. The Act is still waiting to be fully implemented.

Asian Sheltered Residential Accommodation (ASRA)
155 Kennington Park Road
London SE11 4JJ
793 0959
General information and advice. Leaflets for disabled people in Hindi, Urdu, Gujarati and Bengali. ASRA also provides door-to-door transport for their residents. Active in Ealing, Lambeth, Haringey and Greenwich. Contact ASRA Dial-A-Ride 928 9379.

Disability Alliance
25 Denmark Street
London WC2H 8NJ
240 0806
Publish the Disability Rights Handbook, *an indispensable information source (£3.75 post free).*

DHSS Free Telephone Advice Line
0800 666555

ACCESS

'Access: Regulations and Guidelines', a leaflet from GLAD gives an outline of what regulations exist. There is no single piece of legislation governing access to buildings by disabled people.

Centre on Environment for the Handicapped
35 Great Smith Street
London SW1P 3BJ
222 7980
An information service on technical matters and design relating to disabilities.

Some areas have local access guides available from Social Services Departments or disability associations giving detailed information about shops, lavatories etc. A book entitled *Access in London* gives details of restaurants, hotels and leisure venues in central London. It is published by Nicholson (£3.50) and available from bookshops.

HEALTH

If you need to get treatment of any kind from the health service but are unsure whom to contact, a useful first port of call is your local GP. S/he may visit you at home if necessary. In any case s/he will either treat you personally or refer you to the correct person. You may not have to pay for medication if you meet certain conditions.

If you do not know your local GP, contact your local Family Practitioners Committee or Community Health Council (in the phone book) and they will send you a list.

Community Health Councils may also be able to help you with both general and specific information, or if you have a problem or a complaint about a doctor. See Health section for more general addresses.

EDUCATION

Kenneth Baker's Education Act has caused more than a little concern among those involved in special education for people with disabilities. ILEA had a fairly good record with children with special educational needs and many organisations and individuals are rightly worried that the abolition of ILEA will lead to a decline in the way these needs are met in the future. The possibility of schools opting out of local authority control might well cause serious problems in the coordination of a thorough approach to the education of those with special needs.

The organisations involved are doing their utmost to ensure that the Act does not have an adverse effect on the provision of education for people with disabilities. They are encouraging the boroughs to continue the work of ILEA once they take over responsibility for education in their locality.

Every local authority has a department to deal with special educational needs. Whenever possible each will try to integrate children with disabilities into ordinary schools. A 'statement of needs' should be recorded by the LEA and a copy given to the parent. It is at present unclear how the new arrangements will affect this procedure.

Information can be obtained from the following addresses:

Advisory Centre for Education (ACE)
18 Victoria Park Square
London E2 9PB
980 4596

Information for parents of children in state-maintained schools.

Centre for Studies on Integration in Education
4th Floor
415 Edgware Road
London NW2 6NB
452 8642
Information on educating children with special needs in ordinary schools.

Voluntary Council for Handicapped Children
8 Wakeley Street
London EC1V 7QE
278 9441
Information service for parents and professionals.

National Bureau for Students with Disabilities (SKILL)
336 Brixton Road
London SW9 7AA
274 0565
General information on further and higher education for potential students, parents and professionals, including advice on grants and benefits. Conferences and other activities arranged.

EMPLOYMENT

The law supposedly enforces a quota system which demands all employers with more than twenty employees to ensure that 3 per cent of its staff are registered disabled. In reality, many employers are either unaware of or ignore the quota regulations and it is not widely enforced. Some employers do have Equal Opportunities policies but discrimination is still widespread.

The Department of Employment is responsible for Job Centres and employment services for disabled people. The Disablement Resettlement Officer (DRO) will help to arrange interviews and advise you on vacancies, training opportunities, practical help and special schemes. The DRO is usually based at the Job Centre.

The Employment Service keeps a register of disabled people seeking work. To be able to register you must have been 'substantially handicapped in obtaining or keeping employment' for at least twelve months. You will be given a 'Green Card' and a registration number. Registration may help you to get some forms of assistance from the Employment Service (ES).

If you have to use a taxi to travel to work, you are entitled to three-quarters of the cost from the ES. The ES can also provide certain aids required at work. Furthermore, it can provide grants of up to £6,000 to employers to make necessary adaptations to buildings so that they are accessible to disabled people. Contact DRO.

Part-time readers for blind people or partially sighted people in employment can be obtained from the RNIB.

Careers Advice for Schools

Most education authorities employ a specialist careers officer. To contact him/her, phone the LEA.

Adviser for Education, Training and Employment
Pathway
MENCAP
115 Golden Lane
London EC1Y 0TJ
250 4105
A scheme to help people with a mental handicap to work with an employer for a trial period. Support once the job has started.

Employment Section, RNIB
(see p. 279)

Opportunities for the Disabled
1 Bank Buildings
Princes Street
London EC2R 8EL
726 4961
A non-commercial employment agency for people with disabilities.

Outset
Drake House
18 Creekside
London SE5 3DZ
692 7141
Training in office skills for people with disabilities and provides a number of employment possibilities.

LEISURE

Many boroughs do not have a fully formulated approach to the provision of leisure facilities for people with disabilities or even staff with specific responsibility for that area of work. Some boroughs have taken initiatives but often problems of inaccessibility and poor publicity remain. First contact for information should be your local disability organisation, your local Social Services Department or the leisure or recreation department.

Sport

British Sports Association for the Disabled
Suite 202, Glen House
200–208 Tottenham Court Road
London W1P
631 3735

UK Sports Association for People with a Mental Handicap
30 Philip Lane
Tottenham
London N15 4JB

See also Chapter 1: Arts and Leisure; many sports organisations, including the Sports Council, offer facilities and advice to disabled people. For details of the many specialist sports organisations for people with disabilities, contact GLAD.

Arts

Artsline
5 Crowndale Road
London NW1 1TU
388 2227
*A free and confidential telephone
advice service to help disabled
people discover London's arts and
entertainments, plays, films,
exhibitions, concerts, classes and so
on.*

Disability Arts in London (DAIL)
London Disability Arts Forum
c/o 5 Crowndale Road
London NW1 1TU
*A monthly magazine including
listings and access guides. Free
subscription to disabled individuals.*

Graeae Theatre Company
The Diorama
18 Park Square East
London NW1 4LH
935 5588
*Professional and amateur
companies of performers with
disabilities. Campaigns for disabled
people in the arts.*

**National Federation of Gateway
  Clubs**
115 Golden Lane
London EC1Y 0TJ
250 4105
*Organises leisure clubs for people
with mental disabilities.*

**(PHAB) Physically Handicapped and
  Able Bodied**
Tavistock House North
Tavistock Square
London WC1H 9HX
388 1963
*Organises social activities through a
network of clubs allowing both
disabled and able-bodied people to
meet on equal terms.*

SHAPE
1 Thorpe Close
London W10 5XL
960 9245
*Working to increase the
involvement of under-represented
groups and individuals in the arts.
Runs a special reduced price ticket
scheme for people with disabilities
or elderly people and free transport
and escorts when required.*

Thames Water
Nugent House
Vastern Road
Reading RG1 8DB
0734 593777
*Has produced a useful leaflet on
recreational facilities for people with
a disability.*

Talking Newspapers and Books

**Alternative Talking Newspapers
  Collective**
c/o Neil Harvey
Flat 7
19 Lee Terrace
Blackheath
London SE3 9TF
318 2002
Produce a tape magazine, Left Out,
*a digest of the left-wing and
feminist press.*

**Feminist Audio Books or Women's
  Tapeover**
52–54 Featherstone Street
London EC1Y 8RT
251 0713

National Listening Library
12 Lant Street
London SE1 1QH
407 9417
Runs a postal cassette library.

**Talking Newspaper Association of
  the UK**
90 High Street
Heathfield
East Sussex TN21 8JD
*Provides tapes of national and local
newspapers.*

HOLIDAYS

Holidays can never be taken for granted by people with
disabilities unless all his/her special needs are catered for. There
are a number of organisations who help with holidays for the
disabled, financially, practically, home and abroad. Space does
not permit a full list, but the main sources of information are:

The Holiday Care Service
2 Old Bank Chambers, Station Road
Horley
Surrey RH6 9HW
0293 774535

RADAR (see p. 278).
*RADAR publishes two booklets
covering holidays in Britain and
holidays abroad.*

RELATIONSHIPS

**The Association to Aid the Sexual
  and Personal Relationships of
  People with Disabilities (SPOD)**
286 Camden Road
London N7 0BJ
607 8851
*Information about disability,
relationships and sexuality. Can
direct you to an expert counsellor if
you would like to discuss something
about a personal problem or
concern.*

Gay Men's Disabled Group
c/o Gay's the Word Bookshop
66 Marchmont Street
London WC1N 1AB

**GEMMA (Lesbians with/without
  disabilities)**
BM Box 5700
London WC1N 3XX

HOUSING

Very little housing is designed with disabled people in mind. If
you are looking for somewhere to live in London and you have a
disability, your choice is likely to be severely limited.

If you are homeless and disabled, your council should put you
in the 'priority need' category (see Chapter 8: Housing). The
council has a duty to find you at least temporary accommodation,
but may claim it has difficulty in finding a place for you. It is
probably true.

If you are not homeless but are looking for permanent accommodation, you may approach your local authority for help. Some boroughs now consider special housing needs more carefully, but there is still a massive shortage of suitable premises. Housing associations are also worth considering and there may be special projects in your area that you can contact through a local advice agency.

If you register with your council when you begin to look for a house and describe your needs fully, they may be able to put you in touch with local housing associations or cooperatives which have special schemes.

The Housing Advice Switchboard
434 2522
Helps you to find the right organisation to assist you.

Carematch
286 Camden Road
London N7
609 9966
Computer-based service giving help in search for residential care.

Centre on Environment for the Handicapped
(see above under 'Access')

Disabled Living Foundation
380–384 Harrow Road
London W9 2HU
289 6111

Disability Alliance
(see above under 'Discrimination')

Support and Housing Assistance for People with Disabilities (SHAD)
13–15 Stockwell Road
London SW9
737 6748
Helps more severely disabled people to live in their own home by arranging the necessary help.

VOLUNTEER WORK

If you would like to help with the work of any of the organisations listed in this chapter or to work with the disabled in some way, there are a number of organisations whom you could contact. Your borough organisations will be particularly helpful (see end of chapter).

Association of Disabled Professionals
The Stables
73 Pound Road
Banstead
Surrey SM7 2HU
0737 352 366
Concerned with the improvement of rehabilitation education training and employment opportunities for disabled professionals.

British Council of Organisations of Disabled People
St Mary's Church
Greenlaw Street
London SE18 5AR
316 4184

Contact a Family
16 Strutton Ground
London SW1P 2HP
222 2695
Brings families with special needs children together.

Disablement Income Group
Millmead Business Centre
Millmead Road
London N17 9QU
801 8013
*Advice and research to prevent
financial hardship as a result of
disability.*

Fair Play
c/o SHAPE
1 Thorpe Close
London W10 5XL
960 9245
*Campaigning within the arts for
better representation of people with
disabilities.*

Good Practices in Mental Health
380–384 Harrow Road
London W9 2HU
289 2034
*Information for health and social
services planners. Stimulates
studies and evaluations in the
mental health services.*

**National Association for Patient
Participation**
13 Manor Drive
Surbiton
KT5 8NF
399 4122
*Information and advice for health
service patients.*

National Citizen Advocacy
2 St Paul's Road
London N1 2QR
253 2056

**National Council for Carers and
their Elderly Dependants**
29 Chilworth Mews
London W2 3RG
724 7776
*Information and advice for carers.
Pressure group for better services
and benefits.*

**National Council for Voluntary
Organisations**
26 Bedford Square

London WC1B 3HU
636 4066
*NCVO also publishes a directory of
700 health and disability
organisations.*

**National League for the Blind and
Disabled**
2 Tenterden Road
Tottenham N17 8BE
808 6030
*A trade union for the blind and
disabled involved in many disability
campaigns, for example the
campaigns against closure of
sheltered workshops, benefit cuts,
and discrimination.*

National Union of the Deaf
167 Yew Tree Drive
Barfield Estate
Guildford
Surrey
*A trade union for the deaf and hard
of hearing.*

Pensioners Link
17 Balfe Street
London N1 9EB
278 5501/2/3/4
*Helps pensioners to lead full and
active lives and maintain
independence.*

People First of London and Thames
Kings Fund Centre
126 Albert Street
London NW1 7NF
267 6111
*Campaigns for the rights of disabled
people and the replacement of
medical by educational words in the
discussion of disability.*

**Union of Physically Impaired
Against Segregation (UPIAS)**
Flat 2
St Giles Court
Dane Road
Ealing W13 9AQ
*Opposes all forms of segregation of
disabled people.*

ADDRESSES

For information on specific disabilities contact a local information centre or one of the following:

The Greater London Association for Disabled People
336 Brixton Road
London SW9 7AA
274 0107

GLAD's primary function is the gathering and disseminating of information to organisations who cater for the needs of disabled people. Offers many publications to individuals and groups a full list of which is available.

Most useful is the *Directory of London Disability Organisations* containing details of 200 London-based organisations, price £3.50. Also useful is 'Information for Disabled People', a 35-page guide to rights, services and sources of information, price 50p to cover p&p; a series of free leaflets covering all the important sources of information on subjects such as transport, holidays, access, information services, sport and general statistics and a monthly newsletter.

RADAR (The Royal Association for Disability and Rehabilitation)
25 Mortimer Street
London W1N 8AB
637 5400

Aims to 'care for, rehabilitate and assist disabled people; promote the education and welfare of disabled people and their integration into the community; promote and support research into the causes, prevention, treatment and cure of disabling diseases; promote and conduct research and surveys on the social welfare of disabled people and raise funds to promote the interests of disabled people'. Also produces a comprehensive list of its own publications and those of related organisations. Particularly useful for Londoners are: British Rail and Disabled Travellers, Heathrow Airport, Gatwick Airport, Access in London, Housing Grants and Allowances, Local Authority Provision of Housing Services for Disabled People, The Directory for Disabled People.

The Spastics Society
London Regional Office
32–38 Osnaburgh Street
London NW1 3ND
387 5505

Head Office
12 Park Crescent
London W1N 4EQ
636 5020

Largest charity working with people with cerebral palsy in Britain, helping them to achieve their goals in life and to make their own decisions about their future. Offers education through specially equipped schools and colleges, residential units and centres to accommodate special needs, work centres to give the opportunity to work and develop their skills, assessment and therapy facilities, advice and support to those with cerebral palsy and their families. Also carries out research into the causes and effects of cerebral palsy as well as advertising campaigns and speaking tours attempting to change attitudes towards all people with disabilities.

John Grooms Association for the Disabled
10 Gloucester Drive
London N4 2LP
802 7272
Runs projects throughout England and Wales, including residential accommodation, employment schemes, holiday schemes and research.

National Association for Limbless Disabled
31 The Mall
London W5
579 1758

Network for the Handicapped Ltd
16 Princeton Street
London WC1R 4BB
831 8031/7740

Outsiders Club
PO Box 4ZB
London W1A 4ZB
499 0900
Helps people who feel emotionally isolated, perhaps because of disability, by bringing them together at club meetings and activities.

Sisters Against Disablement (SAD)
52–54 Featherstone Street
London EC1
251 6332
A group of women with disabilities who meet to discuss feminism and disability. Newsletter available.

Organisations for People with Sight Disabilities

The Royal National Institute for the Blind (RNIB)
224 Great Portland Street
London W1N 6AA
388 1266

Provides schools for the blind and for those who have other handicaps as well as blindness; training colleges for older blind people, a rehabilitation centre to help newly blind people to adjust to their condition; a centre for mobility training; a team of employment officers; sports and leisure advice; a London resource centre; homes, hotels for holidays and a hostel for working blind people; books and sheet music in Braille and

Moon and on tape; financial help; money and research into the prevention of blindness and the improvement of education and employment prospects for those who have a visual handicap.

Greater London Fund for the Blind
2 Wyndham Place
London W1H 2AQ

Raises funds for the blind and visually impaired in all parts of Greater London. Money raised goes towards equipment for schools and factories, Braille and Moon books, tactile toys, radios and so on. Local branches exist. Contact central office for details. A large number of other organisations can be contacted through GLFB.

Association of Blind Asians
322 Upper Street
London N1 2XQ
226 1950

**Jewish Blind and Physically
Handicapped Society**
118 Seymour Place
London W1H 5DJ
260 2003

Royal London Society for the Blind
105 Salusbury Road
London NW6 6RH
Works especially in the field of education.

Organisations for People with Hearing Difficulties

**Royal National Institute for the Deaf
(RNID)**
105 Gower Street
London WC1E 6AH
387 8033
Works with both the hard of hearing and the profoundly deaf, also has a technical department. Contact point for many organisations for the deaf.

Breakthrough Trust
The Hall
Peyton Place
London SE10 8RS
853 5661

**British Association for the Hard of
Hearing**
7–11 Armstrong Road
London W3 7JL
743 1110/1353

British Deaf Association
38 Victoria Place
Carlisle, Cumbria, CA1 1HU
0228 48844

**National Association of Deafened
People (NADP)**
60 St Gabriel's Road
London NW2 4SA

National Deaf Children's Society
45 Hereford Road
London W2 5AH
229 9272/4

**National Network of Deaf Students
(NNDS)**
Bulmershe College
Woodlands Avenue
Reading, Berkshire, RG6 1HY
0734 666506

Royal Association in Aid of Deaf People
27 Old Oak Road
London W3 7SL
743 6187

SENSE (National Deaf–Blind and Rubella Association)
311 Grays Inn Road
London WC1X 8PT
278 1005

Sympathetic Hearing Scheme
7–11 Armstrong Road
London W3 7JL
740 4447
Canvasses support for hearing impaired people who find it difficult to hear in public places (e.g. stations, banks, etc.).

Learning Disability

MENCAP (London Bureau)
(Royal Society for Mentally Handicapped Children and Adults)
115 Golden Lane
London EC1
250 4105

MENCAP has three District Officers working on welfare and rights issues covering central, west and east London. The London Division also has an officer for education, training and employment advice; Pathway officers finding work for people taken out of schools in Wandsworth, Islington, Lambeth, Sutton and Barnet; Gateway Clubs organising sport and leisure activities; a Homes Foundation, currently providing residential accommodation in ten boroughs, as well as schemes for the severely handicapped and the very young.

British Institute of Mental Handicap
Wolverhampton Road
Kidderminster
Worcestershire
0562 850251
Conferences and workshops.

Campaign for Mentally Handicapped People
12a Maddox Street
London W1
491 0727
Campaigning organisation encouraging integration.

Children's Aid Team (CATS)
75–77 Granville Road
London N22
888 4189
Information service for mentally handicapped people and their

families. Runs hostels, a twenty-four-hour crisis service, seminars, drama, dance, art and animal therapy.

Children's Legal Centre
20 Compton Terrace
London N1
359 6251
Legal advice.

Jewish Society for the Mentally Handicapped
Stanmore College
Old Church Lane
Stanmore
Middlesex
954 9433

KIDS
80 Waynflete Square
London W10 6UD
969 2817
A personal service for families with children with developmental or learning difficulties, or who are diagnosed as handicapped. Organises home visits by trained visitors to help parents with direct teaching techniques.

National Library for the Handicapped Child
University of London Institute of Education
20 Bedford Way
London WC1H 0AL
636 1500 ext 599
Assists children whose disability affects their ability to read. Prepares materials and adapts ordinary books to make them more accessible. Provides books on tape, filmstrips, slides and reference materials for adults/carers.

Parents in Partnership
c/o 25 Woodnock Road
London SW16 6TZ
Gives a voice to parents of children with special educational needs.

Steiner House
35 Park Road
London NW1
An alternative approach to the treatment of people with mental disabilities based on Anthroposophy (see Chapter 7: Health).

Local Disability Organisations

Disablement Association in the Borough of Barnet
DABB Advice Centre
4 Oakleigh Gardens
Whetstone
London N20
446 6935

Bexley Association of the Disabled
c/o 18 Eversley Avenue
Barnhurst, Kent

Brent Association for Disabled People
154 Harlesden Road
London NW10
451 3822

Bromley Association for the Handicapped
94 Tweedy Road
Bromley
Kent BR1 1RG
464 1238

Disabled in Camden
7 Crowndale Road
London NW1 1TU
387 1466

Croydon Disablement Association
12–18 Lennard Road
Croydon, Surrey

Ealing Association for Disabled People
EADP Centre
Beyham Road
London W13
840 0977

Borough of Enfield Voluntary Association for the Disabled
42 St George's Road
Forty Hill
Enfield
Middlesex
363 4296

Enfield Disablement Information Service
Old Porter's Lodge
Highlands Hospital
World's End Lane
Winchmore Hill
Enfield
360 8151

Greenwich Association for the Disabled
Christchurch Forum
Trafalgar Road
SE10 9EQ
305 2221

Hammersmith and Fulham Action for Disability
The Pavillion
1 Munds Street
London W14
385 2156

Haringey Disability Association
c/o Tottenham Town Hall
Town Hall Approach
London N15 4RY
801 5757

Harrow Association for Disability
The Lodge
64 Pinner Road
Harrow
Middlesex HA1 4HU
427 5569

Havering Association for the Handicapped
1a Woodhall Crescent
Hornchurch RM11 3NN
04024 76554

Hillingdon Disablement Association
St John's Hospital
Kingston Lane
Uxbridge UB8 3PL
0895 31677

Advice and Rights Centre for the Handicapped (ARCH)/Islington Disablement Association
90–92 Upper Street
London N1 0NP
226 0137/359 6535

Kensington and Chelsea Action for Disability
19–27 Young Street
London W8 5EH
937 7073

Kingston-upon-Thames Association for Disabled People
c/o United Reformed Church
Eden Street
Kingston-upon-Thames
Surrey
549 8893

Lambeth Disabled Advice Service
115 Clapham Road
London SW9
582 4352

Lewisham Association for People with Disabilities
67 Engelheart Road
Catford
London SE6 2HN
698 3775

Merton Association for the Disabled
326 London Road
Mitcham, Surrey CR4 3ND
685 1618

Newham Association for the Disabled
Durning Hall
Earlham Grove
London E7
519 8595

Handicapped Help Line (Newham)
c/o Community Links
81 High Street South
London E6 4EJ
472 6652

Redbridge Association for Handicapped People
Bridge House
6 Mildmay Road
Ilford
Essex
514 2703

Redbridge Bridgeline
Telephone Information Service
551 6877

**Richmond-upon-Thames
  Association for the Handicapped**
Secretary
Flat 36, Isabella Court
Kingsmead
Richmond
Surrey, TW10 6JP
940 7061/979 7210

**Southwark Disablement
  Association**
Room 48, Aylesbury Day Centre
Bradenham
Boyson Road
London SE17
701 1391

Sutton Association for the Disabled
Sutton West Day Centre
Robin Hood Lane
Sutton
Surrey
643 6059

Out and About (Tower Hamlets)
Neighbourhood Church
Bruce Road
London E3 3HN
980 3056

**Waltham Forest Association for
  People with Disabilities**
Old School Buildings
1a Warner Road
London E17
509 0812

DIAL Waltham Forest
Disability Resource Centre
Address as above
520 4111

**Wandsworth Disablement
  Association**
1c Yukon Road
London SW12 9PZ
675 6521

**Wandsworth Disablement Advice
  Service**
305 Garrett Lane
London SW18 4DU
870 7437

Disability Action Westminster
41 Chippenham Road
London W9
289 2258

Westminster Information Service
10 Warwick Row
London SW1
630 5994

12

RELIGIOUS AND SPIRITUAL BELIEF

It would be an impossible task in a publication of this size to provide either a full list of all the places of worship in Greater London, or a full description of the relative positions and strengths of all the religions and spiritual disciplines practised in the capital. Suffice to say that all major and many minor world religions and spiritual disciplines have contact points in London, most of which are listed below.

Those who practise certain beliefs often suffer abuse and discrimination as a result. In many cases, this is closely linked with questions of race but inter-religion abuse and the abuse of religion as a concept is also frequently apparent. The first port of call if you suffer discrimination as a result of your religion should perhaps be someone from your own religious community. Otherwise, contact Minority Rights Group, Amnesty International, National Council for Civil Liberties, Commission for Racial Equality (all listed in the chapter entitled Citizens' Rights), a senior person in your school, college or workplace, or a trade union representative.

ADDRESSES

Afro-West Indian United Council of Churches
Caribbean House
Bridport Place
London N1 5DS
729 0986

Anglo-Jewish Association
Woburn House
Upper Woburn Place
London WC1
387 5937

Anthroposophical Society
Rudolf Steiner House
35 Park Road
London NW1
723 4400

Assemblies of God in Great Britain and Northern Ireland
106–114 Talbot Street
Nottingham NG1 5GH
0602 474525
Information on Pentecostal churches in London.

Association of Grace Baptist Churches
139 Grosvenor Avenue
London N5 2NH
226 9140
Information about independent local Baptist churches.

Baha'i Faith
27 Rutland Gate
London SW7
584 2566

Baptist Union/Baptist Union Youth
4 Southampton Row
London WC1
405 9803

Bible Society
Stone Hill Green
West Lea
Swindon SN5 7DG
0793 617381
Christian helpline 6–8pm Monday
0793 511148

British Buddhist Association
11 Biddulph Road
London W9
286 5575

British Council of Churches
Interchurch House
35–41 Lower Marsh
London SE1
620 4444

British Evangelical Council
113 Victoria Street
St Albans,
Herts, AL1 3TJ
0727 55655

Buddhist Society
58 Eccleston Square
London SW1V 1PH
834 5858

Catholic Chaplaincy
111 Gower Street
London WC1
387 6370

Catholic International Students Chaplaincy
802 9673

Catholic Truth Society
38–40 Eccleston Square
London SW1V 1PD
834 4392
Bookshop, publishers, film and video hire.

Centre for Pagan Studies
34 Kincaid Road
Peckham
London SE15
639 9372

Central Church of World Methodism
Westminster Central Hall
Storey's Gate
London SW1H 9NU
222 8010

Chinese Overseas Christian Mission
4 Earlsfield Road
London SW18
870 2251

Christian Community
Temple Lodge
51 Queen Caroline Street
London W6
748 8388
*Bookshop, vegetarian restaurant,
art, counselling, accommodation.*

Christian Feminist Network
131 St George's Road
London SE1

**Church of All Saints Greek
Orthodox Church**
Pratt Street
Camden Town
London NW1

**Church of Christ Scientist (Christian
Science Church)**
108 Palace Gardens Terrace
London W8
221 5650

Church of England
London Diocesan House
30 Causton Street
London SW1
821 9351

Church of England
Diocese of Southwark
94 Lambeth Road
London SE1
928 6637

Church of England Enquiry Centre
Great Smith Street
Dean's Yard
London SW1
222 9011

**Church of Jesus Christ of the Latter
Day Saints**
Visitors' Centre, 64 Exhibition Road
London SW7 2PA
584 8868

Danish Church
5 St Katherine's Precinct
Regent's Park
London NW1
935 7854

Dzogchen Community
29 Jeffery's Street
London NW1
485 3108
Tibetan Buddhism.

**Eagle's Wing Centre for Shamanic
Studies**
58 Westbere Road
London NW2 3RU
435 8174

**Evangelical Alliance and Evangelical
Missionary Alliance**
186 Kennington Park Road
London SE11 4BT
582 0288

Federal Student Islamic Society
38 Mapesbury Road
London NW2 4JD
452 4493
A non-Arab Muslim society.

**Fellowship of Independent
Evangelical Churches**
136 Rosendale Road
London SE21
670 5815

Friends Religious Society (Quakers)
Friends House
Euston Road
London NW1
387 3601

Greek Cathedral Agia Sophia
Moscow Road
London W2 4LQ
229 4710

**Greek Orthodox Metropolis of
Thyatira and Great Britain**
5 Craven Hill
London W2 3EN
881 0789

Guru Granth Gurdawa Sikh Temple
Villiers Road
Southall
574 7700/5609/0037

Hillel House
1–2 Endsleigh Street
London WC1
388 0801
Meeting place for Jewish students.

Hindu Centre
39 Grafton Terrace
London NW5
485 8200

Humanist Association
13 Prince of Wales Terrace
London W8 5PG
937 2341

**International Society for Krishna
  Consciousness**
10 Soho Street
London W1
437 3662

Islamic Cultural Centre
London Central Mosque
146 Park Road
London NW8

Jehovah's Witnesses Headquarters
Watchtower House
The Ridgeway
Mill Hill
London NW7
906 2211

Kokani Muslims
127 Hamilton Road
London NW11 9EG
458 4677

**Lesbian and Gay Christian
  Movement**
BM 6914
London WC1N 3XX
283 5165
Counselling Referral Service: 587
1235
*An ecumenical lesbian and gay
Christian movement, open to all,
regardless of sexual orientation.
'Offering Gay liberation to the
Church and Christ to the Gay
Community.'*

Liberal Jewish Synagogue
152 Londoun Road
London NW8
722 8872

Liu Academy of T'ai Chi Ch'uan
13 Gunnersbury Avenue
London W5
993 2549
*Taoist studies, philosophy and I-
Ching.*

London Buddhist Centre
51 Roman Road
London E2 0HU
981 1255

London Buddhist Vihara
5 Heathfield Gardens
Chiswick
London W4
995 9493

**London Guide to Mind, Body and
  Spirit**
c/o Brainwave Publishers
33 Lorn Road
London SW9
*A comprehensive guide to religious
and spiritual practices, mind and
body therapies.*

London Kagyu Centre
Unit 21F, Perseverance Works
38 Kingsland Road
London E2
609 8951
Tibetan Buddhist group.

London Mennonite Centre
14 Shepherds Hill
London N6 5AQ
340 8775

London Soto Zen Group
23 Westbere Road
London NW2
794 3109

London Sufi Centre
21 Lancaster Road
London W11 1QL
221 3215

London Zen Society
10 Belmont Street
Camden
London NW1
485 9576
Rinzai sect Zen group.

Lutheran Services
St Anne and St Agnes Church
Gresham Street
London EC2V
373 5566

Manjushri London Centre
10 Finsbury Park Road
London N4
359 1394
Tibetan Buddhist.

Muslim Information Service
233 Seven Sisters Road
London N4 4DA
272 5170

Open Gate
6 Goldney Road
Clifton, Bristol
0272 734 5952
*Shamanism and other workshops
held in London and Devon.*

Order of the Cross
10 De Vere Gardens
London W8
937 7012
*Reinterpretation of Christian
teachings to include mystical
dimension of attainment of
Christhood.*

**Pentecostal Church Assemblies of
God**
141 Harrow Road
London W2
286 9261

Protestant Truth Society
184 Fleet Street
London EC4
405 4960
Bookshop and publisher.

Rationalist Press Association
88 Islington High Street
London N1
226 7251

RIGPA Buddhist Meditation Centre
44 St Paul's Crescent
London NW1
485 4342

**Roman Catholic Archdiocese of
Southwark**
Archbishop's House
St George's Road
London SE1
928 2495

**Roman Catholic Archdiocese of
Westminster**
Archbishop's House
Ambrosden Drive
London SW1
834 4717

Russian Orthodox Church
All Saints
Ennismore Gardens
London W6
584 0096

**St Andrew Bobola's Polish Catholic
Church**
1 Leysfield Road
London W12
743 8848

St Peter's Italian Church
4 Back Hill
London EC1

Salvation Army
101 Queen Victoria Street
London EC4P 4EP
236 5222

School of Meditation
158 Holland Park Road
London W11 4UH
603 6116

School of T'ai Chi Ch'uan
5 Tavistock Place
London WC1
459 0764

Scripture Union Bookshop
5 Wigmore Street
London W1H 0AD
493 1851

Sikh Divine Fellowship
132 Eastcote Avenue
Greenford
Middx UB6 0NR
903 7143

**Sikh Cultural Society of Great
  Britain**
88 Mollison Way
Edgware
Middlesex, HA8 5QW
952 1215

**Spiritualist Association of Great
  Britain**
33 Belgrave Street
London SW1
235 3351

**The Greater World Christian
  Spiritualist Association**
3–5 Conway Street
London W1V 5HA

**Study Centre for Christian–Jewish
  Relations**
17 Chepstow Villas
London W11 3DZ
727 3597

Subud House
c/o Richard Rogers
52 Knightsbridge Court
9–16 Sloane Street
London SW1
968 3096
(National Office 0825 872223)
*Started in Indonesia by Bapak
Subuh Sumohadiwidjojo. A
movement bringing together people
of many faiths.*

Theosophical Society
50 Gloucester Place
London W1H 3HJ
935 9261
*Courses and workshops in
theosophy, yoga, meditation.*

United Reformed Church
86 Tavistock Place
London WC1H 9RT
837 7661

United Synagogue
Woburn House
Upper Woburn Place
London WC1
387 4300

University Church of Christ the King
Gordon Square
London WC1
387 0670

Vishwa Hindu Temple
2 Lady Margaret Road
Southall
Middlesex
574 3870

Wadada Educational Magazine
c/o Flat 6
147 Coningham Road
London W12 8BU
740 7115/749 3252
*Promoting understanding of
Rastafarianism.*

Zebra Project
1 Merchant Street
London E3 4LY
980 3745
*Brings together black and white
Christians and aims to combat
racism.*

Zoroastrian Association of Europe
88 Compayne Gardens
London NW6
328 6018

13

SOCIAL SERVICES, BENEFITS AND TAXATION

Welfare benefits and entitlements can be very difficult to understand without help. The rules governing them are often highly complex and inter-related. This chapter provides a brief but disturbing insight into recent experiences of social services users in London, and also an easy to understand general guide to individuals' rights to benefits.

The increasing difficulties of obtaining a hearing from London's hard-pressed Benefits and Social Services Offices are described in the chapter. If it is impossible for you to spend a whole day at the Benefit Office to make your claim (for example), or if your claim office is located out of London and you cannot contact them, an *advice centre* may be able to help you. Benefits and services are your rights, but it can often be very hard to find out exactly what they are.

A vast array of changes has been made in recent years to social rights, including benefit entitlements. As a result more and more people find that one of their most important rights is to free, independent advice and advocacy from advice centres. Advice centres employ trained staff who can help individuals find a way through the maze of what benefits they may claim and what services they may use.

Advice centres can help you make your case clear to the authorities, negotiate on your behalf if you wish, and represent you at appeals. There are many different kinds of advice centre, with different names and offering different kinds of services. You can find out about the ones near you from your local council or library, or from the Federation of Independent Advice Centres, the Greater London Citizens Advice Bureaux Service, or the Law Centres Federation (see Appendix).

Christine Thornton
Management Development Advisor,
Federation of Independent Advice Centres (FIAC),
author of Managing to Advise,
a manual of good practice for advice centres.

The views expressed in the guide are not necessarily those of the Federation of Independent Advice Centres (FIAC).

SOCIAL SERVICES

It would be easy to take the view that social services in London are in a permanent state of crisis. Offices are often closed and there are never enough social workers to deal with all the problems that exist. The turnover of social workers in London is remarkable. In June 1989, the vacancy rate for non-residential social workers in Greater London was 16.4 per cent. A total of 20.1 per cent left jobs within a year. There is a particular shortage of mental health specialists and occupational therapists. Poor pay and high levels of stress, physical violence and verbal abuse are most often cited as reasons for such staff shortages.

The services in London are geared to respond to particular crises such as the recent focus on child abuse after the Cleveland report. This means that other groups such as those with physical disabilities or elderly people are given lower priority. (For details of services available, see also Chapter 2: Children and Young People; Chapter 10: Older People; Chapter 11: People with Disabilities; and Chapter 15: Women.)

A particular problem clear to anyone who has had direct contact with a social services department is the lack of coordination between boroughs coupled with a lack of funds and staff necessary to carry out the functions required. Many social workers or office staff do not have the authority to deal with many of the problems facing them. This inevitably results either in a bottleneck while everybody waits for the availability or directive of a senior officer, or in a mass of red tape.

The government has encouraged social services departments wherever possible to allow people who have been in institutionalised care to return to the community. The number of residential places for mentally ill people, for example, is declining, partly as a result of local councils having government limits placed upon spending on essential areas.

Recently, a woman who had been mentally ill was resettled in a house divided into six flats, two rented to private tenants and four to the neighbouring borough council, which in turn employed a housing association as agents to house people from its long-term waiting list. The woman clearly required supervision. Symptoms of her illness included shouting for long periods, often during the night, either at other residents, passers-by or nobody in particular; throwing furniture around her flat; verbally abusing and physically attacking other tenants.

Despite several visits from the police, the housing association had no powers to find the woman more suitable accommodation since the responsibility lay with the council social services department. Nor did any social workers have the authority to gain access to the flat. After a court hearing the woman was evicted because she had been offered alternative accommodation and refused it. It seems likely that she did not understand that she was in danger of being put on to the streets. She spent several nights on the streets until she was finally taken into hospital.

Nevertheless, despite shortages, cuts and pressures, the London boroughs still manage to offer a range of services to their residents. Boroughs usually offer the following to local residents to some degree depending on available funds: day and residential care for elderly and disabled people; support for vulnerable people in their own homes; residential care and social education for mentally handicapped people; adoption; fostering and residential services for children in care; aids and adaptations to help people live at home; transport schemes for handicapped people; meals on wheels and lunch clubs; holidays; short-term respite care and support for carers. To find out about services in your borough, contact the Social Services Department directly. (See Appendix for borough council addresses and for more details of services available, see Chapter 2: Children and Young People; Chapter 10: Older People; and Chapter 11: People with Disabilities.)

BENEFITS

In the area of welfare benefits, the overall picture is of a steadily declining provision of funds for those who are most in need of help. Over £11 billion has been cut from social security benefits nationally since 1979 and yet people at the top end of the wage scale are receiving massive tax handouts.

After recent changes in the law, under 25s now receive a lower rate of benefit in many cases and 16 and 17 year olds are only entitled to benefits in exceptional cases. Students have already had their right to housing benefit and other financial help reduced and more changes are likely, going hand in hand with cuts in grants and the introduction of loans.

In theory, the system of welfare benefits attempts to prevent poverty as well as alleviating existing need. We pay for these benefits through our taxes. Successive governments, but especially the current one, have not provided adequate funds for the social security system. This has resulted in a visible increase in poverty on the streets of London. In addition, the Department of Social Security (DSS) offices are themselves suffering from government attempts to dismantle the Welfare State and cut jobs in the DSS.

After the 1986 Social Security Act came into force in 1988, the social security benefit system went through a major upheaval. The present government has changed the names and kinds of benefits available as well as eligibility for many of them. Benefits as a whole have been cut and those in most need of assistance are most likely to be worse off as a result. Pensioners, people under 25 (especially those under 18), low-paid workers, mothers/expectant mothers, people with disabilities and the unemployed are all likely to receive less in real terms after the recent reforms.

A particular problem with the new benefit arrangements is a loss of flexibility. For example, somebody with a serious disability on Supplementary Benefit could previously push up his or her income with additional requirements payments and single payments, whereas under Income Support there is a fixed amount for serious disability. This could result in one person with a disability being better off under the new scheme while another loses out.

To make matters worse, benefit offices are regularly understaffed by poorly paid workers, often with insufficient training and no authority for many of the tasks they are called upon to carry out. Waiting for a senior officer causes friction and frustration for officer and claimant alike. The DSS as a whole is underfunded and tied up in petty bureaucracy and as a result often slow and inefficient in the distribution of urgently needed benefits. Clearly, an injection of funds and a reform of the entire system is necessary but with the government attempting to cut back in the field of benefit provision, this seems unlikely.

Benefits are often poorly publicised. The government saves millions of pounds every year on unclaimed benefits. Contact a Citizens Advice Bureau or other advice centre (see Appendix) to ensure you are getting your due. If you suspect you might be eligible for a benefit, claim it. Don't be put off by complicated jargon and regulations. Advice centres employ trained staff who can help you make claims and appeal against wrong decisions.

Benefit rights and eligibility are far too complex to deal with fully in the few pages available here, and I propose to give a small amount of basic information along with a list of organisations to contact for further, more detailed, help. The Child Poverty Action Group's *National Welfare Benefits Handbook* and *Guide to Non-Means-Tested Benefits* are probably the most detailed guides to benefit provision.

NB 1: Unless otherwise stated, the term 'couple' refers only to heterosexual couples, as benefit regulations do not recognise homosexual relationships.

NB 2: If you are not eligible for one benefit, it does not necessarily imply that you are not eligible for other benefits. For instance, if you are unwaged or on a low income you can always apply for Income Support or Housing Benefit. Claim all benefits you think you might be entitled to – it may add up to several.

NB 3: Certain people's immigration status might be threatened by applying for certain benefits. People in this situation should check with a CAB or other advice centre.

Means-tested Benefits

How to claim:
With the exception of the non-means-tested Unemployment Benefit (see p. 301) you should go to your local Department of Social Security benefit office in order to claim benefits. Forms are also available from Post Offices.

Income Support (IS)

Income Support (IS) is an income-related (means-tested) benefit which replaced Supplementary Benefit. It is taxable but only claimants who have other income, such as income from employment, will pay tax. It consists of a system of personal allowances plus flat-rate premiums for certain groups of people, such as people with disabilities, families with dependent children, lone parents and pensioners. Income Support does not depend on National Insurance contributions.

There are basically two groups of people who are entitled to IS: those who receive IS because they are unemployed and available for work, and those who do not have to be available for work. People over 60, single parents, people incapable of work as a result of sickness or disability, people working less than twenty-four hours a week may all be entitled to benefits.

You cannot claim Income Support if you or your partner is working twenty-four or more hours per week. If that is the case you may be eligible for Housing Benefit and/or Family Credit.

The second major test is savings: if you have more than £6,000 in savings you cannot receive IS. If you have between £3,000 and £6,000 your savings will be taken into account in assessing benefit; a 'tariff income' of £1 per week is assumed for every £250 you have over £3,000 (1989 figures).

People under 18 can only claim Income Support in exceptional circumstances. This particularly affects young people coming to live in London. The two broad categories of under 18s who can claim are:

1 People who would not be expected to be available for work, such as single parents or people with a disability.
2 People living away from home for a good reason can get Income Support for a limited period, and perhaps a discretionary hardship payment. Since benefit is only received for a limited period, a common result is that young people are forced on to poorly paid YTS schemes in order to be entitled to any money at all. From the government's point of view this is a positive state of affairs since it improves the unemployment figures.

IS also covers the interest element of mortgage repayments made by owner-occupiers but for people under 60, only 50 per cent is paid for the first sixteen weeks. Claimants will, however, have to pay 20 per cent of rates or Poll Tax (Community Charge) from their personal allowance. (See also section on Community Charge Benefit.)

IS contributes towards personal expenses and meal allowances for people in residential care, but no longer for people living in hostels.

Family Credit

Family Credit is a means-tested, non-taxable benefit for people with one or more children; one or both of the partners working twenty-four or more hours per week but the family income being below a certain level. It is a weekly benefit payable to the mother of a family, or to single parents of either sex.

Family Credit has replaced the Family Income Supplement. In general, families who receive Family Credit will receive more than they did on Family Income Supplement, but the government admits that it is only likely to reach four out of ten of those entitled to it. What is more, the increase is likely to be swallowed up by the cost of school meals – those receiving Family Credit will no longer be entitled to free school meals for their children. Housing Benefit for rent and rates will also be reduced for those receiving Family Credit.

Housing Benefit

This is also a means-tested, non-taxable benefit. If you are not eligible for Family Credit, you may still be eligible for Housing Benefit. To qualify you have to be responsible for payment of rent and/or rates whether as a tenant, subtenant, boarder or owner-occupier. Housing Benefit covers payments for rent and for rates. In some areas, you will have to fill in two separate forms.

A total of £550 million in cuts means that around 1 million people nationally will have had Housing Benefit cut altogether since April 1989 and 5 million people will receive less. Pensioners will be particularly hit because of a new rule stating that anyone with savings over £8,000 will not qualify for Housing Benefit. For savings between £3,000 and £8,000, £1 per week income is assumed for each £250 over £3,000, and is taken into account in calculating benefit.

Furthermore, everyone is forced to pay at least 20 per cent of their rates bill (or of their poll tax bill) out of this reduced benefit. (See also section on Community Charge Benefit below.)

Community Charge Benefit/Rebate

Rebates are payable on personal and collective, but not standard, community charge. The maximum rebate is 80 per cent. People on Income Support are automatically entitled to a maximum rebate. A person can claim a rebate even if s/he has not been informed how much community charge s/he will have to pay. S/he should ask for a claim form from the local authority. People receiving Income Support but not Housing Benefit will be sent a claim form by the DSS.

Clients receiving housing benefit before 1 April 1990 will automatically be assessed for a rebate. The amount will depend on their circumstances and the local level of the community charge. If a local authority does not have enough information, a claim form will be sent. After 1 April, people who begin to receive Housing Benefit will not automatically be assessed; they will have to claim personally.

A person not receiving Housing Benefit or Income Support but who has a low income may be entitled to a partial rebate of the personal community charge. Claim forms from the local authority should in theory be returned before you receive a poll tax bill.

The Social Fund

The Social Fund was introduced in 1988 to replace the former system of single payments and urgent needs payments available for Supplementary Benefit claimants. Payments under the Social Fund are divided into six types under two broad categories.

1 Regulatory Payments

These are governed by regulations and claimants have the right of appeal against negative decisions. If a claimant meets the criteria laid down in the regulations, s/he is entitled to the benefit. The following benefits fall into this category:

(i) *Maternity payments* If you are expecting a baby and are receiving Income Support or Family Credit, you are entitled to a single payment which does not have to be repaid.

(ii) *Funeral expenses* for which you are responsible will be covered if you are receiving Income Support, Family Credit or Housing Benefit, but payments from insurance policies, charities or relatives will be taken into account. The old Death Grant has been abolished.

(iii) *Cold weather payments* may occasionally be paid to people on Income Support, depending on rulings by the Minister at the time of the cold weather.

2 Discretionary Payments

These will only be paid at the discretion of the Social Fund Officer out of a finite budget, with no independent right of appeal (although there is a review procedure in certain circumstances). Claimants might be refused simply because the office in question has gone over budget. The following fall into this category:

(i) *Budget Loans* (interest free) are sometimes allowed to people who have been on Income Support for twenty-six weeks or more and are faced with an urgent need such as a cooker, bedclothes or electricity reconnection. The loan will be repaid by deduction from future Income Support.

(ii) Crisis Loans (interest free) may be available to cover emergency costs resulting from fire or flood, for instance, even to people not receiving benefit. Crisis loans are only given to avoid serious risk to physical or mental health or safety. Unfortunately, an assumption is sometimes made that young people are fit and healthy and not in danger and therefore do not need help, even if they meet the letter of the eligibility requirements. Crisis loans are very hard to get.

(iii) Community Care Grants are available in exceptional cases, for example to reinstate people returning to the community after a stay in institutional care, or to help someone remain in the community rather than going into institutional or residential care.

Overall the Social Fund is likely to mean a cut in claimants' weekly income because it has not fully compensated for the loss of the old single payments system, or for inflation. As a result individuals will be forced to turn to the already overpressed local authority social services departments and charities for help. Many have already turned to commercial money lenders and run up unpayable debts. Even if they accept interest-free Budget or Crisis Loans, the money still has to be paid back.

NB: Income Support and Housing Benefit can be claimed by anyone on a low income (or not working more than twenty-four hours a week), as long as they do not have savings of greater than £8,000 (£6,000 for those on Income Support). Therefore, a person receiving, for example, Severe Disablement Allowance or Invalidity Benefit can also receive Income Support and/or Housing Benefit. You can always apply for Housing Benefit to help with housing costs and Income Support to supplement low income.

Non-Means-Tested Benefits

Non-means-tested benefits have been under attack for some time. Child Benefit, for example, was not increased in line with inflation for a number of years and has now been frozen. Rights to Unemployment Benefit have been restricted. Furthermore, some of these benefits do contain elements of means-testing.

NB: All non-means-tested benefits are counted as extra income in the calculation of Income Support, with the exception of Attendance Allowance and Mobility Allowance (see below).

Unemployment Benefit

In order to qualify for Unemployment Benefit you have to have paid a certain amount of National Insurance Contributions. You should claim the benefit even if you are unsure about your NI record. Once you have registered as 'available for work' your NI record will be assessed to decide whether you are entitled to Unemployment Benefit or Income Support. Unemployment Benefit can be paid for a maximum of one year.

Additional payments may be available for a spouse who is not working or a child (if you are over pension age).

The 1989 Social Security Act made major changes to the regulations relating to availability for work. As well as proving that you are available for work, it is now necessary to demonstrate that you are 'actively seeking employment'. The Act also introduced the 'permitted period', during which people can look for specific types of work. After this time, they are not allowed to be so selective. A claimant must prove that s/he has 'good cause' for turning down a job.

When a person signs on, s/he will be given a leaflet explaining the rules on being 'Available for and Actively Seeking Work'. The rules have become much stricter in this area and a person may now be asked at any time to show that they have been seeking work in any given week. Claimants must therefore keep job advertisements they have responded to, letters from employers, and record or take copies of their application letters. Claimants must also be able to show in which week job applications were made.

Unemployed people will have to face regular interviews to assess their job seeking. During such interviews, they are likely to be offered a job vacancy or a place on a scheme. This might happen when the claimant first signs on and the claimant is interviewed by a 'New Client Advisor', or it might be after six months of unemployment when they are called for an interview by a 'Restart' counsellor. However, it could happen at any time a Claimant Advisor decides it is necessary to talk to the claimant.

At each counselling interview, including the initial meeting with a New Client Advisor, the claimant will have to fill in a

UB671 form asking questions about their background and job-seeking activities.

If the 'permitted period' for seeking a specific type of job has expired (the length of this period depends on the claimant's usual occupation and accustomed rate of pay and ranges from one to thirteen weeks), the claimant will 'be encouraged to consider jobs which are less familiar or less well paid if the work is otherwise appropriate to their skills and capabilities'. They may also be 'encouraged to consider training or going into a Jobclub'.

There may be circumstances when a claimant will find it difficult to show that s/he has been actively seeking work, such as when there has been a death in the family. Nevertheless, Nicholas Scott, the Social Security Minister responsible for the new legislation has said 'short periods of absence (from home) perhaps due to family emergency, can be catered for within the normal arrangements. Provided the claimant is available for work, he should have time during the week to undertake some job search to satisfy the condition.' Two weeks in a year are allowed to a person to be excused from seeking a job, provided the Unemployment Benefit Office is informed, and provided the person remains available for work.

If a claimant's job-seeking activities are not deemed to be adequate they will be warned in writing that they might be subject to a benefit penalty. The warning letter will outline five steps that they should take in order actively to seek work. They must then attend an 'Actively Seeking Review' interview two to four weeks later. If the claimant has failed to take the five steps, benefit may be suspended for one or two weeks. Nicholas Scott described this as a 'shock to the system' to ensure that claimants look for work. After two more weeks, during which the case is referred to adjudication, the claimant will be reassessed and if the counsellor feels that the claimant is still failing actively to seek work, warning will be given that benefit is at risk.

If benefit is suspended, Unemployment Benefit will be stopped and Income Support reduced by up to 40 per cent of the personal allowance. If the claimant is not receiving Income Support, s/he can apply on the grounds of hardship and it may then be paid at the reduced rate.

As for training schemes, the government has claimed that it does not wish to make them compulsory. These include Employment Training (ET), Jobclubs or Restart Courses.

However, the 'Actively Seeking Work' requirement will force many claimants into such schemes. Although claimants will not be directly forced on to such a scheme they will be able to prove that they are 'actively seeking work' by doing so.

If you are sacked from your job for misconduct or have to give up work for some reason or 'leave work voluntarily' you are likely to be disqualified from Unemployment Benefit for up to a maximum of six months, but you can appeal. If you have contributed in any way to losing your job, the maximum applies. Tribunals can and often do reduce this period. An advice centre (CAB, Law Centre or other agency – see Appendix) can help you prepare your case and represent you at the hearing. However, you may still be able to get Income Support which will be payable at a reduced rate.

The result of the new regulations is that the government improves the appearance of the unemployment figures, especially the long-term unemployed statistics, because people are either disqualified from benefit or given short-term jobs or training schemes. Meanwhile, the unemployed person is subject to a system of constant policing that can only damage self-esteem and lead to constant humiliation and exploitation rather than a satisfactory job.

How to claim:
To claim Unemployment Benefit you should go to your local Unemployment Benefit Office (UBO) on the first day you are unemployed (Post Offices, libraries, telephone directories, CABs and other advice centres all have addresses of UBOs). Take along your P45 form if you have one, a note of your National Insurance number, and some means of identification. Details and/or proof of your address and of any savings may also be asked for.

People under 18 must also register at a careers office or Job Centre. The 'availability for work' rules force many young people to accept places on YTS schemes, especially those people who have come to London seeking work and need to have a regular income in order to find a place to live, thus avoiding the familiar and increasingly common spiral that leads to homelessness and vagrancy.

Anyone under 25 is now considered the responsibility of their parents in welfare benefit terms and therefore receives

304 LONDON: A LIVING GUIDE

less money in the government's attempts to cut the benefit bill.

If the claimant is unable to manage on the income received from Unemployment Benefit s/he should also claim Income Support and/or Housing Benefit. Once the period of Unemployment Benefit has run out, Income Support and/or Housing Benefit can still be claimed.

NB: Most areas have Unemployed Centres that are listed in the local telephone directory or which can be contacted through your borough council offices, Trades Council, Citizens Advice Bureau or other advice centre (see Appendix). They can give you advice and information on all topics relating to unemployment, counselling, voluntary work, etc.

Statutory Sick Pay and Sickness Benefit

If you become ill while employed and earning more than a certain amount per week you should be entitled to Statutory Sick Pay (SSP). SSP covers any period of illness up to twenty-eight weeks after which Invalidity Benefit can be paid, providing you have paid enough NI contributions. Some people are not entitled to SSP, e.g. people on short-term contracts, people on strike, people who are self-employed or those on a low income. If you are not entitled to SSP you may still be entitled to sickness benefit (SB) (see below).

Invalidity and Disability Benefits

(i) Invalidity Benefit

A person will qualify for Invalidity Benefit if s/he has been claiming SSP or Sickness Benefit for twenty-eight weeks and at the beginning of that period has satisfied the conditions for sickness benefit. In order to continue receiving Invalidity Benefit, the claimant must show that s/he is unable to work because of sickness or disability by sending medical certificates to the local Department of Social Security.

(ii) Severe Disablement Allowance

If you are unable to work because of sickness, disability, industrial injury or disease for twenty-eight weeks *and* are not eligible for invalidity benefit *and* have lived in the UK for twenty-four of the last twenty-eight weeks *and* ten of the last twenty years *and* are over 16 and under pensionable age *and* pass a disablement test, you are entitled to receive this benefit. No NI contributions are needed.

(iii) Industrial Disablement Benefit

People with a disability caused by an accident at work or an industrial disease, including accidents while travelling in the course of work, are entitled to this benefit. Young people aged 13–16 can also claim. Self-employed people do not qualify. No NI contributions are needed. The amount to which you are entitled depends on the degree of disablement. Extra allowances can be paid on top of this benefit:

Reduced Earnings Allowance: (see below).

Constant Attendance Allowance: Paid to those who are so seriously disabled that they need constant care and attention and who are getting 100 per cent Disablement Benefit. It is paid at different rates dependent on the amount of attendance needed.

Exceptionally Severe Disablement Allowance: Paid to those who get Constant Attendance Allowance at a higher rate where the need for attendance is likely to be permanent.

Invalidity Pension: (see above). Can be paid on top of maximum disablement benefit.

(iv) Reduced Earnings Allowance

Paid to people who cannot earn as much as they could before a work-related illness or disablement occurred and who are assessed by the DSS as having a disablement of 1 per cent or more. However, people retiring after April 1989 will find REA replaced by a new retirement allowance which will be worth a good deal less. No NI contributions are needed and it is paid until the claimant retires.

(v) Invalid Care Allowance

Can be claimed by women aged 16–60 and men aged 16–65 spending at least thirty-five hours a week caring for a person with a disability who is getting Attendance Allowance or Constant Attendance Allowance. No NI contributions are needed.

(vi) Attendance Allowance

This can be claimed by people aged 2 and over who have attendance needs, such as help with washing, dressing, eating, using the toilet. Attendance Allowance is not payable to a claimant living in residential care, hospital or accommodation where costs of care are covered by public funds.

The claimant must have been in the UK for six of the last twelve months and normally live in the UK and be in the UK at the time the claim is made. This allowance has two rates: those who need care day *and* night and those who need care day *or* night. It is paid for as long as the claimant requires care. This may be for a fixed period or for life.

Attendance Allowance is payable on top of all other benefits. It is a difficult benefit to get but appeals against the DSS to pay it are often successful, particularly when independent advice is sought beforehand.

(vii) Mobility Allowance

Mobility Allowance can be claimed by people over 5 and not more than 66, provided they qualified before the age of 65 *and* are virtually unable to walk *and* are likely to be in this position for at least a year. In addition, you must have lived twelve of the last eighteen months in Britain, *and* normally live here *and* live here at the time of claiming. No NI contributions are needed. It is paid for a fixed period or until the age of 80, unless the claimant has given up a DSS vehicle, in which case s/he will receive the allowance for life.

NB: Unlike the rest of the non-means-tested benefits,

Attendance Allowance and Mobility Allowance are *not* taken into account when calculating Income Support. Indeed, eligibility for one of these two benefits may act as a passport to one of the Income Support Special Premiums.

The Disability Alliance (see p. 315) produce an excellent publication entitled the *Disability Rights Handbook*, available from their office.

Maternity Benefits

There are two kinds of weekly maternity benefit: Statutory Maternity Pay, which is payable to women who are in employment and whose earnings are above a certain level; and Maternity Allowance, which is payable to women unable to get SMP. The Maternity Grant no longer exists. As a result of the change in maternity benefits, around 100,000 women receive less benefit.

(i) Statutory Maternity Pay (SMP)

SMP is paid by your employer at two different rates; the higher rate, 90 per cent of your weekly pay is paid for six weeks provided you have worked at least two years for your current employer as of fifteen weeks before the baby is due, and for at least sixteen hours a week. These six weeks are followed by twelve weeks paid at the lower rate. If you have worked for between twenty-six weeks and two years, all eighteen weeks will be paid at the lower rate (about 35 per cent). Tax and NI are payable on SMP. In order to claim SMP you must stop working by the sixth week before the baby is expected, although it can be paid from the eleventh week before the baby is due.

(ii) State Maternity Allowance (SMA)

Payable for eighteen weeks including the six weeks before the baby is due. You will receive SMA if you are not entitled to SMP and are not disqualified for some other reason.

(iii) Social Fund Maternity Payment (see p. 299)

Child Benefit

A tax-free benefit payable in respect of all children under 16 or under 19 if in full-time secondary education (not further or higher education). It is usually paid every four weeks. An additional amount is payable to single parents. It is counted as extra income in the calculation of Income Support. Child Benefit was not increased in line with inflation for several years in the 1980s and is now frozen. The Child Poverty Action Group in particular have campaigned long and hard to have the Child Benefit set at a realistic level. It is possible that the government may move to make Child Benefit a means-tested benefit and its future is far from safe.

If you have taken an orphan child into your family for whom you are entitled to claim Child Benefit, you may also be entitled to an additional Guardian's Allowance.

One-parent Benefit

An extra payment sometimes available to lone parents.

Widows' Benefits

Widows under the age of 60 might be entitled to one of three benefits: Widow's Payment, Widowed Mother's Allowance, Widow's Pension. Widow's Payment will be received whatever the claimant earns. The others will be reduced according to your level of income from other sources.

Retirement Pension

Men approaching the age of 65 and women approaching 60 should make sure of their right to a pension even if they are not planning to retire immediately. A form should be sent from the Department of Social Security in advance of your sixty-fifth/sixtieth birthday which you should complete immediately.

Retirement Pension has three basic elements: Basic Pension, depending on National Insurance contributions, State Earnings Related Pension Scheme (SERPS) dependent on earnings since

April 1978 (many people have now opted out of SERPS and taken up an occupational or personal pension scheme), and Graduated Pension, derived from contributions paid above a certain minimum between 1961 and 1975.

Since October 1989 Retirement Pension has become payable at the age of 60 (women) or 65 (men) whether the claimant has retired or not. That is, the claimant can continue to work and earn money without this affecting her/his retirement pension.

APPEALS

If you are dissatisfied with what you have been awarded for any benefit you have claimed, contact a Citizens Advice Bureau or other advice agency (see Appendix), or a trade union representative to help you make an official appeal to the DSS or Department of Employment. It is very important to appeal; a very high number of people who are entitled to benefit get turned down on their first application. An appeal must be made within three months of the date on the letter from the DSS giving the decision.

FRAUD/FALSE INFORMATION

When claiming a benefit, always read the leaflets and forms carefully. Officially, you can be charged if you knowingly give false information.

For example, when claiming Unemployment Benefit remember that the form asks whether you are doing any paid or unpaid work; this is to find out whether you are actually available for work. If you are doing even a small amount of voluntary work it is possible that you will be penalised if you cannot prove your availability for work.

The forms and leaflets tend to put the onus on the claimant to prove that s/he is eligible for a benefit. For instance, you may even be considered to be cohabiting if an inspector decides that your food or toiletries are shared, especially if a male and a female are sharing accommodation.

OTHER PROBLEMS

Racism

In order to claim Income Support you have to pass a residence test and/or have immigration status. Therefore, some immigrants can only gain access to benefits by putting themselves at risk of being reported to the Home Office.

The Social Fund has now become a discretionary benefit and like all other discretionary benefits, its application is open to abuse and personal prejudices, even unconscious prejudices.

Administration of Benefits

In its wisdom, the Department of Social Security has decided to relocate London benefit administration offices to places like Wigan, Glasgow and Belfast. So far Ealing, Acton and Notting Hill have lost their benefit offices and the others will follow over the next couple of years. All processing and calculation will now take place using a computerised system in a remote location.

From now on claimants will only be able to speak to the person dealing with their claim by phone. Clearly, this will discriminate against those who have literacy problems or those for whom English is not the first language. Even if an interpreter is provided (it has been suggested that a three-way telephone conversation might take place, with the interpreter in a third location !) there will be no face to face contact between claimant and administrator. The administrator will no longer have any local knowledge or feeling for the kinds of problems experienced in a particular part of London.

There will still be a local social security 'branch office' but the person to whom a claimant speaks in this office will have no responsibility for their claim. The branch office will have a free phone for contacting the relevant office.

TAXATION

Basic Types of Personal Taxation

(a) Income Tax

The most common tax on incomes, charged on earnings, occupational pensions and most social security benefits. Most people pay income tax on the PAYE (Pay As You Earn) scheme, whereby tax is deducted automatically from pay before we receive it.

PAYE for London is usually dealt with in offices a long way away, such as Manchester, Southampton or Shipley, but there are PAYE Enquiry Offices all over London and they can be found in the telephone directory.

(b) Capital Gains Tax

A tax on large profits from selling property or goods, over and above income tax.

(c) Inheritance Tax

From 18 March 1986 most gifts made during a person's lifetime are not taxable. If the gift was made within seven days of death it will be taxable. This replaces the old Capital Transfer Tax.

For information on how tax is worked out, tax allowances, taxable types of income, tax relief and rebates and all other tax-related problems, contact your local Tax Enquiry Office, Citizens Advice Bureau or other advice agency (see Appendix).

The Poll Tax

The Community Charge or 'Poll Tax' is a system of local taxation due to replace domestic rates charged by local authorities on 1 April 1990. Most people over 18 will be obliged to pay the charge.

Many people are opposed to the Poll Tax, claiming it is a return to a system of taxation last seen in the 1300s, where every individual pays the same amount regardless of ability to pay. Local councils, political parties and community-based pressure groups have organised anti-poll tax campaigns. It is widely seen as an unfair, unjust and undemocratic charge which will gravely damage the interests of the community and the poorest within it.

Basic objections are as follows. As a rule it is those who are already in the highest wage-earning bracket who stand to gain most from the introduction of the Poll Tax, since they will be paying the same as people much less well off, and certainly much less than they would have been paying in rates.

Those most likely to be worse off are large families or people living in small, poor quality or crowded accommodation. It is a sad fact that those families forced by other forms of discrimination (in employment and in housing), namely ethnic minorities, are the most likely, though by no means the only, people to be living in such accommodation. This housing tends to be found in poorer areas where local social services expenditure, and therefore the rates, are higher. Thus the Poll Tax bill will be correspondingly higher and more poverty will be added to existing hardship and racial discrimination.

What is more, control will be moving from the local authorities to central government, once again undermining local democracy.

Quite apart from the huge expense involved in registering, checking and collecting, the Poll Tax represents a tremendous potential invasion of basic rights to privacy. Election registers will be used to check who has not registered for the Community Charge. This will encourage poorer people in particular to refrain from registering for elections so as to avoid paying a charge they cannot afford. (And yet it may well become an offence to avoid electoral registration.) Furthermore, there will be legal consultation between local authorities across the country and cross-checking with water, gas and electricity suppliers, the vehicle licensing office, libraries, DSS and concessionary bus/train pass application lists.

Even people receiving Income Support or Housing Benefit will have to pay at least 20 per cent of the charge. Others who will suffer from the new regulations will be young people saving for a deposit on a mortgage or older people with savings, since savings will be taken into account when calculating any possible rebates. It is also likely that the government will eventually recoup unpaid Poll Tax bills from people on welfare benefits by making deductions from benefit payments.

In a nutshell, the Poll Tax will hit hardest those who can least afford to pay and will lead to potential infringements of personal rights. The majority of people will be paying a greater amount in Poll Tax than they did in rates.

There are three kinds of Poll Tax:

1. Personal Community Charge

A flat rate payable by individuals aged 18 or over, unless exempt for one of the reasons listed below, and who have their only or main home in the local authority area. The flat rate is set by the local authority. Married or cohabiting couples pay the tax as individuals, but each partner in a heterosexual relationship is liable for the other's payment.

2. Standard Community Charge

A flat rate paid by owners of second homes not used as a permanent home by someone else.

3. Collective Community Charge

Payable by owners or landlords of property where residents only stay for a short time, or where it is too difficult to collect a personal community charge, such as short-stay hostels, HMOs or lodging houses.

Those exempt from the charge are: people under 18, people over 18 still covered by Child Benefit, residents in treatment hostels (e.g. drug or alcohol abuse hostels), resident hospital patients, residents of residential care homes, people with severe mental handicap, convicted prisoners and prisoners on remand, foreign diplomats, members of religious communities such as monks and nuns, homeless people with nowhere to live, certain care workers, residents of certain crown buildings, residents of some emergency short-stay accommodation such as Salvation Army hostels.

Students will be liable for 20 per cent of the poll tax bill, but will receive no rebate.

At each address, one person will be assumed as a 'responsible person' who will be responsible for filling in Poll Tax forms and for payment of the charge. A Community Charge Register will be compiled by each local authority.

Rebates will be payable to certain people such as those on Income Support. The maximum rebate is 80 per cent but a

Citizens Advice Bureau or other advice agency will provide more detailed information (see Appendix).

Failure to provide requested information or deliberately providing false information can result in a fine. (Currently, £50 for a first offence and £200 for each subsequent failure to provide requested information.)

Community Charge Benefit

See above under 'Means-Tested Benefits'.

Campaign Against the Poll Tax Resource and Information Centre
60b St George's Road
London SE1 6ET
928 7636 or 219 6566

Poll Tax Forum
1–5 Bath Street
London EC1V 9QQ
A consortium of larger voluntary groups opposed to the Poll Tax.

ADDRESSES

Action (A Voice for Long-term Unemployed People)
100 Park Village East
London NW1 3SR
387 2171
Working for and with the long-term unemployed to find new approaches and solutions to long-term unemployment.

Action for Benefits
124–130 Southwark Street
London SE1 0TU
928 9671
Campaigns for a fairer and improved benefit system. Run by a steering group from organisations such as trade unions, SHAC, Shelter, Low Pay Unit. Not an advice service to individuals.

Age Concern
54 Knatchbull Road
London SE5 9QY
737 3456
Information and advice on benefits for older people.

Bootstrap Enterprises
18 Ashwin Street
London E8 3DL
254 0775

Helps unemployed people create their own jobs in workers' coops. Workshops, loans, business training.

British Pensioners and Trade Unions Action Association
Norman Dodd's House
315 Bexley Road
Erith, Kent
0747 61802

Campaign for Work
45 Cholmley Park
London N6 5EL
341 7771
Campaigns to encourage positive action on unemployment.

Central London Social Security Advisers Forum
Basement
37–40 Great Pultney Street
London W1R 3DE
287 5111
Information for social security advisers and agencies. Do not usually deal with individual public inquiries.

CHAR (The Housing Campaign for Single People)
5–15 Cromer Street
London WC1H 8LS
833 2071
Tend not to deal with individual cases.

Child Poverty Action Group
4th Floor
1–5 Bath Street
London EC1V 9PY
253 3406
Reports, researches and campaigns on benefits, welfare and poverty, especially with relation to children and families.

Church Action with the Unemployed
Holywell Centre
1 Phipp Street
London EC2A 4PS
729 1434
Encourages and helps churches to work with the unemployed.

Commission for Racial Equality
10–12 Allington Street
London SW1E 5EH
828 7022

Department of Employment
(Public Enquiry Office)
Caxton House
Tothill Street
London SW1H 9NF
273 6969

Department of Social Security
266 Euston Road
London NW1 3DN

DSS Free Advice Line
0800 666555
For general information on benefits.

Disability Alliance
25 Denmark Street
London WC2H 8NJ
240 0806
Information on many areas. Produce an excellent guide entitled Disability Rights Handbook.

Employment Institute
Southbank House
Black Prince Road
London SE1 7SJ
735 0777
Promotes study and debate about methods of reducing unemployment. Publishes a number of related leaflets.

Equal Opportunities Commission
Overseas House
Quay Street
Manchester M3 3HN
061 833 9244

Federation of Claimants Unions
296 Bethnal Green Road
London E2
739 4173
Will give you the address of your local claimants union, who will in turn give you advice and information on social security and related topics.

Gingerbread
35 Wellington Street
London WC2E 7BN
240 0953
Support, advice, information and social activities for lone parents.

Greater London Association for Disabled People
336 Brixton Road
London SW9 7AA
274 0107
Information on many subjects including benefits for people with disabilities.

Help the Aged
16–18 St James's Walk
London EC1R 0BE
253 0253

Low Pay Unit
9 Upper Berkeley Street
London W1
262 7278
Investigates, publicises, advises and campaigns on low pay, poverty and related issues.

Maternity Alliance
15 Britannia Street
London WC1X 9JP
*Campaigns for better health care,
social and financial support for
parents to be and young babies and
their families.*

**National Council for Civil Liberties
(Liberty)**
21 Tabard Street
London SE1 4LA
403 3888

**National Council for One-Parent
Families**
255 Kentish Town Road
London NW5 2LX
267 1361

SHAC (London Housing Aid Centre)
189a Old Brompton Road
London SW5 0AR
373 7276

**Shelter – National Campaign for the
Homeless**
157 Waterloo Road
London SE1 8XF
633 9377

Social Security Leaflets Unit
PO Box 21
Stanmore
Middlesex HA7 1AY
*Provide information leaflets on all
social security benefits. These can
also be picked up at DSS offices,
Post Offices, Citizens Advice
Bureaux and Independent Advice
Centres (see Appendix).*

Unemployed Workers Centres
can be contacted through your local
Trades Council (see telephone
directory).

Unemployment Unit
9 Poland Street
London W1V 3DG
734 5948
*Promotes awareness of problems
facing the unemployed, particularly
long-term and recurrently
unemployed people and their
families. Publishes bulletins,
statistics and briefings.*

Youthaid
9 Poland Street
London W1V 3DG
439 8523
*Studies effects of youth
unemployment and campaigns for
its alleviation and reduction.
Produces information to help the
young unemployed.*

Unions

**Civil and Public Services
Association**
160 Falcon Road
London SW11 2LN
924 2727

**NALGO (National and Local
Government Officers Association)**
1 Mabledon Place
London WC1H 9AJ
388 2366

**National Union of Civil and Public
Servants**
124–130 Southwark Street
London SE1 0TU
928 9671

National Union of Students
Mandela House
461 Holloway Road
London N7 6LJ
272 8900

**National Union of Students –
London**
University of London Union
Malet Street
London WC1G 1HY
631 3541/637 1181

Trades Union Congress
Congress House
Great Russell Street
London WC1 3LS
636 4030

14

TRANSPORT

On an average weekday in London, the Department of Transport
(DTp) calculates, there are 8.3 million car journeys (but only
166,000 car commuters into Central London), 2.3 million bus
journeys, 8.3 million walking journeys (over 50 yards), 1.1
million 'other' journeys, which include cyclists, and 2.1 million
rail journeys. The last figure seems strangely low, for London
Underground say they carry some three million passengers a day,
and increasing, while the DTp's own 1987 Roads White Paper
put the figure for rail journeys (BR and Underground) at 3.5
million. Seven million of these journeys are for work; 15.1
million are non-work journeys.

We all know the effects; crowded roads where traffic crawls
slower and slower, subject to 'superjams' which may last ten
hours and gridlock an area 6–7 miles across; crammed rush-hour
trains where commuters may stand all the way from Gatwick or
Woking, where if you want space to breathe you may have to let
five tube trains go past, where the barriers at Victoria and Angel
stations must be closed to incoming passengers to prevent a
Hillsborough style crush on the platforms beneath.

Equally, we know the effects on our homes and neighbour-
hoods of the pressure of through traffic for which our local
shopping centre is simply an annoying bottleneck, our quiet
residential street a speedy 'rat-run' short-cut. We know that the
soil in our garden is too loaded with heavy metals for us to grow
vegetables safe to eat, we would not dream of hanging washing
outside to grow grey in the diesel particulates from passing lorries
or buses. We may even have found the fine black soot of diesel
particulates coating the inside of windows kept closed against
traffic noise and dust.

It isn't as if no one's doing anything about it; indeed Transport 2000 last year counted up to twenty-five major transport or transport-related developments going on in London, all run by different bodies with little evidence that any were taking into account the effects of the others; Channel Tunnel rail link, King's Cross redevelopment, Canary Wharf and other docklands, a possible light rail system around Croydon, Central London Rail Study, four major 'corridor assessment studies', and so on. The DTp, in response to critics, has issued a 'Transport for London Strategy' and formed a London coordinating unit. But doubts remain as to whether it is looking at the right problems, let alone coming up with the right solutions. A dead giveaway is the observation that despite the (surprising?) fact that as many journeys are made by walking as by car, pedestrians get just thirteen lines out of the twenty-seven page report.

Building major radial roads is no solution to London's transport problems, ministers have acknowledged. But for orbital journeys, where public transport is poor, major road building may be needed. Yet when the consultants conducting the four orbital corridor 'Assessment Studies' asked local people what they perceived as the major transport problems in their areas, the answers were overwhelmingly: too much through traffic funnelled on to their local roads, poor public transport. What they wanted was more frequent and better local public transport services, and traffic restraint.

Public transport improvements are needed, ministers acknowledged, and commissioned the Central London Rail Study which recommended new lines to relieve central area tube congestion, but passengers must bear the costs through fares. Only for 'non-user benefits', such as relief to road congestion, and perhaps pollution and accident reductions, might public grants be made. Quantifying the social and environmental benefits of public transport, together with similarly quantifying the social and environmental costs imposed by motor traffic, is to be welcomed. As other countries recognise, efficient and attractive public transport is essential infrastructure, necessary to the health of a city.

The arguments that an integrated, environmentally sound transport policy should encourage public transport, walking and cycling while restraining motor traffic have hinged on the assumption that at present car use imposes costs which motorists do not pay: pollution, accidents (500 road deaths a year in

London, 50,000 serious injuries); land-take for roads and parking; noise, smell, and dirt; time demanded to escort or drive children to school because the roads are so dangerous; loss of freedom to children or old people who can't go out because of traffic danger; delays to pedestrians; one-third of walking time spent waiting for a chance to cross the road; damage to gas, water, electricity pipes and cables. Simply, cars are an extravagant mode of transport, in energy used, space occupied, and use of raw materials.

How can we solve the massively complicated transport problems of the 'megapolis'? Reducing the need to travel, by encouraging location of facilities like shops, schools and medical centres close to the people they serve or at public transport foci is a basic preventive step. Consolidating local facilities into giant out-of-town hypermarkets or regional hospitals may serve internal administrative costs, but it imposes extra travel costs of time, fuel or fares on those who must come from further to use it.

As individuals, we can avoid unnecessarily long trips, especially at peak hours, and realise the value of local shops. Hypermarket prices may look cheaper, but what is the cost of the petrol and time taken to drive there, the land (perhaps taken out of green space) occupied by it and its parking area? How much do you value having neighbourhood shops, open for those perhaps rare times you do want to use them, rather than boarded up? More local employment available also reduces the number of people having to commute long hours and distances at peak hours when travel imposes most costs on the system, and the person travelling. Transport isn't an end in itself, but a connection, a means of getting somewhere, for some activity. We can't solve transport problems in isolation from the activities and locational patterns that produce travel demands.

We can look outside London for hopeful examples. Increasingly, European cities show us the possibilities held out by 'traffic calming' for residential and suburban streets, with the most densely packed city centres going 'car-free'. We see patches of these 'streets for people' around London: brick paving and street landscaping around the Covent Garden/Soho area, suburban centres like Woolwich, Harrow, almost every local authority in the country seems to have at least one pedestrianised showpiece high street. But most of our roads remain traffic-choked, dangerous and far from pleasant. In Europe, high quality, low fare public transport ensures that clearing the streets of motor traffic actually makes it easier to get about, in the cleaner, more attractive centres. Not surprisingly, local shops and business boom. As environmentalists have always said: good environment is good economics.

Judith Hanna
Assistant Director, Transport 2000

GENERAL INFORMATION

As Judith Hanna's introduction shows, traffic can turn our environment into a nightmare. Congestion makes conditions worse for everyone whether they have a car or not. Mechanised transport causes pollution, wastes fuel and land. The programme of road building in London is gradually eroding the countryside surrounding London, not to mention the damage it is doing to parks, woodlands and buildings in Greater London itself.

The road-building programme is based on the fact that we rely on the least energy efficient forms of transport, namely cars and lorries which use up fuel reserves and increase dependence on oil. Declines in public transport quality and provision have forced up both fares and car ownership. Unpleasant road conditions discourage cyclists and pedestrians are constantly at risk.

Clearly, things must improve. There should be genuine public participation in transport decision-making. There should be reliable and accurate information on public transport services which must themselves be improved. The transport of freight should where possible be transferred to rail or water. Location of industry could contribute to this. Road safety should be a political priority with special attention to services for cyclists and pedestrians.

A constant theme in London's transport policy-making is the incredible lack of public accountability. Local people, vulnerable groups such as people with a disability, elderly people, women and young people, all feel they have little say in the formulation of policies that directly affect them. In the words of 'The Big Choke', a report by Transport and Environment Studies (TEST) on approaches to transport provision in London: 'The disposition of housing, jobs, schools, shopping and support services should determine transport provision – not the other way round. In other words, we should decide how we want to live first, and what we want to have within easy reach, before deciding on transport hardware – roads, rail, footways and cycleways and so on.'

What's more these decisions should be made by those who will be using or affected by their outcome. Public inquiries, when they happen, are marked by devious tactics from the DTp, banning certain representative groups from participating and by civil servants whose task appears to be to hinder rather than to help. Furthermore, it is the DTp that takes the final decision on its own plans.

ROADS AND ROAD TRAVEL

In 1984, the Department of Transport embarked upon four London Road Assessment Studies, on the South Circular; in West London; in East London between the A1 in Islington and the A102 Tower Hamlets and Hackney; and in South London in the A23 corridor, focusing on links to the M25. They have been the cause of resentment, opposition and campaigning ever since they were made public in 1988.

Up to 20,000 homes all over London are affected by the studies, either through threat of damage or because the planned roads will lower the value and desirability of the properties and cause stress and worry to the tenants.

Nevertheless, the studies provided some embarrassing information for the DTp. To quote from the West London Study, 'There was virtually no acceptance by residents in any district that commuters or heavy commercial traffic had no option but to pass through residential districts. It was generally felt that more commuters should use public transport and that freight should be carried on roads which by-passes built-up areas.' This was not what the DTp wanted to hear and therefore has apparently been largely ignored.

ILEA estimated that more than 250 education premises would be at risk from the schemes and the horrendous threats to London's green spaces is covered in Chapter 6: Green London. More than 100 local protest groups have grown out of the protests against DTp plans to improve 'orbital movement' and serve 'developing areas', as well as supposedly relieving congestion.

The DTp is renowned for its bias towards road traffic and road building as opposed to public transport improvements. In February 1986, in London, the DTp employed 86 staff on highways policy and programmes, 142 on highways contracts and maintenance, 182 on highways engineering and 176 on traffic and Greater London roads. Only 22 were employed to cover London's public transport (and that of the other metropolitan authority areas). The powerful 'road lobby' consisting of road builders, car manufacturers, oil companies, lorry operators and motoring clubs has tremendous influence in the DTp. (It is worth noting, though, that members of motoring organisations are often involved in protests against road plans. There is no consultation with the membership on the subject of policy.)

Many, including Friends of the Earth, point out that new roads will only suck in more traffic and worsen an already massive congestion problem. All London boroughs, no matter what political colour, have agreed that improved public transport would be preferable and would encourage people off the roads, thus easing congestion far more effectively than building more roads.

The example of the M25 has clearly shown that new roads do not necesarily improve congestion. Parts of the road designed to take 80,000 vehicles a day are faced with up to 130,000 and the supposedly faster route is becoming more and more congested as more people are encouraged to use it. Too many access roads, especially in the Surrey stockbroker belt, were a temptation to local traffic.

Sean O'Neill in *City Limits* magazine (11 May 1989) outlined other common opinions held both by transport experts and by campaigners against government plans. If tax subsidies were removed from company cars (80 per cent of morning rush hour cars are company cars) at least £800 million would be saved; enough to create a major system of bus lanes and to halve bus fares. By contrast, in France it is public transport that is eligible for tax concessions because of the wider benefits it brings to towns and cities. Higher penalties for illegal parking would prevent hold-ups and obstructions.

Most people entering central London come by public transport – 921,000 per day – with BR taking 421,000, London Underground 381,000 and buses and taxis 119,000. Cars bring in only 166,000 yet cause the most congestion. Oxford Street is used by more than 60,000 people an hour at peak times. Plans have been proposed to turn it into a no-stopping, no-turning through-way, but little progress has been made. Approximately 5,000 vehicles a day ignore the street's no entry regulations.

The need for a London-wide body to plan and coordinate traffic policy and develop public transport facilities has never been more apparent. It is often forgotten that the GLC did a good deal towards wooing people away from private cars and on to public transport. The introduction of the combined bus/tube 'Travelcard' led to a great increase in users of public transport facilities. In just two years, 1983 and 1984, bus use in London increased by 13 per cent, tube use by 44 per cent and car commuting decreased by 21 per cent.

Despite government criticisms that the GLC was wasteful on

transport spending, GLC spending was in fact very low in comparison to other European cities. Indeed, in many if not most major European cities, the concept of large-scale car commuting into cities is considered as inefficient, expensive and out of date. Similarly, the GLC's efforts to introduce a proper cycle network was no more than modest compared to other cities where cycling ways are the norm.

Motorway Routes into and out of London

Midlands, North Wales, Northern England and Scotland:	M1
East Anglia:	M11
South-East England:	M2 or M20
South Coast:	M3 (Hampshire) M23 (Sussex)
South Wales, West and South-West England:	M4

TAXIS

Officially, the 15,670 registered black cabs are the only taxis that can be flagged down in the street, although radio cab firms often buy old black cabs and use them in central London. Technically this is illegal although people can rarely tell the difference.

There are a number of 'radio circuits' but these often give preference to credit accounts. A few radio cab firms have been known to close down phone lines at busy times and just work on account business. There will always be a list of local firms in the Yellow Pages.

Registered black cabs that stop for you must take you to your requested destination if it is within six miles of Charing Cross. Otherwise they have the right to refuse, but rarely do.

You may find, however, that empty taxis drive past without their 'for hire' lights on. This is often because drivers are looking out for the more lucrative tourist passengers from whom they might expect larger tips and possibly shorter journeys (so that they can do more journeys in total).

There is a limited scheme of shared taxis, introduced in 1987, whereby certain designated and labelled taxis will carry passengers on a shared-fare basis. Fares are calculated as a proportion of the total fare on the meter.

Taxi Fares

Extra charges are made at certain times and on certain days. On weekday evenings, at weekends, and on public holidays (except Christmas and New Year) you will pay between 40p and 60p extra. From 8pm on Christmas Eve until 6am on 27 December and from 8pm on New Year's Eve until 6am on 1 January £2.00 is the set extra charge. Small charges are also made for extra passengers and for luggage.

Public Carriage Office
278 1744
Information on all aspects of taxi policy, fares and regulations.

Licensed Taxi Drivers Association
286 1046

Safe Women's Transport
The Albany
Douglas Way
London SE8
692 6009

Ladycabs
57 Stoke Newington Church Street
London N16
254 3501/3314
All-woman taxi company charging standard fares. Operates all over London but mileage due from Stoke Newington.

London Taxicard Users Association
c/o 5 Mapleton Road
London SW18 4AH
874 7058

LONDON UNDERGROUND

Need for Improvements

London Underground has 462 trains, 251 miles of track, 274 stations and 2,500,000 people use it every day. It is renowned for overcrowding, inefficiency, dirty stations, crime and lack of adequate safety measures. The King's Cross fire had been warned against for years. Failure to spend money where it mattered, namely on improving old and worn out escalators, providing proper safety training to LU staff, having clearly labelled escape routes and fire equipment led to a situation where a catastrophe was bound to happen sooner or later. For a number of reasons, including the refusal of government to provide money for these improvements (preferring to spend vast sums on dubious road schemes), the failure of LRT to accept that its job goes further than simply keeping trains running; poor management, poor training procedures and poor working conditions have led to a system that is a source of shame when compared to other European cities.

Only after lives were lost was anything done about the

disgusting state of the tube system. Now, of course, it will be necessary to cause major disruption to passengers in order to carry out the necessary improvements.

Sadly, lessons have still not been learned. Stories in the London press about potentially dangerous situations have if anything increased since the King's Cross tragedy. A letter in the *Evening Standard* shortly after the fire told how passengers were asked to leave a tube train and evacuate a station because of a bomb alert, only to find that passengers were still swarming into the station because nobody had bothered to tell staff to prevent people entering. Luckily the alarm was false.

After the long drawn out inquiries following the King's Cross tube disaster, 157 recommendations were eventually made to LRT. Most were already being implemented by February 1989, if LRT officials were to be believed. Examples of improvements to be made include replacement of wooden sides on escalators, better communications with the emergency services and complete replacement of all wooden escalators by August 1989. Stiffer fines for people caught smoking have also been instituted and there is now a ban on the sale of tobacco at stations. Fire Brigade reports on progress and safety of individual stations began in April 1989.

There are already hints that increased fares may be used to pay for the cost of improvements. The government is wedded to the idea that the London Underground should pay its way and is reluctant to subsidise it, despite the clear economic benefits of doing so: property prices and concentration of businesses are affected by access to and quality of tube services, not to mention the fact that London would grind to a halt without an underground system.

Ticket Barriers

New automatic ticket barriers, whose ability to speed up exit and access to platforms is far from certain, are in the process of being introduced at all LU stations. Fears abound as to what would happen if the barriers failed during an emergency. Up to now it has been common for the machines to get stuck. In any case they are too narrow for, for example, large people, pregnant women, people with cases, etc. Indeed, fire chiefs have already ordered a number of modifications. It has been suggested that a system like that used in Moscow would be far more suitable. Passengers pay a set fee on entering the system, then there are no further checks, no bottlenecks, and no barriers. Another possibility is the introduction of frequent random spot checking on trains with a very large fine for fare dodging. This is also a system used in some European cities.

Overcrowding

A siren was introduced in 1989 to indicate when train doors are about to close. LRT officials have said that they hope it will encourage people to move more quickly inside the trains and stop people jumping doors. Unfortunately, in the majority of cases, the tube commuter's brain ceases to function as soon as it leaves the workplace. Passengers steadfastly refuse to move along the gangways of tube trains, meaning that the crowding in the doorways is ridiculously uncomfortable not to mention dangerous. And, of course, some joker will always decide, just as the doors are closing, that it is after all possible to squeeze into that last remaining centimetre of space, forcing all the other passengers who have carefully wedged themselves into position to mutter and tread on each other's toes.

Many problems remain; stations that are too small to cope with the number of passengers using them, platforms that are too narrow, poor signposting in stations, too few entrances and exits, and so on. Overcrowding is now at very dangerous levels at many stations especially Victoria, used by 73 million passengers a year. In rush hours, platforms are so full that staff have to keep passengers behind temporary barriers usually, as is normal on the Underground, with little or no explanation as to what is going on. Passengers are frequently afraid, especially in the wake of King's Cross. Victoria is perhaps one of the worst cases but similar problems exist at most stations in the rush hour and other times. Failure to invest in improving the system will only increase congestion and encourage more even more people to use London's roads.

Crime

Only around 400 police work on London Underground. Of these only 200 are actively involved in patrolling but shift rotas, court appearances and absences mean that usually there are no more than fifty officers on the system at any one time. Crime is common, usually pickpocketing or mugging. The danger to drivers, too, is often forgotten. There is little that a driver can do to prevent an attack from taking place on a train, especially if it is one-person operated with no guard. Clearly, the drivers themselves are constantly faced with the possibility of violence. However, an advantage of the random spot checking for fare dodgers mentioned above is that there would be a more regular presence of staff on trains for both safety and information purposes.

Three police stations are to be opened on the Underground at Hammersmith, Wembley Park and Finsbury Park, joining the one already in operation at Stockwell. It is hoped that this will allow police to reach the scenes of crimes more quickly than was possible from the old bases at Baker Street and Mansion House in Central London.

There are often complaints about the attitude of LRT staff towards the public. There is no doubt whatsoever that staff are often at best uninterested and at worst downright rude when questioned by the public. On the other hand, as far as dealing with crime is concerned, it is wrong to criticise the LRT staff too strongly as they have no powers of arrest and are often just as likely to be attacked as members of the public.

Inefficiency

My own experience of the apparent degree of incompetence in LRT came to a head when I wrote for some general information for use in this book. I received the following reply:

'Thank you for your letter . . . Please find enclosed, with our compliments, a selection of maps and leaflets which I hope you will find useful.'

Fine, I thought, until I reached into the envelope to pull out my pile of 'useful' literature and found . . . a District Line timetable! Nothing else, just one District Line timetable. I don't even live on the District Line. Need I say more?

Regular users of the Underground know to their cost that inefficiency goes far beyond petty examples like the one above. True, it is usually a matter of annoyance rather than danger, but how many times have you sat in a tube train, in a tunnel, stationary for ten minutes with no announcement as to what is going on, why you have been delayed and whether you will be moving soon? How many times have you been forced to leave a train before your destination, despite the fact that the train was advertised as going to the end of the line? Indeed, this became so common on the Northern Line that passengers started sit-ins, refusing to move until the train continued to its advertised destination.

I carried out an unofficial 'survey' which found that during the period from January 1989 (when I began work on this book) to June 1989 (when I began work on this particular chapter) only once did I find a tube station where all the escalators or lifts were working at the same time. Such examples are too numerous to mention. Suffice to say that it is common knowledge that LU is nowhere near as efficient as it could be.

If you wish to make a complaint, the normal procedure is to complain first directly to London Underground Limited and if you are not satisfied with the response, to take the matter to:

London Regional Passengers Committee
8 Duncannon Street
London WC2N 4JF
839 1898
A statutory body representing the interests of LRT passengers. Deals with complaints and inquiries.

Practical information

LRT produce a free leaflet giving details of bus and underground travel, tickets, travelcards (weekly, monthly or annual tickets), etc. The leaflet includes a tube map and a map of central London bus services. Further information can be given at Travel Information Centres, listed below. Alternatively, a twenty-four-hour Travel Information Service can be contacted by calling 222 1234.

Travel Information Centres

	Mon–Sat	Sun
Heathrow Terminals 1, 2, 3 station	07.15–18.30	08.15–18.30
Terminal 1 Arrivals	07.15–22.15 (21.00 Sat)	08.15–22.00
Terminal 2 Arrivals	07.15–21.00	08.15–22.00
Terminal 3 Arrivals	06.30–13.15	08.15–15.00
Terminal 4 Arrivals	06.30–18.30	08.15–18.30

Victoria station	08.15–21.30	08.15–21.30
Piccadilly Circus station	08.15–18.00	08.15–18.00
Oxford Circus station	08.15–18.00	closed
Euston station	07.15–18.00 (19.30 Fri)	08.15–18.00
King's Cross station	08.15–18.00 (Mon–Thur) 07.15–19.30 (Fri) 07.15–18.00 (Sat)	08.15–18.00

The London Tourist Board has information centres at Victoria station, Heathrow Airport, Harrods, Selfridges and the Tower of London.

LONDON BUSES

Like the Underground, red buses are ultimately responsible to London Regional Transport, although operational responsibility falls to eleven separate operating companies belonging to London Buses Limited. Buses tend to be criticised less than the underground service, although workers' pay and conditions are frequently the subject of controversy.

London Transport was removed from GLC control in 1984 and became the responsibility of the DTp. It was subsequently divided into London Underground Limited and London Buses Limited.

Successive reductions in grant have led to a considerable deterioration in standards of service. There have been many redundancies, many as a result of switching to one-person operated buses as opposed to the more popular and faster conductor-staffed Routemaster buses. The theory behind the switch to one-person operated buses was that it would save money. Unfortunately, this only goes to show the short-sightedness of the planners. Traffic is delayed behind buses at bus stops, bus journeys take longer and people tend to feel less safe particularly at night, not to mention unable to ask for information. One-person buses have proved so unpopular that London Buses are now considering a new model of buses with crews.

Quite apart from the constant and apparently increasing threat of violence on public transport to passengers and drivers alike, especially on one-person operated buses, it is often overlooked that women are particularly heavy users of buses which are offering an increasingly unsatisfactory service in many parts of London, in terms of safety, regularity and accessibility. Struggling on to a bus with a pram and shopping bags and then pay your fare from your purse which may be at the bottom of your bag is not easy – try it!

Buses are used more for local journeys than for longer distances, yet most bus routes follow the radial main roads. There is a tremendous need for more local routes to take people to shops, stations, etc., especially for women, children and older people who are the most regular users of buses.

Buses are seen by some as the key to unblocking traffic congestion in London. If this is to be proved, priority must be given to the development of a swift, reliable and efficient service. There has been a fall in the number of bus users mainly as a result of unreliability of the service. Buses account for 30 per cent of all road travellers in London and yet make up only 1 per cent of the vehicles on the roads. It seems likely, then, that a better used bus service would clear many vehicles from the roads.

Deregulation

The deregulation of bus services outside London has had mixed effects. More buses appear to be on the roads but the services offered vary in usefulness. For instance, in some areas it has become almost impossible to plan a journey where you need to use two or more bus companies because of the peculiarities of timetabling, not to mention the added expense for the passenger of not being able to buy one return ticket to cover the whole journey. What is more, many of the buses used by smaller companies are old, slow and uncomfortable. The likely effects of deregulation in London are uncertain. As yet, only the 24 service from Hampstead to Pimlico has been sold off, to Grey Green buses, and it is not clear how many routes are likely to follow suit.

Practical Information

Central London and local bus route maps and timetables are available from the Travel Information Centres listed on p. 329, otherwise you can phone 371 0247 or write to:

London Buses
A&P Freepost
London SW1H 0YH

London Regional Transport
55 Broadway
London SW1H 0BD
*Same address for London
Underground Ltd, London Buses Ltd
and LRT Unit for Disabled
Passengers.*

Airbus

A frequent service from the major hotel areas in central London calling at all Heathrow terminals. The A1 runs from Victoria and the A2 from Euston/Russell Square. The service is considerably more expensive than the forty-five-minute tube journey to Heathrow, costing £4 (adults)/£2 (children).

There is also a coach service between Gatwick and Victoria but this is not a London Buses Limited service.

BR LONDON REGION/NETWORK SOUTHEAST

Despite its relative environmental benefits compared to road transport, money for the rail network in and around London has been progressively cut back by the government. The result, when coupled with a degree of inefficiency, is the familiar story of breakdowns, cancellations and staff discontent as an already overloaded system attempts to cope with a task for which it is receiving inadequate financial and political support. Trains continue to be cramped and uncomfortable especially at peak times. Conditions on the network have declined to such an extent that simple maintenance of stations is hailed as a remarkable example of progress.

As for 'real' progress, such as the refurbishment of Liverpool Street BR station, the incredibly slow pace of work and the associated hold-ups have increased passenger frustration to ever higher levels. The continuing failure of BR staff to 'get there' as their adverts suggest they are doing, despite supposedly being given special training in passenger relations, means that rudeness and 'couldn't care less' attitudes towards passengers do nothing to encourage sympathy for strike action and pay/conditions claims which are in themselves more than justified. With this in mind the high degree of public sympathy for the summer 1989 train strikes especially with regard to overtime and rest day working and union concerns about safety and overcrowding on trains, was remarkable.

Network SouthEast is the only part of British Rail with set loading standards for passenger trains, and yet these are set at 135 per cent and treated as normal for rush-hour trains. The volume of passengers is difficult to cope with and it is not just better train services that would help. More flexi-time working and more investment in local employment would certainly help decrease the burden.

Of course, BR itself has its hands tied to a certain extent. BR's objectives, including financial objectives, are set by the government. BR cannot make investments in the service unless it can prove an 8 per cent commercial return.

Network SouthEast
British Rail
Euston House
24 Eversholt Street
London NW1 1DZ

Getting into and out of London by British Rail

Blackfriars: 928 1500
Broad Street: 387 7070
Cannon Street: 928 5100
Charing Cross: (SE England and local services) 928 5100
Euston: (The North) 387 7070
Holborn Viaduct: 928 5100
King's Cross/St Pancras: (The North and Scotland) 278 2477
Liverpool Street: (East Anglia) 928 5100
London Bridge: 928 5100
Marylebone: 387 7070
Paddington: (Wales and SW England) 262 6767
Victoria: (Kent and Sussex) 928 5100
Waterloo: (Southern England) 928 5100

Thameslink

A new service through the heart of London from Bedford and Luton to Orpington, Sevenoaks and Brighton, passing through King's Cross, London Bridge and Gatwick Airport.

Docklands Light Railway

A service linking Docklands to the centre of London. Plans are under way to extend it. The line is already overused at peak times and there have been many complaints about the design of the train, for instance, inward-opening doors. The service was supposed to be quickly expanded to run evenings and weekends – this plan has now been shelved until at least 1992.

The Channel Tunnel Rail Link

Nothing has outraged the NIMBY protesters (Not-In-My-Back-Yard) more than the Channel Tunnel rail link and its likely impact on houses, countryside and environment in Kent and South London. If present plans remain in place, not only will it destroy parks and nature reserves like Camley Street (see Chapter 6: Green London), but it will require the building of some thirty-three ventilation tunnels as high as a two-storey house. BR claim that these shafts will be disguised, but what exactly they are going to do is unclear. They will be built at 750-metre intervals in streets, playing fields, parks and sports grounds.

Under present plans five major construction sites will bring disruption for several years in South and South-East London and Kent, at Hither Green, Lewisham, Peckham, Bexley and Swanley, Kent. The line will run from King's Cross Station (BR have frequently refused to reconsider what many saw as a more suitable site for the terminal at Stratford) under Britannia Street and Derby Lodge and the proposed East-West Cross rail link at Farringdon. Then it will pass under the proposed Jubilee Line extension just north of the Thames, under the river and Bankside Power Station. Next it will turn under the New Globe Theatre, Borough High Street and Warwick Gardens, Peckham, continuing towards Hither Green, Watery Lane (Bexley) or Scadbury Park (Bromley), then to the tunnel entrance east of Swanley village, Kent, off the M25. A small number of concessions relating to the proximity of Swanley village and certain other parts of the tunnel were accepted in August 1989. The 'final route' was then announced in September at which point concern over the increasing cost of the project rose to the surface once more. It was even suggested in some quarters that the entire project was threatened by spiralling budgets. In December 1989, it was announced that BR was to re-examine its plans and that there would be a twelve-month delay in seeking parliamentary approval. The extra time will give rival contractors, such as those supporting the Stratford option, the chance to pursue their alternative proposals.

The need for the rail link has been questioned by many who suggest that the existing lines to the coast could be improved more cheaply and with less lasting effect to the public or the environment, even allowing for the need to free some lines for freight trains. So far this has cut little ice with BR and the developers. Bill Oddie, who has been heavily involved in campaigning against the Chunnel terminal at King's Cross, told me: 'BR is ripping up vast amounts of countryside so that a few businessmen can get to London twenty minutes earlier. It's immoral!'

TRAVELCARDS AND BUS PASSES

Travelcards are valid for bus and London BR travel as well as on the Underground. They also cover the Docklands railway and Thameslink within Greater London. They can be bought from all underground and BR stations in London and any London Transport or BR Travel Information Centre.

Passes for use on buses only are also available on a zonal basis (i.e. the more zones you wish to travel in, the more expensive the ticket). Full details from 222 1234. Special passes are available for children and young people, and for elderly people (see Chapter 10: Older People). Before buying any bus pass or travelcards, you will require a photocard (except for one-day tickets). Provided you have a passport-sized photo with you, a photocard will be issued at the same time as your first pass or travelcard.

VIOLENCE AND FEAR ON PUBLIC TRANSPORT

A report carried out in November 1988 at Liverpool Street and Fenchurch Street stations showed that women, the young and the elderly travel in fear of violence, especially sex attacks. BR officials told the police not to publish the results. All the 1,000 questionnaires completed, mostly by women, expressed concern about safety.

'Lager louts' were cited as a particular problem – many of

those questioned had seen or been involved in incidents. There was found to be a great deal of pestering and direct assaults by men. The report says only a small number of incidents are reported. The reason given for this is that passengers can rarely find an official or policeman to complain to. Many even said they would not travel outside rush hours. This, of course, does nothing to ease overcrowding. A total of 250,000 people per day travel on Eastern region commuter trains.

British Rail is the paymaster for the transport police but there is a clear crisis of confidence in their ability to deal with crime on trains and in stations. In early 1989, a good deal of publicity surrounded the arrival in London of the Guardian Angels, a group of self-appointed vigilantes from the USA. They claimed that their presence on the US subway acted as a deterrent to crime and they had the overwhelming support of the police and public. They did not find things so easy in London. Police opposition to their presence was clear although it did seem to spur them into increasing, marginally, the number of police on the tube. They attracted a number of recruits from London but many remain dubious of the morality and benefits of having vigilantes on public transport. Nevertheless, they were welcomed by many tube travellers as they appear to want to do a job the police seem unable to do.

CYCLING

Despite a steady rise in the number of cyclists in London over the last ten or so years, the level of provision for them is at best in its infancy. The combination of pollution (see also Chapter 6: Green London), lack of cycle paths and weight of traffic means that cycles only account for 3 per cent of London traffic, whereas in similar flat continental cities it is quite common for this figure to reach 30 per cent.

London Cycling Campaign
3 Stamford Street
London SE1
928 7220
Has local groups. Organises events, campaigning and lobbying and produces a bimonthly magazine, The Daily Cyclist. *Also gives free legal advice, free insurance, and organises discounts in cycle shops.*

PEDESTRIANS AND ROAD SAFETY

Friends of the Earth run the London Road Safety Alert, an information service giving advice on having pedestrian crossings installed, getting pavements or potholes mended, making routes to school safer, promoting facilities for cyclists, stopping commuter rat runs, diverting heavy traffic, preventing illegal parking, slowing down speeding traffic, combating drink driving, and so on. The FoE Cities for People campaign and the Transport 2000 Feet First campaign, started in 1989, have resulted in a higher level of publicity for the rights and requirements of pedestrians.

There has been discussion of measures such as 'traffic calming' in cities whereby more areas are pedestrianised and other streets have ramps built to slow down those vehicles that must use the street for deliveries, and so on. It is quite wrong that so little attention is paid to the needs of pedestrians. After all the vast majority of journeys are short ones undertaken on foot. Apparently simple measures such as replacing cracked paving stones and sweeping away slippery leaves can save lives; around 400 people die every year as a result of falling on pavements.

The Pedestrians Association
1 Wandsworth Road
London SW8 2LJ
Campaign for the provision of safe, convenient and attractive ways for people on foot. Information and advice.

WOMEN AND TRANSPORT

Most transport is designed with the 'average man' in mind, often ignoring the special needs, vulnerability or fear of women. A GLC survey in 1984–5 showed that only 37 per cent of women felt safe travelling on buses, and only 16 per cent on underground or BR trains. About a quarter of those questioned never travelled on public transport at night. A Harris survey in October 1988 backed up some of the earlier survey's findings. In a transport police survey carried out during 1988 the main concerns of women on British Rail were drunkenness, disorder, assault and indecency.

Studies by CILT (Campaign to Improve London's Transport) have shown that other concerns include unsafe, unpleasant, unstaffed stations, long waits, high fares, long staircases causing major obstacles for those women with pushchairs or small children, or for those with a disability. The Harris survey also showed that women did not like travelling on trains whose carriages were completely separate from one another and not linked by a corridor.

On the underground stairs and escalators are again cited as major obstacles, as well as distances to be walked to get to trains. Lifts and escalators being frequently out of service is a constant problem and one which shows no sign whatever of improving despite the post King's Cross 'improvements'. New automatic ticket gates are alarming for parents travelling with small children who can easily get caught in the gate if it closes between them and their escort. Overcrowding (exposing women to molesting) and lack of staff to help with pushchairs or simply inquiries are also common complaints. Of course, London Underground have no incentive to make access easier for more women or elderly people and people with disabilities, because they are already struggling to cope with an overused and inefficient system. Without diversion of public resources, improvements in the near future are unlikely.

Buses are the most commonly used form of public transport by women, but there are still problems, such as long waits at bus stops with small children on large roads and one-person operated buses. The latter is a twofold problem: supervision of passengers who may be threatening or frightening a woman is very difficult and when getting on to the bus a woman may have to hold a pushchair, carry a baby and search for her fare all at once. In the Harris survey 42 per cent of those women questioned said there should be more space for baby buggies and luggage. A particularly worrying complaint, and something which I have seen myself many times on both buses and tube trains, is the closing of automatic doors before women and children, or older people have finished leaving the vehicle. I have seen more than one person get hurt and more than one driver find the whole thing very amusing . . .

Door-to-door transport is clearly the preference of most women. The price of taxis is obviously too high for most women to use regularly, but there are a number of community transport schemes, dial-a-ride schemes and so on mentioned elsewhere. In certain boroughs, Safe Women's Transport schemes provide low cost door-to-door transport in the evenings for women, with a woman driver and escort. Local authorities in Hammersmith and Stockwell fund such schemes, although one in Lewisham closed after a cut in its funding.

London Women's Safe Transport Group c/o CILT (see below) have produced some useful work on the subject of women and transport, including a report on 'Women's Transport Needs in London' and a guide to setting up safe transport schemes entitled 'On the Safe Side'.

**Hammersmith and Fulham
  Women's Safe Transport**
Palinswick House
241 Kings Street
London W6 9LP
748 6036

London Women's Safe Transport
c/o CILT
(see below)

Stockwell Women's Lift Service
46 Kelper Road
London SW4
274 4641

Women's Environmental Network
287 City Road
London EC1
490 2511

Women for Improved Transport
12 Bartholomew Villas
London NW5 2LL
267 8136
Call attention to the special needs of women using London transport, particularly safety and access.

See also Taxis (p. 325).

PEOPLE WITH DISABILITIES

See Chapter 11: People with Disabilities.

OLDER PEOPLE

See Chapter 10: Older People.

ADDRESSES

**ALARM (All London Against the
  Road Menace)**
c/o Rupert Harwood
26–28 Underwood Street
London N1 7JQ
490 1555
A loose association of 120 groups campaigning against road schemes in and around London.

Campaign for Lead-free Air (CLEAR)
2 Northdown Road
London N1 9BG
278 9686

**Campaign to Improve London's
  Transport (CILT)**
3rd Floor
Universal House
88–94 Wentworth Street
London E1 7SA
247 1302
Campaigning for improved, democratically run transport systems that are efficient, convenient and accessible. Contact for London Women's Safe Transport Group.

Capital Transport Campaign
308 Gray's Inn Road
London WC1
833 4022
Similar aims to CILT. Particularly good on women's issues and how to channel complaints.

Central Transport Users Consultative Committee
First Floor
Golden Cross House
Duncannon Street
London WC2N 4JF
839 7338/7339

Child Accident Prevention Trust
75 Portland Place
London W1
636 2545

Department of the Environment
As DTp

Department of Transport
2 Marsham Street
London SW1P 3EB
276 3000

Dial-A-Ride Users Association
25 Leighton Street
London NW5 2QD
482 2325
Coordinates local schemes for those unable or unwilling to use public transport. Will tell you about local schemes. Publishes the invaluable 'Dial-A-Ride Directory'.

Friends of the Earth
26–28 Underwood Street
London N1
FoE have a Transport Campaign working on all aspects of transport in London.

London Amenity and Transport Association
3–7 Stamford Street
London SE1
928 1440
Has a list of local residents and amenity societies concerned with transport issues.

London Centre for Transport Planning
Address as above.

London Community Transport Association
Finsbury Business Centre
837 0081
Can provide a list of community transport schemes.

London Boroughs Transport Committee
Regal House
London Road
Twickenham, TW1 3QB
891 1411
Responsible for running the London lorry ban.

London Planning Advisory Committee
Havering Town Hall
Main Road
Romford
Essex RM1 3BD
0708 46040
Statutory London-wide Transport and planning borough committee.

London Strategic Policy Unit Transport Group
20 Vauxhall Bridge Road
London SW1V 2SB
633 3524
Joint borough committee of nine labour boroughs.

London Transport Technology Network
16 Warren Lane
London SE18
316 5659

National Association for Community Transport
Tavistock House North
Tavistock Square
London WC1H 9HX
388 6542
Advice and support for those wishing to set up schemes.

Royal Society for the Prevention of Accidents
Cannon House
Priory Queensway
Birmingham B4 6BS

Secretary of State for Transport
Department of Transport
Marsham Street
London SW1

SERA (Socialist Environment and Resources Association)
11 Goodwin Street
London N4 3HQ
263 7424

Transnet
16 Warren Lane
London SE18 6DB
854 5425
Transport technology network. Press cuttings service available, research, briefings and Transnet News *magazine.*

TEST (Transport and Environment Studies)
177 Arlington Road
London NW1 7EY
267 7711

Transport 2000
Walkden House
10 Melton Street
London NW1 2EJ
388 8386

Transport 2000 London
5 Pembridge Gardens
London W5
727 4689
National federation of environmental and consumer groups, trade unions and industry concerned about the impact of transport on our environment and society and the formulation of a coherent, far-sighted national transport policy.

Transport Unions

Transport and General Workers Union
Transport House
Smith Square
London SW1
828 7788

National Union of Railwaymen
205 Euston Road
London NW1
387 4771

ASLEF
9 Arkwright Road
London NW3 6AB
431 0275

TSSA
Walkden House
10 Melton Street
London NW1 2EJ
387 2101

15

WOMEN

Women account for nearly 52 per cent of London's population. Our experiences vary according to our race, age, religion, abilities, class and sexuality. We face discrimination in many areas of our lives but we are striving to organise to fight back. The last three years, since the abolition of the Greater London Council, has seen a number of women's organisations lose their funding and be forced to dissolve. However, others have survived and women are still coming together to provide services, resources, support and to campaign and challenge. Included here is a list of groups. It is not exhaustive but it will provide women with a first step to finding what they are looking for.

Women should telephone their local town hall for information on facilities for women in the area. They should either ask for the women's unit or equality officer, or otherwise the general information desk. If you cannot find the information you require, phone us at Wesley House London's Women Centre and we will try to help.

Marie Gabriel
Centre Coordinator
Wesley House London Women's Centre

GENERAL INFORMATION

Local council provision for women varies tremendously. The attitude of a council towards women's issues such as violence, discrimination and equality can often, though not always, be discerned from the existence or otherwise of a women's unit at the council. Money spent specifically on women's needs has been reduced dramatically since the demise of the GLC. The GLC Women's Committee funded more than 500 women's groups around the capital. Many of these have now gone to the wall.

The prioritising of women's issues is no longer on the agenda of many of the borough councils. Even some of those Labour councils that have had a good profile on women's issues are closing down women's units or facilities. A combination of the need to cut back on spending forced upon them by government legislation and apparent climbdowns by the London Labour leadership on equal opportunities policies, perhaps for the cynical electoral reason of divesting themselves of the 'loony left' label, has led to the closure of a unit in Lewisham and threats to facilities in Camden, Hackney, Haringey and Hounslow among others.

VIOLENCE AGAINST WOMEN AND WOMEN'S SAFETY

There are thousands of cases of rape and violent assault in London every year committed against women of all ages. One in seven of all sex attacks committed in England and Wales takes place in London. Nationally, there was a rise of 6 per cent in sex attacks in 1989 as compared with 1988.

Although police treatment of women who report rape is believed to have improved, there are still many stories of women who say they have been made to feel guilty for being raped, treated unsympathetically by duty officers and so on. Complaints against the police can be made through the official complaints procedure. A Citizens Advice Bureau, Law Centre or other independent advice centre can advise you on how to go about it (see Appendix).

As many a (white, male) judge has proved, rape within marriage may not be an offence in the eyes of the law. In reality, a husband can rape his wife and a boyfriend his girlfriend, just as a stranger can rape a women walking along the High Street but the law does not recognise this.

An excellent book covering the law relating to rape, police and the courts, medical information, harassment at work and how to take action was published by the London Rape Crisis Centre (Women's Press) entitled *Sexual Violence: The Reality for Women*. Liz Kelly's book, *Surviving Sexual Violence* (Polity) is also a valuable publication.

The organisations below can offer help and support to victims of rape and other forms of violence. Some may direct you to a refuge if necessary.

Domestic Violence

Domestic violence is every bit as much of a constant threat to women as violence on the streets. Statistically, women are more likely to be attacked or sexually assaulted by men they know in their own homes, and in many cases the perpetrators are men with whom they are involved in a relationship. Domestic violence tends to refer to the latter.

The scale of the problem of domestic violence against women in London is a grave cause for concern and certainly deserves more attention than it has received in the past. Rape, other physical abuse and mental cruelty are all common forms of domestic violence. Every year 100,000 women in London receive medical treatment as a result of domestic violence. A survey of crime in Islington, in 1986, gave a figure of 2,500 incidents of domestic violence over a year, only 694 of which were reported. This would give a rough figure of 750,000 per year for the whole of London. (Source: T. Jones *et al.*, *Islington Crime Survey*, London, Gower, 1986.)

Over 1,000 women call the police every week in London to report domestic violence. The real number of incidents is considerably higher because, for various reasons, many do not report incidents. For example, women are so physically and mentally drained by the experience of escaping from a violent relationship that they feel unable to carry through a prosecution. Others withdraw statements to the police as a result of bullying or threats from their partner.

It has been claimed that in as many as 90 per cent of cases, women retract their statements while a case is being prepared. They stay in violent relationships because they believe they have nowhere to go and are financially dependent. Others remain because they believe their partners' claims that there will be no further violence.

Another common reason for not informing the police is simply the belief that it would not do any good. In the Islington survey, 45 per cent of those who did not report violence stated this reason. Of those who did report domestic violence to the police, 66 per cent said they were satisfied with the response. A survey in *Woman* magazine found that 75 per cent of the respondents went to relatives, 59 per cent to friends and only 28 per cent to the police to report domestic violence. Indeed, there remains a fairly low opinion of the police's willingness or ability to deal satisfactorily with the problem. To quote from 'Police Response to Domestic Violence', a report by the London Strategic Policy Unit: 'At present the police use a jaundiced view of women's willingness to pursue complaints as an excuse for taking no action themselves. In our view the police should pursue charges against a man who is alleged to have committed a criminal offence against his wife or partner, unless the woman is sure she does not want any action taken.'

It is worth comparing the processes used in Britain with a successful scheme in London, Ontario, Canada. In Britain, if you saw a bank robbery, the police would not allow you to withdraw your statement as it is the police who are charging the criminal and the Crown who is prosecuting. In the case of domestic violence, statements can be withdrawn because it is the individual victim who is prosecuting. Clearly, this is an inconsistent system.

In the Canadian example, police will charge an attacker if they have enough evidence. The charge once made cannot be dropped and the Crown prosecutes, even if the woman will not or cannot give evidence. Men who are charged with domestic violence in London, Ontario are made to attend counselling and to pay for it. The money then goes to women's refuges.

In Britain, distrust of the legal process also stretches to the courts. Stories like that of a 27-year-old woman from Camden who said she felt as if she had been 'raped in court' by the lawyer questioning her, are all too common. The *Camden and St Pancras Chronicle* reported that the woman lodged a complaint about the lawyer's behaviour and offensive line of questioning and said that she had been made to feel as if she was herself on trial.

In London, women entering refuges have suffered an average of thirty-five assaults but only 390 cases per year result in prosecution. The Islington report showed 92 per cent of the women reporting violence were punched or slapped, 57 per cent were kicked, 22 per cent were attacked with a weapon, including bottles, glasses, knives, scissors, sticks, clubs and other blunt instruments. Ninety-six per cent of those attacked suffered bruises to the skin or eyes, 45 per cent cuts and 10 per cent broken bones.

Self-defence

Self-defence classes can usually be traced via your local council or via London Women's Aid, Wesley House Women's Centre or one of the other organisations listed below.

Criminal Charges

Although police have been reluctant to arrest men for domestic violence, a recent directive from the Metropolitan Police told officers to treat domestic violence as a serious offence. If there are visible signs of injury, the police should arrest and charge the man. If not, it is up to the woman to decide whether to press charges. Legal advice should be sought.

Legal Aid

Certain categories of people will receive Legal Aid if required, for instance the unemployed or low paid. Your solicitor will apply for you. (See also Chapter 3: Citizens' Rights.)

Injunctions

A court order can be used to prevent your attacker coming near you. Women's centres, Law Centres, Citizens Advice Bureaux or other independent advice centres (see Appendix) can help you with this.

Leaving Home

If you have to leave your home because of violence it is advisable to take the following with you if possible: birth and marriage certificates, benefit books, rent book, passports, savings books, cheque books, cheque cards and credit cards, driving licence, clothes and valuables. If you have to leave in a hurry, refuges will usually pay your fares. Refuge workers can return at a later date to pick up larger items you are unable to bring with you.

Children

Usually refuges will cater for your children's needs as far as possible, although cramped conditions may be a problem. Underfunding of refuges and their consequent lack of resources is a constant problem. However, refuges will look after your children and give you advice on their rights and welfare.

For further information, London Women's Aid can provide a booklet entitled 'Untold Pain' from which some of the information in this chapter was culled, and which gives a great deal of practical information on refuges, legal help, ethnic minority women and more. For information on the abuse of children and young women see Chapter 2: Children and Young People.

London Women's Aid
251 6537
(Twenty-four-hour answering service)
Coordinates the work of refuges, refers women to refuges, offers advice and support.

Asian Women's Resource Centre (ASHA)
27 Santley Street
London SW4 7QF
274 8854 or 737 5901

Chiswick Family Rescue
PO Box 855
London W4 4JF
995 4430 (twenty-four-hour crisis line) 747 0133 (office)

Refuge, help and advice for women of all ages who are in difficulty and need to leave home.

Incest Crisis Line
422 5100 or
890 4732

Rape Crisis Centre
PO Box 69
London WC1
278 3956; 837 1600 (twenty-four hours)

Women's Anti-violence Organisation
73–75 Stockwell Road
London SW9
326 1228

Violence or Relationship Breakdown and Leaving Your Home

If violence forces a woman to leave her home immediately, and she has no family or friends with whom to stay, she should contact a women's refuge via Women's Aid or ASHA. If the police have been called, the woman can insist that they contact Women's Aid on their behalf. Women's Aid refuges may be a short-term solution especially if violence is involved. They will also help with claiming benefits, solicitors and legal problems or with finding accommodation.

There are about thirty women's refuges around London, although for obvious reasons the addresses cannot be listed here. Refuges will welcome any woman providing there is space and providing there is no drug or alcohol problem. There are also refuges catering specifically for black women, Asian women and women with disabilities.

Provided that no violence is involved and the male partner refuses to leave, there may well be no immediate solution, although divorce proceedings may transfer the tenancy.

If you are what the council calls 'priority need' (see Chapter 8: Housing) you should be given emergency council accommodation.

However, if you can afford it, bed and breakfast is another option. Most important, tenancy should not be given up until advice is sought.

If a partner has been violent towards a woman and/or her children, the woman should apply for an injunction. A legal advice centre, Citizens Advice Bureau (see Appendix) or Women's Aid will give assistance and provide general information on legal rights. Nevertheless, women should not be pushed into taking out an injunction if it is felt it would make the violence worse.

There is a complex system of regulations relating to rights to stay in a home.

(a) Unmarried Women

If a woman is not married and is the sole tenant or owner of the home, the male partner has no legal right to stay in the home. A woman need only give 'reasonable notice'. If there is violence or the man refuses to leave, it may be possible to obtain a court order or apply to the council under the Homeless Persons Act.

If the tenancy is in both names the situation is far more complex since both partners have equal rights to stay. They must either mutually agree on who leaves or else a temporary exclusion order may be sought against the partner. Independent advice should be sought, for example, from the council, Citizens Advice Bureau, Law Centre (see Appendix) or Women's Aid.

If there is violence, an injunction may be sought. If there are still problems after divorce proceedings, you should apply for a management transfer. Some councils are more helpful than others.

For an unmarried woman whose partner is sole tenant/owner there are limited rights. Temporary exclusion is possible if violence or mental cruelty is involved, while you look for permanent accommodation.

(b) Married Women

For a woman who is sole tenant/owner the male partner has some rights to stay. Legal advice should be sought, via Women's Aid, ASHA, Citizens Advice Bureau, Law Centre or other independent advice centre (see Appendix).

If a married couple are joint tenants/owners they have equal rights to stay and to a share of the property in the event of a divorce, separation or nullity. An injunction may be possible if violence or cruelty is involved. Tenancy may be transferred as part of divorce proceedings.

If the male partner is sole tenant/owner, the woman has a right to remain. In council or housing association property or fully protected private rented accommodation, it may be possible to have the tenancy transferred to you. Advice should be sought.

(c) Lesbian Couples

Lesbian couples are not usually recognised by law as a couple. It may be possible to get tenancy as single sharers, otherwise the normal rules about single or joint tenancy apply.

NB: A council is not obliged to put a tenancy into both names if a lover moves in, although it may be possible.

SHAC produce two valuable books on the subject. *A Woman's Place: Relationship Breakdown and Your Rights* (for married women) and *Going It Alone: Relationship Breakdown and Your Rights* (for unmarried women), both £3.95.

DISCRIMINATION

Education

It is still true that young women obtain fewer and different qualifications than their male counterparts. Far more females than males study arts subjects and far more males study scientific or 'practical' subjects. Choices, if they can be described as such when so much pressure is involved for teenagers trying to plan their future, are often based as much on others' expectations as on personal wishes. The problems start at an early age with sex stereotyping in books and other teaching materials, not to mention by the teachers themselves.

White middle-class boys are the most likely group to go on to further or higher education. Similarly, there are fewer women in positions of authority on school, college or university teaching staffs.

It is illegal under the Sex Discrimination Act to prevent children taking a subject at school on the grounds of sex. It is illegal to discriminate against someone on the grounds of sex with regard to entrance into further, higher or adult education or vocational training.

**Campaign to Impede Sex
  Stereotyping in the Young
  (CISSY)**
177 Gleneldon Road
London SW16 2BX
677 2411

Women Writers Network
52 Park Chase
Wembley Park
Middx HA9 8EH

Employment

Under the provisions of the 1975 Sex Discrimination Act, direct sex discrimination at work means being treated less favourably than a person of the opposite sex is or would be treated in similar circumstances. An example of this would be a policy of appointing only men to management positions.

Direct marriage discrimination means being treated less favourably than an unmarried person of the same sex is or would be treated in similar circumstances. An example would be not appointing a married person to a post requiring time to be spent away from home.

Indirect sex discrimination means being unable to comply with a requirement which on the face of it applies equally to both men and women, but which in practice can be met by a much smaller proportion of one sex. For instance, an organisation may be indirectly discriminating against women if access to certain jobs is unjustifiably restricted to particular grades which in practice are held only by men.

Indirect marriage discrimination is similar to indirect sex discrimination, such as being denied a job because it is only open to people with no family responsibilities.

Victimisation

If someone is treated less favourably as a result of having made allegations in good faith under the Sex Discrimination or Equal Pay Acts, that person is being treated illegally.

The Sex Discrimination Act also applies to discrimination against men and has been used to support allegations made by male employees. However, the vast majority of cases involve discrimination against women.

The Act applies to both part-time and full-time employees, self-employed people who undertake contract work, apprentices, partners in firms, contract workers, pregnant women. (NB: Maternity rights are a complex topic and advice should be sought from a Citizens Advice Bureau, Law Centre or other independent advice agency – see Appendix.)

The Act also covers training and qualifying for a job, employment agencies and job centres, promotions, transfers, redundancy, dismissal and retirement.

Sexual Harassment

Such things as unreciprocated or unwelcome comments, looks, physical contact or suggestions such as requests for sexual favours are all classed as sexual harassment, and may be actionable under the Sex Discrimination Act. Trade unions, staff representatives or colleagues may be able to help or advise you.

Taking Action

Any complaint under the Sexual Discrimination Act must be lodged within three months of the action in question having taken place. You should first contact either a trade union representative at work, LAGER (Lesbian and Gay Employment Rights) or Rights of Women (addresses below). Otherwise, contact the EOC who will advise you and treat your inquiry in confidence. The next step will be to get an IT 1 form from the EOC, a job centre or UB Office, fill it in and send it to the Central Office of Industrial Tribunals whose address appears on the form.

The EOC will tell you how industrial tribunals work and the whole process will cost you nothing provided you have made the complaint in good faith. There are a few exceptions to the Act such as matters covered by the Equal Pay Act or other legislation. The EOC will provide full information and can offer a wide range of materials on issues relating to discrimination at work.

Despite the Sex Discrimination Act, women are still concentrated in certain types of job. At school, girls and young women are encouraged to study certain subjects and careers advice still has a reputation for advising girls to go into secretarial work and other 'conventionally female' jobs.

Equal Pay

The Equal Pay Act as amended in 1984 enables a woman to claim equal pay for work of equal value to that done by a man employed by the same employer (or an associated employer under common terms and conditions of employment). The terms of the Act are quite complicated. A booklet from the EOC explains how the Act works and how to make a claim if you think you are not receiving 'equal pay for work of equal value'.

In April 1987, full-time female workers in Greater London were earning an average weekly wage of £184.90 as opposed to £280.50 for men. The figures for the whole country were £148.10 and £224.00 respectively. For manual workers in the South East the figures were women: £126.20; men: £185.50. Disparities exist in every kind of work, manual or otherwise. Clearly, the Equal Pay Act has not led to pay equality and appears to be a long way from doing so.

Housing

As a rule it is unlawful to discriminate against a woman (or a man) in the sale or letting of premises and in the treatment of those occupying premises. This applies to local authority and private housing (though lodgers in private households are excepted).

Goods, Facilities and Services

Discrimination in provision of the above or refusal to provide them on the grounds of sex is unlawful. This includes financial facilities provided by banks, credit card agencies, stores, etc., access to public places like hotels, pubs and discos; educational facilities, e.g. for training or adult education; public transport or local authority services. Exceptions to this include the activities of political parties, religious organisations, non-profit-making voluntary bodies and genuinely private clubs, so far as treatment of their own members is concerned.

Insurance

It is not unlawful to discriminate in relation to certain insurance policies, if it can be justified by referring to reliable figures that there is a difference of risk for men and women.

Advertisements

Any published advertisement suggesting an intention to discriminate, such as a job advertisement, would be unlawful. Complaints to a publication or publisher are possible but only the EOC can take action under the Sex Discrimination Act.

General

Despite legislation, advertisers still get away with sexist advertising, often quite blatant. The building of stereotyped images of women is bolstered by TV and the media. Everything from stereotyped female characters in soap operas and page three girls to hard porn, is part of a network of image making which years of complaining and campaigning have highlighted but by no means wiped out.

Discrimination is not simply a matter of legislation. Social attitudes and pressures still lead to many forms of discrimination that cannot be legislated against. Inability to walk safely alone at night or to wear the kind of clothes one wants without being accused of 'asking for it' is itself discrimination, and one which, like stereotyping in young children, particularly at school, requires education and changes of attitude which will only be achieved by constant pressure and campaigning in a context that spreads far wider than the subject of discrimination alone. Many groups exist, a number of which are listed in this chapter.

The Equal Opportunities Commission

The EOC was set up by Parliament in 1975 to prevent unfair treatment on the grounds of sex and to prevent discrimination against employed married people. Particularly concerned with the areas of work, education, consumer rights and welfare benefits, EOC helps both individuals and groups such as a particular factory or schools. The commission bases its work on three Acts of Parliament: the Sex Discrimination Acts of 1975 and 1986 and the Equal Pay Act of 1970.

Every case brought to the commission will be treated independently and this may result in the EOC fighting your case for you and covering legal costs. In every case advice will be given free of charge.

The EOC strives to 'persuade, advise, inform' and to accept that using the power of the law is not always the best way to achieve cooperation. The commission helps employers, insurance companies, schools, and so on to formulate and implement equal opportunities policies and to encourage employment of women in traditional male jobs.

The EOC carries out a research and investigation role, advising on how policies – both government and other – might be improved. Grants may be awarded to individuals or organisations wishing to carry out educational and research projects that help towards achieving equal opportunities.

The EOC has a library and information centre and publishes leaflets and guides. When possible it works with the press and voluntary organisations and provides exhibitions, conferences, seminars and training.

The Equal Opportunities Commission
Overseas House
Quay Street
Manchester M3 3HN
061 833 9244

LAGER (Lesbian and Gay Employment Rights)
Room 205
Southbank House
Black Prince Road
London SE1 7SJ
587 1636 (Lesbians)
587 1643 (Gay Men)

Rights of Women
52–54 Featherstone Street
London EC1
251 6577

HEALTH

Changes in NHS care currently under discussion will have an effect on all users of the service. However, certain problems specific to women are likely to increase.

The provision of women-only care for those women who wish it is already poor; special provision is bound to suffer as a result of the generally declining state and changing priorities of the NHS. Older women's health needs in particular are and will remain underfunded. A further piece of bad news is that the merger of the Soho Women's Hospital and the Elizabeth Garrett Anderson Hospital means that the EGA is now lost as a hospital for women, staffed only by women.

Local Community Health Councils (CHCs) or The Family Planning Association (636 7866) can tell you the location of your nearest Well Woman Clinic. These clinics provide free medical check-ups including cervical smear tests, pelvic examinations, breast examinations, blood tests, urine tests and tests for rubella and sickle cell anaemia. CHCs can also provide information about all aspects of NHS care. CHCs are listed in the phone book.

Anorexia Anonymous
24 Westmoreland Road
London SW13
748 3994
Advice and counselling.

Anorexia and Bulimia Nervosa Association
12 Geneva Court
Manor Road
London N16

Black Women's Health Action Project
Wickham House
10 Cleveland Way
London E1
790 2424

CLASH (Central London Action on Street Health)
734 1794

Healthline
c/o College of Health
PO Box 499
London E2
980 4848

A confidential telephone information service giving tape recorded advice and information 6pm to 10pm.

National AIDS Helpline
0800 567123

Praed Street Project
(Genito-urinary Clinic)
725 1549

Sangam Society of Asian Women
235–237 West Hendon Broadway
London NW9
202 4629
Counselling and advice centre on health and other matters.

Women's Alcohol Centre
66 Drayton Park
London N5
226 4581

Women's Health Information Centre
52–54 Featherstone Street
London EC1
251 6580

A London-wide information source on women's health issues and groups.

Women's League of Health and Beauty
Rooms 29–31
18 Charing Cross Road
London WC2H 0HR
240 8456

Women's National Cancer Control Campaign
1 South Audley Street
London W14 5DQ
499 7532

Information on cancers of the breast and cervix.

Women's Natural Health Centre
1 Hillside, Highgate Road
London NW5 1QT
482 3293
Offers a variety of alternative therapies for women and children living on low income.

Women's Therapy Centre
6 Manor Gardens
London N7
263 6200
Therapy, workshops and training.

NB: See also Chapter 7: Health.

PREGNANCY, ABORTION AND CHILDCARE

Pregnancy

Active Birth Centre
55 Dartmouth Park Road
London NW5 1SL
267 3006

Association for Improvements in Maternity Services
163 Liverpool Road
London N1 0RF
278 5628
Support and advice on parents' rights, complaints procedures, etc.

Association for Post-natal Illness
c/o 7 Gowan Avenue
London SW6 6RH
Advice from mothers who have recovered from such illness and from medical experts.

Association of Radical Midwives
79 Halesworth Road
London SE13
692 8590
Campaigning for radical changes in maternity services.

Birthright (National Fund for Childbirth Research)
27 Sussex Place
Regent's Park
London NW1 4SP
723 9296/262 5337
Funds medical research for the better health of women and babies. The appeal arm of the Royal College of Obstetricians and Gynaecologists.

Cervical Stitch Network
15 Mitcham Road
London E11 3LE
555 5248
Information and support.

Foundation for Study of Infant Deaths, Cot Death Research Support
4–5 Grosvenor Place
London SW1X 7HD
235 1721

Independent Midwives Association
65 Mount Nod Road
London SW16 2LP
677 9746

La Leche League
BM 3424
London WC1
242 1278
*Advice on breastfeeding and
mothering.*

Maternity Alliance
15 Britannia Street
London WC1X 9JP
837 1265
*Campaigning for maternity rights
and welfare.*

**National Association of Maternal
and Child Welfare**
1 South Audley Street
London W1Y 6JS
493 2601
*Actively promotes health education
in schools. GCSE equivalent
examinations are arranged for
16–19 year olds.*

National Childbirth Trust
Alexandra House
Oldham Terrace
London W3 6NH
992 8637
*Promotes education about
childbirth and parenthood and
supports choice in childbirth.*

Contraception and Family Planning

Birth Control Trust
27–35 Mortimer Street
London W1N 7RJ
580 9360
*Research on all aspects of birth
control.*

British Pregnancy Advisory Service
7 Belgrave Road
London SW1V 1QB
222 0985
*Family planning and contraception
advice.*

Brook Advisory Centres
153a East Street
London SE17 2SD
708 1234
*Free contraceptives, advice and
counselling.*

Family Planning Association
27–35 Mortimer Street
London W1N 7RJ
636 7866
Leaflets and phone-in inquiries.

Marie Stopes House and Annexe
108 and 114 Whitfield Street
London W1
388 4843
*Advice on family planning and
abortion.*

Pregnancy Advisory Service
11–13 Charlotte Street
London W1
637 8962
*Advice on pregnancy, abortion and
fertility. Diagnosis, counselling and
information. Family planning
advice, post-operative counselling,
examination and surgery,
pregnancy testing, post-coital birth
control ('morning-after' care),
sterilisation, cervical smears, breast
and other gynaecological
examinations, artificial
insemination. Separate advisory
service for women from overseas.*

Women's Health Concern
Ground Floor
17 Earl's Terrace
London W8
602 6669
*Promotes research and gives advice
to women with gynaecological and
obstetric disorders.*

Adoption and Fostering

**British Agencies for Adoption and
 Fostering**
11 Southwark Street
London SE1 1RQ
407 8800

Fosterfacts
34 John Adam Street
London WC2N 6HW
*Information and advice on
fostering. Information can also be
obtained from local councils
fostering sections.*

Independent Adoption Service
123 Camberwell Road
London SE5
*Working with black families, single
women and children.*

National Adoption Society
Hooper Cottage
Kimberley Road
London NW6 7SG
624 3411
*Arranges legal adoption of young
babies, comprehensive service for
the unmarried mother including
mother and baby hostels.*

Single Parents

Gingerbread
35 Wellington Street
London WC2
240 0953
*Advice and support for single
parents.*

**National Council for One-Parent
 Families**
255 Kentish Town Road
London NW5
267 1361

Parents Alone
Caxton House
St John's Way
London N19
263 3151/2

Single Parent Project
Mary Ward Centre
42 Queen Square
London WC1
831 7711

Working Mothers Association
23 Webbs Road
London SW11 6RU
228 3757
Information, advice and support.

Abortion

After years of campaigning by groups such as the Abortion Law
Reform Society, the Abortion Act was passed by government in
1967. The Act allows a woman to have an abortion if two doctors
believe that continuing her pregnancy would involve a greater
risk to the life of the woman, injury to her physical or mental
health, or injury to the health of her existing children than if she
had an abortion. Two doctors may also grant an abortion if there
is a substantial risk of the child being seriously handicapped.

Since 1967 abortion rights have come under attack both in
Parliament and elsewhere. The James White Bill (1977), Benyon

Bill (1977), Corrie Bill (1979/80) and most recently the Alton Bill (1987–8) were all defeated as a result of successful public campaigns instigated and led by women. An unsuccessful attempt was made by Conservative MP Ann Widdecombe to introduce a new anti-abortion bill in 1989.

Yet abortion rights are still limited. The central premise of most groups campaigning for improved abortion rights is that it is the woman's right to choose when and if to have children and whether or not to have a termination. Adequate day care facilities for early and safe abortion under the NHS, improved ante-natal care to identify foetal abnormalities in mid-term pregnancy, and a change in the law requiring the say-so of two doctors are thus all fundamental aims of abortion rights groups.

Unfortunately, there are organisations which advertise themselves as abortion advice centres but are in fact anti-abortion groups with the aim of campaigning against abortion. They will try to persuade women not to have an abortion rather than offer balanced advice based on the individual woman's circumstances and the woman's right to choose. It is rarely easy to identify such organisations other than the more well-known anti-abortionists such as LIFE or SPUC, so it is worthwhile checking before going to any agency not listed below.

A new campaigning umbrella organisation, the Pro-Choice Alliance, has been launched by the Abortion Law Reform Association and the National Abortion Campaign.

Abortion Law Reform Society
88a Islington High Street
London N1 8EG
359 5200
Campaigning for further liberalisation of the law on the basis of a model bill for a woman's right to choose about abortion.

National Abortion Campaign
Wesley House Women's Centre
4 Wild Court
London WC2B 5AU
405 4801
Campaigns for every woman's right to choose for herself whether or not to continue with a pregnancy; for freely available contraception and fertility treatment for all women on the NHS, and for adequate sex education, public information and counselling services.

CO-ORD (Co-Ordinating Committee in Defence of the 1967 Act)
27–35 Mortimer Street
London W1
580 9360

Doctors for a Women's Choice on Abortion
157b Dunstans Road
London SE22

Fairfield Nursing Home
88 Russell Road
Buckhurst Hill
Essex
505 4651
Abortion advice and free pregnancy tests.

Labour Abortion Rights Campaign
PO Box 110
London SE21 8ND

P&G Advisory Service
26 Fouberts Place
London W1V 1HG
437 7125
Abortion advice, pregnancy testing while you wait, morning-after pill, contraception.

Pregnancy Control Centre
72 Tottenham Court Road
London W1
580 4847
DSS registered. Pregnancy testing while you wait.

The Preterm Centre
40 Mortimer Street
London W1
580 9001

Pregnancy testing and abortion advice.

Support After Termination for Abnormality
22 Upper Woburn Place
London WC1H 0EP
388 1382
Support for couples who have undergone termination due to a foetus's abnormality.

Tories for a Free Choice
2 Hyde Court
78 Elsinore Road
London SE23

Women's Reproductive Rights Campaign
52–54 Featherstone Street
London EC1
251 6332

Childcare

National Childcare Campaign
c/o Wesley House London Women's Centre
4 Wild Court
London WC2B 5AU
405 5617/8

Childcare Now
As above
831 6632

Health Visitors

Health visitors are available on the NHS to all children under 5. The visitor will come to your home to talk in private. They will either help you themselves or tell you where to go for the help you need. To contact a health visitor, phone the local clinic, doctor's surgery or Community Health Department at the local council.

Childminders

Childminders approved by the Social Services can be contacted via the council Social Services Department. Lists are often available in clinics or local libraries. Childminders are not free.

National Childminding Association
8 Masons Hill
Bromley
Kent, BR2 9EY
464 6164

Playgroups

Part-time places during school term time for 3 to 5 year olds.
Fees are usually low. Libraries and newspapers usually advertise
local groups.

Pre-school Playgroups Association
61–63 King's Cross Road
London WC1X 9LL
833 0991

Nursery Schools

Run by local education authorities, providing part-time and full-
time places in school hours for 3–5 year olds. No fees.

Day Nurseries

Local authority Social Services Departments offer full-time places
from 8am to 6pm for children aged 3 months to 5 years. Fees
vary. Demand always exceeds supply.

GENERAL ADDRESSES

London Women's Aid
52–54 Featherstone Street
London EC1Y 8RT
251 6537
(affiliated to Women's Aid Federation England)

Provides refuge if you need to leave home due to psychological,
physical or sexual abuse from a partner, or due to your children
being abused. Provides information, advice and refuge for
women who have suffered domestic or other violence. There are
a number of refuges in London where women who have been ill-
treated by a man can live with their children. Your local refuge
can be contacted through the Samaritans, Social Services,
Citizens Advice Bureau, other advice centres or the police, or by
ringing the central office number of Women's Aid.

Women at the refuge will help you with claiming social security benefit if necessary and with making school or nursery arrangements for your children. The centre will also provide information about how to take legal action, how to return to your house or find alternative housing, and continue to provide help and support even after you leave the refuge. Most of all the centre will listen and provide support when you most need it.

Wesley House London Women's Centre
4 Wild Court
London WC2B 5AU
831 6946

Set up in 1984 by the GLC Women's Committee. Passed to the London Residuary Body and subsequently to the Borough of Camden in May 1987. The centre, like many other things, has suffered because of government restrictions on local authority expenditure, which if anything are likely to increase. Despite its funding problems, the centre manages to provide a range of facilities that are being used by more and more women.

For example, rehearsal space, video edit suite, performance space, cervical and breast screening clinics, courses in association with the City Lit (see education section), a computer centre, workshops, and much more. (The centre is for all women but especially targets black and ethnic minority women, lesbians, disabled women, working-class women, older women and younger women.)

There are many groups based at the centre:
Akina Mama Wa Afrika/*African Woman* journal (405 0678)
Asian Women's Network (no phone, please write)
Beach Project 831 7377 (education project working with Bangladeshi homeless)
Black Women Healers (no phone, please write)
Camden Black Sisters (831 7897)
Clean Break 405 0765 (ex-offenders theatre group)
Creative and Supportive Trust (CAST) (working with ex-offenders – please write)
Fleet Street Nursery (831 9179)
Kingsway Children's Centre (831 7460)
Lesbian Archives (405 6475)
Lespop (833 4996)
London Women's Centre Administration (831 6946)
Microsyster (430 0655)
National Abortion Campaign (405 4801)

National Childcare Campaign (405 5617/8)
Women's Computer Centre (430 0112)
Women's Sports Foundation (831 7863)
Women's Training Link (242 6050)

Feminist Library
5–5a Westminster Bridge Road
London SW1
*Books, pamphlets, articles, journals
and unpublished papers on many
topics, information service,
newsletter for members.*

**National Federation of Women's
 Institutes**
39 Eccleston Street
London SW1W 9NT
730 7212

The Samaritans
17 Uxbridge Road
Slough
Berks SL1 1SN
0753 32713
London numbers in Chapter 7:
Health.

*A twenty-four-hour confidential
telephone service for the suicidal,
depressed and despairing.*

South London Women's Centre
55 Acre Lane
London SW4
274 7215

Women's Royal Voluntary Service
234–244 Stockwell Road
London SW9 9SP
733 3888
*A community service working
independently and with government
departments, carrying out a vast
range of welfare and
emergency work.*

Black and Ethnic Minority Women

**ASHA Asian Women's Resource
 Centre**
27 Santley Street
London SW4 7QF
274 8854
737 5901

Bangladesh Women's Association
91 Highbury Hills
London N5 1SX
359 5836

Black Women's Centre
41 Stockwell Green
London SW9
274 9220

**Chinese Information and Advice
 Centre**
152–156 Shaftesbury Avenue
London WC2
836 8291

**Joint Council for the Welfare of
 Immigrants**
115 Old Street
London EC1V 9JR
251 8706

London Irish Women's Centre
59 Stoke Newington Church Street
London N16
249 7318

**National Federation of Cypriots in
 Great Britain**
4 Porchester Terrace
London W2
402 8904

**Pakistan Women's Welfare
 Association**
20 Blackstock Road
London N4 2DW
226 4427

Union of Turkish Women in Great Britain
110 Clarence Road
London E5
986 1405

West Indian Women's Association
71 Pound Lane
Willesden
London NW10 2HU
459 4961

See also Chapter 5: Ethnic Minorities.

Legal

Rights of Women
52–54 Featherstone Street
London EC1
251 6577
Have a list of recommended women solicitors and give advice over the phone. Citizens Advice Bureaux, Law Centres or women's refuges can also offer help.

Criminal Injuries Compensation Board
Whittington House
19 Alfred Place
London WC1E 7LG

Law Centres Federation
Duchess House
18–19 Warren Street
London W1P 5DP
387 8570

Pornography

Campaign Against Pornography
9 Poland Street
London W1

Marriage Guidance

London Marriage Guidance Council
76a New Cavendish Street
London W1
580 1087

Financial Problems

Child Poverty Action Group
1–5 Bath Street
London EC1
253 3406

DSS Freephone
0800 666555

National Federation of Claimants Unions
296 Bethnal Green Road
London E2
739 4173

Lesbians

Lesbian Line 251 6911

See also Chapter 9: Lesbians and Gay Men

Bookshops

Silver Moon Women's Bookshop
68 Charing Cross Road
London WC2 0BB
836 7906

Sisterwrite
190 Upper Street
London N1
226 9782

16

CONCLUSION – PAST, PRESENT AND FUTURE

The preceding fifteen chapters leave one with mixed feelings. On the one hand, I am appalled at the way London has been allowed to become the laughing stock of European cities. With its dirty streets, inefficient transport, filthy and overcrowded stations, thousands sleeping rough and begging for food, hospitals closing, social services and citizens' rights declining – London has much to be ashamed of.

On the other hand, I am encouraged by the work of the hundreds of organisations and thousands of people – many working voluntarily, most others working for low wages – offering support, advice, information and facilities.

Yet these organisations run on shoestring budgets and increasingly they are providing services which local authorities can no longer afford to fund themselves. The boroughs have been given more responsibilities without sufficient funds to carry them out. At the same time, the funding and responsibilities given to local authorities rarely take fully into account the specific needs and priorities of the differing local populations; as a result, these populations are left at the mercy of the whims of their borough leaders, whatever their political colour.

In the past, rate capping has prevented the boroughs from providing essential services; in future, they will have to choose between cutting services further or setting massive poll tax bills in order to fund their requirements. At the same time, political and legislative powers have been severely undermined as local authority representation on health, education and transport planning bodies is reduced and more and more power shifted to central government.

The need for a democratically elected London-wide authority has never been greater. As cleaning and waste disposal, traffic-calming initiatives, and education are planned on a piecemeal and area-specific basis, it is becoming clear – if it were ever in doubt – that services need to be planned and coordinated on a London-wide basis by authorities which are accessible and accountable to the population.

Yet we have a government obsessed with free enterprise and market forces. Privatisation and profit take precedence over people's needs. What good is a local policy of housing improvements by private contractors if the refurbished homes are too expensive for local inhabitants and affluent young people from the home counties move in, forcing the original tenants to move to other boroughs thus worsening the housing crisis and creating ghettos of the less well-off?

Just like the affluent and upwardly mobile young people who come here to make their fast buck before moving on, so planners and policy-makers fix their eyes on short-term profit instead of considering long-term social priorities.

So what of the future? Will London continue to decline at the current alarming rate until it really becomes the 'third world city' it is already called by other countries? Or will London's population refuse to be pushed into submission by increasing poverty, homelessness and decay?

Unfortunately, it is not simply a question of public outrage leading to a reversal of the current disastrous government policies and corporate irresponsibility that plagues the capital, its people and its environment. There has to be a new perspective but new attitudes and approaches do not magically appear with a change of government, however committed that government might be to restoring an elected London-wide body to replace the GLC and ILEA and to reversing the tide of decline in living standards and service provision.

In the future, planning must take place in consultation with all local populations if real needs are to be met. Small cliques of white upper middle class men in ivory towers do not create policies which answer the needs of a multicultural, multifaceted city; rather they answer their own political and financial priorities. Londoners know what services they need, if only they had the opportunity to decide their own fate.

London's future hangs in the balance and I have no doubt that it will survive and flourish again as it has done for centuries. But at what cost? Even if a new government begins to confront homelessness, poverty and the multitude of mounting crises, it is too late to help the patients who have died because hospital waiting lists are too long, the teenagers who ended up in the gutter with a hypodermic in their arm when unemployment, poverty and homelessness finally became too much, parks and buildings irreversibly damaged by pollution and neglect, rivers and the remaining precious green spaces buried under developers' concrete and short-sightedness.

For these it will be too late. Surely, it is the responsibility of all of us to make sure the London of the future is based on the meeting of needs, social responsibility and fulfilling at least some of everybody's expectations; not on profit, power and personal gain.

Despite everything, London is still full of life, culture and beauty – we should *all* have the right to enjoy them.

John Grounds
Editor

APPENDIX

LONDON BOROUGH COUNCILS

Borough councils usually have departments covering the following areas: Housing and Property, Education, Recreation/Arts, Finance, Technical Services/Engineering and Works, Planning, Social Services, Environmental Health. Some also have departments and/or officers dealing with women's issues, lesbians and gay men, ethnic minorities, people with disabilities, older people, children and young people. If there is not a separate department covering the issue you are pursuing, contact the general information office or council switchboard.

Inner London Boroughs

City of London
PO Box 270
Guildhall
London EC2P 2EJ
606 3030

Camden Borough Council
Town Hall
Euston Road
London NW1 2RU
278 4444

Greenwich Borough Council
24–27 Wellington Road
London SE18
854 8888

Hackney Borough Council
Town Hall
Mare Street
London E8 1EA
986 3123

Hammersmith and Fulham Borough Council
Town Hall
Hammersmith
London W6 9JU
748 3020

Islington Borough Council
Town Hall
Upper Street
London N1 2UD
226 1234

Kensington and Chelsea Borough Council
Town Hall
Hornton Street
London W8 7NX
937 5464

Lambeth Borough Council
Town Hall
Brixton Hill
London SW2 1RW
274 7722

Lewisham Borough Council
Town Hall
Catford
London SE6 4RU
695 6000

Southwark Borough Council
Town Hall
Peckham Road
London SE6 8UP
703 6311

Tower Hamlets Borough Council
Town Hall
Patriot Square
London E2 9LN
980 4831

Wandsworth Borough Council
Town Hall
Wandsworth High Street
London SW18 2PU
871 6000

Westminster Borough Council
City Hall
Victoria Street
London SE1 6QP
828 8070

Outer London Boroughs

Barking and Dagenham Borough Council
Civic Centre
Dagenham
Essex RM10 7BN
592 4500

Barnet Borough Council
Town Hall
The Burroughs
London NW4 4BG
202 8282

Bexley Borough Council
Civic Offices
Broadway
Bexleyheath
Kent DA6 7LB
303 7777

Brent Borough Council
Town Hall
Forty Lane
Wembley
Middlesex HA9 9HX
904 1244

Bromley Borough Council
Civic Centre
Rochester Avenue
Bromley
Kent BR1 3HU
464 3333

Croydon Borough Council
Taberner House
Park Lane
Croydon
Surrey CR9 3JS
686 4433

Ealing Borough Council
Town Hall
Ealing
London W5 2BY
579 2424

Enfield Borough Council
Civic Centre
Silver Street
Enfield
Middlesex EN1 3XA
366 6565

Haringey Borough Council
Civic Centre
PO Box 264
High Road
London N22 4LE
528 9020

Harrow Borough Council
Civic Centre
Harrow
Middlesex HA1 2UW
863 5611

Havering Borough Council
Town Hall
Romford
Essex RM1 3RD
0708 46040

Hillingdon Borough Council
Civic Centre
Uxbridge
Middlesex UB8 1BW
0895 50111

Hounslow Borough Council
Civic Centre
Lampton Road
Hounslow
Middlesex TW3 4DN
570 7728

Kingston-upon-Thames Borough Council
Guildhall
Kingston-upon-Thames
Surrey KT1 1EU
546 2121

Merton Borough Council
Crown House
London Road
Merton SM4 5DX
543 2222

Newham Borough Council
Town Hall
East Ham
London E6 2RD
472 1430

Redbridge Borough Council
Town Hall
Ilford
Essex IG1 1DD
478 3020

Richmond-upon-Thames Borough Council
Municipal Offices
Twickenham TW1 3AA
891 1411

Sutton Borough Council
Civic Offices
St Nicholas Way
Sutton SM1 1EA
661 5000

Waltham Forest Borough Council
Town Hall
Forest Road
London E17 4JF
527 5544

INDEPENDENT ADVICE AGENCIES

Law Centres Federation
Duchess House
18–19 Warren Street
London W1P 5DB
387 8570
Can tell you the location of your local Law Centre.

Federation of Independent Advice Centres (FIAC)
London Unit
13 Stockwell Road
London SW9 9AV
274 1839

Can tell you where to go locally for independent advice and support.

National Association of Citizens Advice Bureaux (NACAB)
115–123 Pentonville Road
London N1 9LZ
833 2181

Greater London Citizens Advice Bureau Service (GLOCABS)
136–144 City Road
London EC1V 2QN
251 2000
Can direct you to your local CAB.

AMENITIES

London Electricity Board
733 1930

Gas
346 8668

Water
741 1500 (day)
837 3300 (night)

Plumbing Helpline
468 7767

Local emergency numbers are to be found in telephone directories or libraries.

POLITICS AND PRESSURE GROUPS

**Communist Party of Britain
(*Morning Star*)**
3 Victoria Chambers
Luke Street
London EC2A

**Communist Party of Great Britain
(*Marxism Today*)**
16 St John Street
London EC1M 4AY

Conservative Party
32 Smith Square
London SW1
222 9000

Green Party
10 Station Parade
Balham High Road
London SW12 9AZ
673 0045

Labour Party
150 Walworth Road
London SE17
703 0833

Social Democratic Party (SDP)
25 Buckingham Gate
London SW1E 6LD
821 9661

Liberal Democrats
4 Cowley Street
London SW1P 3NE
222 0861

Socialist Workers Party
PO Box 82
London E3 3LH

Many small parties and groups of the left, as well as anarchist organisations, sell literature through Collets or Central Books. Anarchist organisations also sell literature through Freedom Bookshop.

Collets International Bookshop
129–131 Charing Cross Road
London WC2 0EQ
734 0782/3

Central Books
37 Gray's Inn Road
London WC1X 8PS
242 6166

Freedom Bookshop
84b Whitechapel High Street (Angel
    Alley)
London E1 7QX
247 9249

Books for a Change
52 Charing Cross Road
London WC2H 0BB
836 2315
*Besides its extensive range of books
on ecology, peace and
disarmament, aid and development,
literature, etc., BFAC also stocks
publications, t-shirts and other
products from a large number of
organisations such as Friends of the
Earth, War on Want, United Nations
Association, CND, Nicaragua
Solidarity, Palestine Solidarity, Anti-
apartheid Movement, Amnesty
International, Peace Pledge Union,
Campaign Against the Arms Trade,
Lifeline, etc.*

BIBLIOGRAPHY

Alternative London, Georganne Downes, Kathy Holme and Max Handley (Otherwise Press, 1982).
Basic Information Pack, vols 1 and 2 (NACAB, 1989).
Bending the Rules: The Baker Reform of Education, Brian Simon (Lawrence & Wishart, 1989).
The Big Choke (TEST, 1989).
Black People, Human Rights and the Media (Black Rights UK, 1989).
Bookshops of London, Diana Stephenson (Lascelles, 1986).
Capital Schemes (Friends of the Earth, 1987).
Children of the Future, Frances Morrell (Hogarth, 1989).
Citizenship for Some: Race and Government Policy, 1979–1989, Paul Gordon (Runnymede Trust, 1989).
City Wildspace, Bob Smyth (Hilary Shipman, 1987).
Civil Liberty: The NCCL Guide, Malcolm Hurwitt and Peter Thornton (Penguin, 1989).
Floodlight, ILEA/Capital Radio (ILEA, 1989).
Green Pages, John Button (Optima, 1988).
Guide to Ethnic London (Michael Haag, 1986).
A Guide to London for Young Irish People (Action Group for Irish Youth, 1988).
Housing Rights Guide, Geoffrey Randall (SHAC, 1989).
Kids' London, Elizabeth Holt and Molly Perham (Pan, 1985).
London Government Handbook, Michael Hebbert and Tony Travers (Cassell, 1988).
London Guide to Mind, Body and Spirit, Kate Brady and Mike Considine (Brainwave, 1988).
London Women's Handbook (GLC, 1986).
National Welfare Benefits Handbook, Beth Lakhani, Jim Read and Penny Wood (Child Poverty Action Group, 1989).
Race in Britain, Paul Gordon (Runnymede Trust, 1988).
Sexual Violence, London Rape Crisis Centre (Women's Press, 1984).
The South London Handbook, Celie Parker (Stockwell Press, 1986).

Springboard (A directory of women's businesses and organisations in the London area) (Springboard, 1987).

Time Out Student Guide (Time Out, 1989).

Voluntary Agencies Directory (Bedford Square Press, 1989).

Wild in London, David Goode (Michael Joseph, 1986).

INDEX

To help readers looking for the address of one of the organisations listed in this index, where there is more than one page reference for any particular organisation, one page reference appears in bold type and denotes a page where the address of that organisation is listed.